Political Journalism

Political Journalism explores the practices of political journalism, ranging from American 'civic journalism' to the press corps covering the European Union in Brussels, from Bangkok newsrooms to French and Italian scandal hunters. The contributors debate three main areas:

- What is political journalism? Who are the main actors in the daily routines and interdependencies of political news production?
- What is the importance of scandals and adversarial reporting in the coverage of politics?
- What is the contribution of political journalism to the functioning of modern democracy?

This edited collection makes a major contribution to the current upsurge of interest in journalism studies. Challenging both the 'mediamalaise' thesis and the notion of the journalist as the faithful servant of democracy, it explores political journalism in the making and maps the opportunities and threats encountered by political journalism in the contemporary public sphere. It contains case studies drawn from the US, the UK, Australia, France, the Netherlands and Thailand among others.

Raymond Kuhn is Senior Lecturer in Politics at Queen Mary, University of London. His research interests are Western European, especially French, politics and the politics of the media. He has edited two books on the media and politics and is the author of *The Media in France*.

Erik Neveu is Professor of Political Science at the Institut d'Études Politiques in Rennes. His publications focus on three main topics: the public sphere, social movements and cultural studies.

Routledge/ECPR Studies in European Political Science
Edited by Jan W. van Deth, *University of Mannheim, Germany on behalf of the European Consortium for Political Research*

The Routledge/ECPR Studies in European Political Science series is published in association with the European Consortium for Political Research – the leading organisation concerned with the growth and development of political science in Europe. The series presents high-quality edited volumes on topics at the leading edge of current interest in political science and related fields, with contributions from European scholars and others who have presented work at ECPR workshops or research groups.

Political Journalism
New challenges, new practices

Edited by
Raymond Kuhn and Erik Neveu

London and New York

First published 2002 by Routledge
2 Park Square, Milton Park, Abingdon, Oxon OX14 4RN

Simultaneously published in the USA and Canada
by Routledge
270 Madison Ave, New York, NY 10016

Routledge is an imprint of the Taylor & Francis Group

Transferred to Digital Printing 2006

Selection and editorial matter © 2002 Raymond Kuhn and
Erik Neveu; individual chapters © the contributors

Typeset in Baskerville by Exe Valley Dataset Ltd, Exeter

British Library Cataloguing in Publication Data
A catalogue record for this book is available
from the British Library

Library of Congress Cataloguing in Publication Data
A catalog record for this book has been requested

ISBN 0–415–25813–8

To Shirley, for all her love and support (RK)

A Mia-Miou L, pour tant de choses, dont la moindre n'est pas de me supporter quand j'écris des livres (EN)

Contents

Illustrations

Tables

Boxes

Contributors

Olivier Baisnée is a doctoral student based at the Institut d'Études Politiques in Rennes. He is currently researching a PhD on the production of EU news, analysing in a comparative perspective the 'pack' of reporters covering the European Union in Brussels. His research interests also include the rise of 'European' media such as Eurosports and Euronews. He has published articles in *Critique Internationale* and *Cultures et Conflits*.

Kees Brants is Director of the MA programme in European Communication Studies at the University of Amsterdam and Professor Extraordinaire of Political Communication at the University of Leiden. He has a broad range of research interests, which include European communications policy; political communication; media, migrants and right-wing extremism; electronic democracy; and the First World War.

Theodore L. Glasser is Professor of Communication and Director of the Graduate Program in Journalism at Stanford University. He is also on the faculty of Stanford's Modern Thought and Literature Program. His recent books include *The Idea of Public Journalism* (1999, edited); *Custodians of Conscience: Investigative Journalism and Public Virtue* (1998, co-authored with James Ettema); and *Public Opinion and the Communication of Consent* (1995, co-edited with Charles Salmon). He was recently elected President of the Association for Education in Journalism and Mass Communication.

Hetty van Kempen is based at the Amsterdam School of Communications Research of the University of Amsterdam where she is working on a PhD project researching cross-national media effects on voting behaviour during the 1999 European elections. Her research interests include election campaigns, media and political attitudes, electoral participation and the role of new media in democracy.

Raymond Kuhn is a Senior Lecturer in Politics at Queen Mary, University of London. He has published widely on the politics of the British and French media, including a single-authored study *The Media in France* (1995).

Francis L.F. Lee is a PhD student in the Department of Communication at Stanford University. He received his MPhil degree at the Chinese University of Hong Kong. His research interests include public opinion, journalism, and political communication. He has previously worked on public opinion in Hong Kong, co-authoring a paper published in the *International Journal of Public Opinion Research*. More recently he has been researching for a project on the politics of opinion polling in Hong Kong, and is currently preparing a study on the use of polls within the movement of public journalism in America.

Duncan McCargo is a Senior Lecturer in Politics at the University of Leeds. He is a Southeast Asia specialist who has worked extensively on media issues. His PhD thesis 'The political leadership of Major-General Chamlong Srimuang' was published in a revised form as *Chamlong Srimuang and the New Thai Politics* (1997). His various books include *Politics and the Press in Thailand: Media Machinations* (2000) and *Media and Politics in Pacific Asia* (forthcoming).

Brian McNair is a Reader in the Department of Film and Media Studies, University of Stirling. He is the author of several books on the media and journalism, including *An Introduction to Political Communication, News and Journalism in the UK* and *The Sociology of Journalism*. His most recent book, *Journalism and Democracy*, was published in 2000.

Erik Neveu is a Professor of Political Science at the Institut d'Études Politiques in Rennes. He teaches on the sociology of journalism, social movements and the construction of social problems. His research interests include the public sphere, journalism and politics, and cultural studies. He has recently published *Sociologie du journalisme* (2001) and co-edited with Bastien François *Espaces publics mosaiques* (1999).

Véronique Pujas is a research fellow at the CNRS-CIDSP unit at the Institut d'Études Politiques in Grenoble. Her thesis, completed at the European University Institute in Florence, studied in a comparative perspective the rise of political scandals in Italy, France and Spain. Her current research focuses on party funding and the fight against political corruption in Europe.

Franca Roncarolo is an Associate Professor at the University of Turin, Italy, where she teaches political communication and political sociology. Her main research interests include the relationship between government and the media, election campaigns, and gender issues in Italian political communication. She is the author of *Controllare i media* (1994) and *I media come arena elettorale* (1997, with Rolando Marini).

Rodney Tiffen is an Associate Professor in Government and International Relations at the University of Sydney. His research and teaching interests include the mass media, Australian politics, comparative democratic politics and Australian relations with Asia. His books include *News and Power; Scandals: Media, Politics and Corruption in Contemporary Australia;* and *Diplomatic Deceits: Government, Media and East Timor.*

Jeremy Tunstall is Research Professor in Sociology at City University, London. He is the author of many books, the most recent of which, all published by Oxford University Press, include *Newspaper Power* (1996), *The Anglo-American Media Connection* (1999, with David Machin) and *Media Occupations and Professions* (2001, edited). He is currently working on two research projects: one on world media and the other on a single television executive producer.

Series editor's preface

'Blaming the messenger' is an old and widely used trick. If increasing numbers of citizens withdraw from the realm of politics and more and more voters are no longer willing to cast a vote, uneasy discussions about the quality of public debates can be avoided by blaming journalists for the way they present political news. By now, the trendy opinion is to express concern about mass media 'reducing' politics to a 'horse race', to complain about an emphasis on 'personal scandals' and about the lack of attention to 'serious issues', and – of course – to point to the 'Americanisation' of political campaigning and the damaging role of the press. Decisions seem to depend on the activities of 'spin-doctors' and not on arguments. In modern democracies, political life is the victim of a 'spiral of cynicism', with hard-boiled journalists as the main villains and culprits.

Common sense is not the best source for sensible and balanced conclusions. Yet it is clear that both politics and journalism have changed tremendously all over the world in the last decades. Usually, the spread of television broadcasting and the rapid expansion of the internet are depicted as revolutionary developments. But journalists' roles and styles might have changed even more fundamentally than these technical supports. Political journalists specially have been searching for new ways to define their tasks and responsibilities, and the consequences of these explorations are most visible for traditional news media like newspapers.

The contributors to this volume all accepted the challenge to move towards innovative approaches to the role and status of journalists in the political communication process. They differ clearly in their research interests, study designs, selected material, and the scope of their analyses, but they all cope with the rapidly changing position of political journalists and the consequences and challenges of this process for democratic decision-making. In their introduction to this volume, the editors summarise this common interest on the basis of what they call a plea for 'Political Journalism Revisited'. This revision is based on a clear rejection of a single approach: 'The study of political journalism does not have to choose between the ethnography of the newsroom, the statistical analysis of news content or the role of journalists as narrative-makers.' The three major parts of this volume address the central questions of this project: the interdependencies between journalists and politicians, the cynical coverage of politics, and the consequences for democratic decision-making.

Before specific analyses dealing with these three questions are presented, Erik Neveu offers a historical overview of the main types of political journalism (Chapter 2). The entry of new generations of more educated and more women journalists has intensified the struggle for jobs in this area. The first part consists of four contributions which address problems of interdependencies between journalists and politicians in various political systems. In a detailed analysis of the first Blair government, Raymond Kuhn shows that the relationships between media practitioners and government officials developed into a process of exchange and mutual dependencies (Chapter 3). Franca Roncarolo presents a wide-ranging analysis on the interdependencies between political crises and crises in political communication in Italy (Chapter 4), while Duncan McCargo challenges Western-centric models in a stimulating discussion of the role of journalists as political actors in Thailand (Chapter 5). An unusual and highly interesting inside view of political journalism is presented by Olivier Baisnée is his analysis of the way journalists function at the EU level (Chapter 6). The next three contributions focus on the much-debated question of a rise of a more cynical coverage of politics. On the basis of an Australian case-study (Chapter 7), Rodney Tiffen starts this part with a systematic discussion of the factors that make some scandals escalate dramatically. Detailed overviews of the exposure of corruption in several countries are presented by Véronique Pujas (Chapter 8). Kees Brants and Hetty van Kempen challenge the popular idea that growing cynical journalism contributes to a more cynical public opinion. Analysing data on developments in the Netherlands, they show that such an interpretation is far too simple to understand the complex developments in politics and journalism in the last decade (Chapter 9). The third part of the volume continues this debate by focusing on the implications for democracy in an era of rapidly changing political communication. Brian McNair argues that the spread of interactive and confrontational forms of political journalism contribute to the mobilisation of popular interest in Britain instead of reducing political engagement (Chapter 10). In a detailed discussion of experiences in the US Theodore Glasser and Francis Lee consider the notion that the purpose of journalism is to promote and improve the quality of public life (Chapter 11). Finally, Jeremy Tunstall returns to the major problems and prospects in his concluding chapter by warning against rather naive interpretations and by presenting the provocative idea that Europe – and not the US – holds the position of world news leadership (Chapter 12).

The days have long gone since Walter Lippmann could observe that 'until quite recently . . . political science was taught in our colleges as if newspapers did not exist' (1922: 320). However, until very recently, many political scientists seemed to favour a kind of caricature of the role of political journalists in the political process and to over-estimate their roles and functions in democratic decision-making processes. The present volume offers much needed critical evaluations of fashionable interpretations and folklore in this area. Scepticism and criticism should not be confused with cynicism. Only realistic approaches to the role and status of political journalism can facilitate a better understanding of governance in an increasingly interdependent and complex world.

Jan W. van Deth
Mannheim, December 2001

Reference

Lippmann, W. (1922) *Public Opinion*, New York: Harcourt.

Acknowledgements

Raymond Kuhn would like to thank his colleagues in the Department of Politics at Queen Mary, University of London, for helping to provide an atmosphere conducive to research. Erik Neveu would like to thank his academic colleagues and research students in the field of journalism for their support, stimulating discussions and understanding.

Both editors owe an immense debt of gratitude to all those who participated in the workshop on political journalism at the joint sessions of the European Consortium for Political Research at the University of Copenhagen in April 2000. In alphabetical order the workshop participants were: Olivier Baisnée, Rosa Berganza, Kees Brants, Christiane Eilders, Frank Esser, Duncan McCargo, Brian McNair, Ralph Negrine, Jim O'Brien, Véronique Pujas, Ludovic Renard, Alexa Robertson, Franca Roncarolo, Wijbrandt van Schuur, Eugenia Siapera, Rodney Tiffen, Jeremy Tunstall, Edurne Uriarte and Claes de Vreese. Without their insightful comments in workshop discussions, the quality of this book would have been much diminished. Unfortunately, despite the very high standard of the papers presented at the workshop, it was not possible to publish them all in this volume. Our sincere apologies to those whose papers we were not able to include. Our thanks are also due to Ted Glasser, Hetty van Kempen and Francis Lee for contributing to this book.

1 Political journalism
Mapping the terrain

Erik Neveu and Raymond Kuhn

One of the most famous paintings by Magritte is that of a pipe painted over the artist's usual blue sky and clouds with a caption which says: 'Ceci n'est pas une pipe' ['This is not a pipe']. Dare we begin with a similar statement – 'this is not just another book on political communication'? Of course, political journalism belongs to the realm of political communication, just as Magritte's flying pipe belongs to a smoker. Our statement does not express a love or abuse of paradoxes, but rather has the aim of challenging the effects of analytical routines on the approach to the study of political journalism by political communication researchers. These routines include the customary focus on the role of journalists during election campaigns as opposed to the periods between elections, the view of journalists as condemned to an endless and hopeless defensive struggle against spin-doctors, and the much greater attention paid to interactions between journalists and politicians rather than to those which develop inside the newsroom itself. The effect of such research routines is often to divert the attention of the researcher away from highly visible dimensions of the object of study. So in answer to our own question we can say, 'this is not just one more book on political communication'. Instead, this book uses the subject of political journalism as a starting point to improve our knowledge of the visible and the unseen in the functioning of the public sphere and the political communication environment.

Putting political journalism at the heart of the political communication process

Towards a re-evaluation of journalism in political communication studies?

Political communication has in recent years been a remarkably prolific research field for political scientists and media researchers. Just to read the articles and books published on this topic since the 1960s would in itself be a full-time job for a newcomer. At the risk of over-simplifying the richness of this scientific literature, one of the basic objectives of this book is to question a kind of routinised 'casting' of political communication actors.

Much of the research to date has emphasised the professionalisation of communication by political actors, both in terms of personal skills and organisational strategy. Another line of research has been devoted, with a strange blend of fascination and repulsion, to the important role assumed by communication consultants and spin-doctors, who are often presented as a new breed of string-pullers. A third area of inquiry has focused on the role of the *demos*, whether in its noble political incarnation as 'public opinion', or in its more common and commercial form as 'audiences'. In both cases the public is regarded as having a powerful influence on journalism.

These lines of research have produced a rich legacy of results and analysis. However, they often ascribe to political journalists a strange role in the political communication castlist. From one perspective journalists are frequently presented as trapped between the quest for audiences and the weight of public opinion on the one hand and the powerful influence of professionalised political sources on the other (Schlesinger 1990). Journalists thus appear as victims, condemned to purely reactive strategies in the face of a combination of forces which are shrinking their professional and intellectual autonomy. From another viewpoint, much research output portrays journalists as the villains of modern political communication (Fallows 1996), or at least as being responsible for an approach to coverage which threatens democratic ideals and weakens the public's interest in politics (Entman 1989).

These rather simplistic visions have recently been challenged by new axes of research on political journalism in several countries, including Germany, France, the UK and the USA. The recent launch in Britain of two journals dedicated to the study of journalism – *Journalism* and *Journalism Studies* – is another symbol of a renewed interest in the study of journalism. Aside from their different theoretical perspectives, all the contributors to this book are participating in this move towards a re-evaluation of the role and status of journalists in the political communication process. Journalists can and do develop proactive strategies in their relationship with audiences and political sources. They are neither the powerless victims of the professionalisation of politics, nor passive cogs in a communications machine. Their contribution to political communication needs to be reassessed in a 'relational' framework which seeks to make sense of the overall power balance between journalists, politicians, spin-doctors and media owners among others. As the sociologist Norbert Elias suggests, to think about complex systems of social interdependencies in a 'relational' framework means both to pay attention to all relevant actors and to remember that most of the time the final result of social interaction – in our case a news bulletin or the political news section of a daily paper – is rarely controlled by only one of the actors in the network.

The theoretical choice of re-evaluating the role of political journalists takes us towards new paradoxes. As any bibliographical investigation shows, no other kind of journalism has been the subject of so much research. Yet at the same time this vast literature contains surprising blind spots, for example with regard to comparative and historical approaches. Three points can be made in this context. First, there is a lack of long-term historical analyses. While there are some remarkable studies on journalism in the 1900s or 1960s, there are few books which – like Chalaby's (1998) – provide a broad perspective on the development of political journalism over time. Second, there has been little research focusing on the particuliarities of political journalism in relation to other specialist output, such as sports, social or crime coverage. Finally, there are relatively few studies which analyse the nature of the questions covered in the 'Politics' section of the media. Many studies have emphasised the trend in political news towards a growing personalisation of coverage, as well as the inexorable shift away from parliamentary reporting towards using the executive or party headquarters as the main source of political information (Negrine 1996). Few studies, however, offer an historical analysis of the changes in the content of the political pages of newspapers, documenting the possible move away from the fixed boundaries between political journalism and other news sections.

The first and last chapters of this book aim to offer some significant pointers to these questions. In Chapter 2 Neveu develops an historical approach expressed in terms of four 'generations' of political journalism since the late eighteenth century. Following the era of publicists came the age of objective political journalists and then a period of 'critical expertise'. Speculating about the possible emergence of a fourth generation of political journalists from the 1990s onwards, Neveu argues that changes in the media environment and communication process are not simply incremental. Political journalism today faces challenges and changes which are sufficiently dramatic to require an in-depth redefinition of its role, skills and formats.

In Chapter 12 Tunstall concludes the book with a stimulating set of questions on current trends in political journalism in a globalised media landscape. One of the most interesting aspects of this chapter is his emphasis on the need to move from a purely national vision of political journalism towards a greater awareness of the 'Russian dolls' structure of political news, which runs the gamut from world news to local reports, embracing the intermediary levels of world-regional, national and national-regional. This new framework suggests the existence of dark corners and blind spots in political news, as shown, for example, in much national coverage of 'European' news. Most 'good stories' in the media are based on national events, yet important stories are increasingly supranational in scope. In pointing to the existence of a multi-levelled political journalism, Tunstall also invites us to make linkages between approaches which in the past have too often been developed in distinct sub-fields of academic research – for example, news as reports of political events and news as the expression of a geopolitics of media companies. What is at stake in

producing reports and narratives of the 'filo pastry' of the different levels
of polities and politics appears then as a weapon in the balance of power
between cultures, states and world regions. Beyond the process of news
globalisation and 'glocalisation', one can identify struggles for influence.
News agencies and international media companies such as CNN or the
Financial Times offer news, but they also act as definers of an international
agenda, working to the international definition and maintenance of representations of nations, leaders and policy stakes. Tunstall's contribution is
basically an invitation to question and perhaps to say farewell to the nation-
centric vision of what constitutes political information.

Let us mention one last paradox. Researchers studying political journalism and communication usually agree on the Weberian principle of 'axio-
logical neutrality'. They practise it too. Nevertheless, one might ask if
academics do not face a challenge in this respect very similar to that faced
by journalists. To put it another way, is the absence of political commitment
sufficient to guarantee a reasonable sense of distance when analysing the
role of political communication actors? We would argue that as academics
we frequently share an invisible agreement with journalists and even
politicians about a 'legitimist' vision of politics. Coined by Bourdieu and
Passeron (1964), this notion of symbolic or cultural legitimacy refers to the
existence of institutionalised representations structured around opposing
dualisms – the noble and the common, highbrow and lowbrow, what is
political and what is not. The peculiarity of these 'legitimate' visions of the
social is to transform hierarchies and classifications which are the products
of history and power balances into natural, indisputable evidence. Symbolic
domination is precisely based on such misunderstandings. It works as a
kind of social magic where important questions can only be those asked by
important people – a search for the common wealth led by the wealthy.

How and why do these remarks apply to academics studying political
journalism? Quite simply. Scholars of political communication usually
share, for academic and/or biographical reasons, a strong interest in politics
which they may consider as normal and universal behaviour. Lacroix (1984)
speaks humorously of 'polit-ism' as a professional disease of political
scientists, who are too easily disposed to imagine, more or less consciously,
that everyone else shares their interest in and knowledge of politics. Like
many journalists and elected representatives, academics are prone to share
a normative vision of political debate, inherited from the Enlightenment,
as a rational exchange of ideas. They tend to limit the realm of politics to
parties and elections, paying less attention to other issues and actors
such as policies, social movements and lobbying. Another expression of this
'legitimism' is a strong tendency to consider that a golden age of politics
existed in the past, as is suggested in the use of concepts such as 'tabloidisation' or 'trivialisation' where description and judgement melt together.[1]

These gaps threaten research with several biases. As McNair suggests
(Chapter 10), they may lead researchers to adopt reluctant attitudes in the

face of any change in the formats of political journalism targeting large or popular audiences. The identification of politics with the core of representative institutions may also explain the fact that so much research focuses on moments of intense mobilisation such as election campaigns and political crises. The frequent adherence to a 'legitimate' definition of politics does not help researchers to pay sufficient attention to the renewal in the coverage of political issues which can develop in other news sections and in the contributions of journalists other than those explicitly dedicated to politics.

Political journalism revisited

The scientific logic of the ECPR workshop that gave birth to this book may become clearer from now on.[2] Beyond the range of their subject matter and their different theoretical perspectives, all the contributors to this book share a common project which can be expressed in terms of four choices and three questions.

First, their approach places journalism and journalists back at the core of the political communication process. To talk in terms of 'core' does not imply an a priori assessment of either the role or power of journalists. It simply means that nearly all the chapters focus on the work, strategies and behaviour of journalists. This first choice implies a second. Our common concern is with the ordinary functioning of the political newsdesk, with the making of political journalism in its 'ordinary' moments rather than during the feverish periods of election campaign and political crisis. As McCargo (Chapter 5) suggests, there is much to learn and understand by paying attention to questions which may seem terribly trite and un-theoretical such as 'Who pays the bill?' when a political journalist has lunch with an MP. A third choice common to all contributors is visible in their desire to make sense of the network of power relationships in which journalists are embedded. However, going back to an approach where attention is focused on political journalists does not mean falling into a new version of the media-centric trap. Instead, to think of political journalism 'in the making' means paying considerable attention to the web of complex relationships journalists have with, for example, sources, colleagues, owners, advertisers and audiences. We might add that a final common feature of the different contributions is their focus more on the press than on the broadcasting and electronic media. This particularity is not the result of a deliberate choice or research programme. Rather it reflects our common desire to highlight the less explored dimensions of political journalism, as the balance of research tends to shift more and more towards broadcasting and new media forms.

The book is organised in three main parts, each of which concentrates on addressing a specific question. Part I explores through four case-studies the complex issue of the nature and balances of the interdependencies in which journalists operate. Part II addresses the question of the 'cynical' coverage of politics. Why are stories about scandal and sleaze such a dominant feature of political news? Can such a development be considered as the explanation for a cynical or disenchanted relationship to politics by citizens? These questions lead logically to Part III, which centres on the current debate about the impact of political journalism on contemporary democracies. Researchers often speak of a 'crisis' of political journalism and communication. They identify new generations, new 'ages' and new trends. How can one make sense, without oversimplifying, of the possible consequences of these changes for representative democracy? These are the overarching questions discussed in this book. The answers to them are provided in a schematic overview in the following two sections of this chapter.

Political journalism as the strategic management of interdependencies

Which interdependencies?

In a much quoted sentence, Durkheim wrote in *The Rules of Sociological Method* that 'One must consider social facts as things'. Commenting on this aphorism, Bourdieu suggests that one should first consider social facts as 'relationships'. While most of the contributors to this book are not addicts of French sociology, they would doubtless agree with Bourdieu's adaptation. Political journalists do not live in a social vacuum; they operate in a web of interdependencies – a term which fits our analytic framework better than the more frequently used concept of interaction. While the latter may lead to an overemphasis on the freedom of manoeuvre of the relevant actors, the notion of interdependency incorporates the idea of dependence and so foregrounds the notion of power balances as an objective reality limiting their autonomy.

Some dimensions of this web can be highlighted here. The most visible is the relationship of journalists with politicians. The forms that this relationship takes can cover a whole spectrum of possibilities from the Italian version of 'political parallelism' between parties and media to the institutionalisation of objective standards of reporting. Beyond the nature of the positioning of journalists, from commitment to distance or adversarial attitudes, one should also investigate the possible forms of pressure and influence. These can follow a short loop when parties or politicians control or own media organisations or outlets or where public media are under de facto political influence. However, as Kuhn notes (Chapter 3), in most Western democracies the relationship between politicians and journalists is mediated and professionalised by the activity of spin-doctors and the ability of political sources to anticipate the needs and formats of journalists. The partners of political journalists are also basically journalists, 'competitor-colleagues' to quote the useful oxymoron of Tunstall (1971).

Journalists may work as a pack, valuing co-operation as they cross-check their notes after an interview. They also face situations of competition, both generally between broadcasting and the press and more particularly among newspaper titles and television channels. Even within the same newsroom, both conflict and co-operation are ever present, especially when political journalists must compete with colleagues from other newsbeats in claiming the right to cover events which may be difficult to pigeonhole in an institutionalised news section – as in the case of which journalists were best qualified and most appropriate to cover the BSE issue. To refer once again to Tunstall's classic study, journalists are also both producers of information and paid workers of a media company. Within the confines of their work-place they must engage in another relationship – this time hierarchical – with management. The trend in this context is clearly driven by commercial pressures to maximise ratings and circulation figures.

This relationship in turn introduces the mediated presence of another actor: the audience/public opinion. Considered from either a commercial or political logic, the situation of the public is paradoxical. They are a powerful actor, whose judgements can be mobilised by journalists to criticise or even damage politicians. In addition, audience ratings and circulation figures can be used by media management to push journalists in the direction of more audience-friendly coverage. Yet, at the same time, the mighty public is an actor more spoken about than speaking. Its influence is mediated via polls and other indices of statistical measurement. This is not to suggest that public opinion can be simply manipulated. Rather it is quite simply a reminder of the variety of strategic objectives which can be supported by reference to the tastes, attitudes and opinions of the public. Politicians, spin-doctors, fellow journalists, owners and managers, and finally the audience – the network of interdependencies is complex and multi-layered. Let us simply add that, notwithstanding strong cross-national differences, the analysis of political journalism is always improved by the additional consideration of its relationship with actors from the cultural and intellectual milieux. This would include references to 'think-tanks' in the UK and USA and the fascination for the status of 'intellectuals' among the elite of French political journalists.

Spin, sources and the microcosm of the journalists' world

The differences in the four chapters in Part I of the book are the product first of all of the countries (Britain, Italy and Thailand) and the special-isation (for example, the pack of EU reporters in Brussels) selected by each author. In addition, these four chapters can also be read in terms of the operationalisation of different research strategies, since each focuses on a different dimension of the interdependencies suggested above.

Kuhn's case-study (Chapter 3) specifically highlights the debate on the alleged growing influence of spin-doctors. His contribution shows the

reality of this trend, highly visible in New Labour's obsession with controlling the media agenda. However, Kuhn also initiates a critical discussion as
a contribution to the British debate on 'primary definers'. Primary definers
undoubtedly exist. However, the status of primary definer clearly appears
in this account as the unstable result of changing power balances, not as
a firmly institutionalised structural reality. Complete control of the agenda
and of the framing of events and issues is clearly no more than a spin-
doctor's dream. In addition to this analysis, Kuhn's chapter is also an
invitation to make sense of the claims and criticisms about the discourse
and power of spin. McNair has previously suggested an interesting
explanation: what he calls the 'demonisation' of spin could be interpreted
as journalists' nostalgia for an imaginary golden age of politics (McNair
2000). Kuhn proposes another reading: denunciation of the spin-doctor
may also be an easy and 'cheap' way for journalists to claim their autonomy
in this particular interdependent relationship. We might further suggest
that such an interpretation could also apply to the academic criticism of
spin-doctoring. One of the strongest resources of communicators and spin-
doctors is to create a belief in the power of communication. The flow of
electoral comments explaining landslides and defeats by the quality or the
weakness of communication strategies – as if voters no longer judged
policies or programmes in making their choices and as if sociological
explanations no longer mattered – is a clear expression of this 'com-
municational' reduction of politics. The theoretical question is clear: do not
academics subscribe to the myth of the all-powerful spin-doctors by the
very excess of influence that they award them? A second important contribution from Kuhn's chapter comes from its attention to the complexity of
the network of influence inside newsrooms and media companies. Political
journalists do not work in a simple face-to-face relationship with politicians.
They must always pay attention, as evidenced by the changes in the
political commitment of *The Sun*, to pressure from proprietors and editors.
The quest for larger audiences and changes inside the newsroom also open
the door to greater pluralism within each newspaper and to more interpretative styles of journalism, clearly visible in the success and prestige of
political columnists.

Based on a study of Italian political journalists during the whirlpool of
changes that have shaken Italian politics in recent years, the particularity of
Roncarolo's contribution (Chapter 4) is its focus on the strategic importance
of political systems on journalism. Roncarolo mobilises two complementary
analytic frameworks: first, that proposed by Blumler and Gurevitch (1995)
for comparing national structures of interdependencies between the state
and politicians on the one hand and the media on the other, and second
Lijphart's (1984) distinction between consociational and majoritarian democracies. The strength of this case-study is to highlight how the relationship
between politicians and journalists is deeply structured by institutional
systems and traditions. Far from being a vague cliché, the notion of

structural crisis is wholly appropriate in this case. The consociational model which characterised the Italian 'first republic' usually combines two logics of political communication. The first is public and conflictual: political journalists behave as supporters of parties and parliamentary cliques. The second is almost silent: major political debates remain locked in insider discussions, managed by whispered conversations in parliamentary lobbies and discreet negotiations in party headquarters. Direct public discussion on all the major political issues fits better with a system of majoritarian democracy. Here the strategy of 'going public' is perfectly adapted to the struggle between two political parties or coalitions. As Roncarolo shows, the basic problem of Italian journalists is to try to deal with an ongoing schizophrenic situation. The old consociational model has crumbled without completely collapsing. The move towards a majoritarian logic is slowed down by remnants of the old system. There remains a need to manage, far away from microphones and television cameras, the process of centrifugal multipartism. But the legacy of the previous model is also lasting control of the press and broadcasting by the state and political parties, symbolised by the two-headed leadership of Berlusconi as both prime minister and media mogul.

This exploration of the Italian crisis also deals with the importance of journalistic culture. Whether due to a real sense of partisanship or because they have had to make a virtue out of necessity, Italian journalists have always been sceptical of the objective style of political reporting. This tradition does not prevent the possibility of change. However, change seems to be driven from outside the newsrooms, for example by judges breaking the previous deferential relationship with politicians and by news anchors or hosts from the 'neo-television' inventing a more fashionable style of political coverage. The strangeness of some changes is also evident in the maintenance of elements of continuity. Shifting from supporters into critical 'crisis entrepreneurs' is a journalistic revolution in the Italian context. Yet it is a revolution which does not change the behaviour of journalists as actors integrated in the political game. Finally, Roncarolo's study highlights both in the political system and journalistic culture the contradictory influences of what Marx called 'the weight of dead generations' on the living.

McCargo's chapter (Chapter 5) is the only one which deals with a developing country. Based on a study of journalist–source relations, it emphasises the strength of an ethnographic approach to political reporting, as exemplified in the research of Padioleau (1985) and Pedelty (1995). Too often social scientists practise a strange division of work. An ethnographic approach and in-depth observation of the newsroom seem to belong to sociologists, while most political scientists focus on the contents, framing and impact of journalists' work. Of course, the division is not so clear cut in practice, but these trends do exist and do not help to combine the knowledge produced in different quarters of the research community. Accompanying Thai reporters in taxis, to press meetings, to restaurants and bars, McCargo allows the reader to understand how the web of these micro interactions can inform the nature of Thai political journalism. His investigation might seem picturesque or exotic to some readers when he describes the 'envelope culture' of bribes and even refers to meetings with MPs in massage parlours! Yet we would tentatively argue that such an 'exotic' approach might be usefully applied to European and North American journalism. The very particularity of Thai journalism, especially the direct (but debated) practices of corruption, could trigger a better understanding of its Western counterparts. The basic point here is not to promote investigations into the 'corruption' of Western journalism, but rather to suggest that the influence of public relations or spin-doctors is also based on similar principles of exchange as analysed by Mauss (1950). Western 'gifts' rarely take the form of bribes.[3] Instead, they consist of an off-the-record statement, a scoop, a free flight in a candidate's plane or time devoted to explaining the background to a decision. Yet these can give rise to a similar spiral of reciprocal exchange, whereby politicians and spin-doctors invite journalists to support them in their coverage or ask them not to engage in adversarial criticism.

Baisnée (Chapter 6) shares with McCargo the same ethnographic approach. His 'tribe' of journalists lives and works at the heart of Europe. Yet, in its daily routines and rituals – the *rendez-vous de midi* and the distribution of Himalayan piles of official reports and statements – the microcosm of the Brussels 'pack' of EU reporters looks strangely exotic. The first lesson of this study is probably to remind us that journalism is not only a job but also a milieu. And when journalists are isolated far away from their newsrooms, they need to re-invent and institutionalise such a milieu and create rituals to share news and experiences. Baisnée also questions the limits of the traditional dichotomy of partisan versus objective journalism. The old generation of French correspondents in Brussels consists of objective supporters of the European project. They offer an almost perfect illustration of what one might term the 'ambassador paradox'. As a result of a long-standing proximity to political actors and/or a commitment to the goals of the institutions that they cover, political journalists run the risk of shifting from being the eyes and ears of their newsroom to acting as the loudspeaker of 'their' political institutions. Watching the Brussels pack operate leads to other central questions. The first is the challenge of the rise of powerful supranational institutions and actors for political journalists. How can they make sense of the EU for their national audiences? By behaving as the deferential heralds of European construction? By 'translating' European issues into mere domestic political debates? And, if neither of these alternatives is desirable, how can journalists explain the internal functioning of a new kind of political entity whose powers are much more important than those suggested by run-of-the-mill reports on safety regulations concerning French cheeses. The last substantial question explored by Baisnée concerns the conditions of change in professional practices. The case-study on the small revolution of investigative reporting among some French journalists clearly shows how and why a close look at the struggles between generations of journalists as representatives of different roles (and media) is essential to explain changes triggered from inside the world of journalism.

It would be pointless to invent a hidden and harmonious coherence between these four chapters. However, three concluding remarks on the chapters in Part I of the book are pertinent. First, they all subscribe to a common approach inasmuch as they suggest the weakness of a linear model of political communication in which spin-doctors package politicians' speeches which are then processed by the gate-keeping activities of journalists and then distributed to audiences. The very complexity of the processes requires a structural and relational approach. Second, most of the chapters reveal that political journalists pay more attention to politics than to policies, even though policies have probably much more practical effects on ordinary citizens. Finally, each case-study makes highly visible the speed and magnitude of the current changes in journalistic practices in varied national and institutional settings, and thus reinforces the need to develop comparative fieldwork.

The age of cynicism or of a media-driven renewal of democracy?

The second and third parts of this book deal with two complementary questions. The first concerns the much debated question of a 'cynical' and adversarial coverage of politics, allegedly evidenced by increasing media attention to scandals. This debate is directly linked to another: are current changes in political journalism an opportunity for, or a threat to, the healthy functioning of representative democracy?

A critical orthodoxy and its critics

Most of the academic research on journalism since the 1960s has emphasised the potentially negative effects of its coverage of politics (Norris 2000). This vision could be expressed in a kind of 'lexicon of threats'. This phrase suggests that many findings and interpretations could be incorporated into a small dictionary whose keywords would include 'adversarial reporting', 'affairs', 'cynicism', 'dumbing-down', 'infotainment', 'newszak', 'populism', 'sleaze' and 'tabloidisation'. The basic findings of this body of research are clearly suggested by Brants and van Kempen in Chapter 9. These can be summarised in four key statements:

1   Faced with more professional and expert sources, journalists tend to react to the threat of manipulation through a more adversarial style of reporting, in which they take pleasure in unmasking staged photo-opportunities and media events.

2   Coverage of politics gives more and more space to the private lives of politicians and to horse-race aspects of political debate, while policies and fundamental issues are pushed to the margins of the media agenda.

3   These trends have been strongly amplified by an increase in commercial pressures. These encourage 'market-driven journalism' which uses shorter formats, values 'soft' news and is more oriented towards audience maximisation than coverage of issues, since the latter are considered dull whatever their substantive importance.

4   All these changes combine to produce a cynical and disparaging coverage of politics, which fuels voter apathy and mistrust. Giving priority to entertainment over enlightenment, this type of journalism cannot help produce an informed and active citizenship.

Being – as researchers – certainly closer to academics such as Franklin or Gans than convinced by their recent opponents, we might be suspected in our editorial role of adopting an overly sympathetic view to the approaches mentioned here. However, we would argue that this research – much more contradictory and less orthodox than it is from now on fashionable to suggest – has brought into the scientific debate a rich harvest of results and empirical studies and a stimulating body of questions both for researchers and citizens. These results can and must be critically examined. The existence of analytical shortcuts between levels of analysis (for example, the best study on framing or bias in news coverage is not sufficient to allow one to draw conclusions about its reception by audiences) and the presence of one-sided approaches to journalism and media do exist in the mainstream literature of the 1970s and 1980s. But we doubt that the one-sided reduction of this complex literature into the mourning of naive believers in a golden age of journalism is the proper way to fight its alleged one-sidedness.

Early in the 1980s, specialists in cultural studies started a paradigmatic revolution. Reacting to a vision of the almighty producers and broadcasters of media messages, authors such as Ang (1985), Morley (1992) and Katz and Liebes (1993) highlighted on the basis of empirical studies the ability of audiences to misinterpret, re-code and negotiate the meaning of cultural products. This debate has sometimes skidded through a methodological populism and campus radicalism, as in Fiske's vision of the unending interpretative victories of popular audiences watching and subversively decoding every soap programme or advertising message. Yet it did bring some fresh air in research and guided the writing of highly stimulating books.

Political communication seems to have undergone a comparable shift. Brants was among the first to argue publicly against the idea of a 'crisis of public communication' as heralded by Blumler and Gurevitch. Then came McNair and Norris. And as a chapter by McNair is included in this book (Chapter 10), there is no need for us to summarise the new basics. His contribution offers a fresh and wide-ranging update of the rising counter-critical paradigm. McNair shakes some clichés and interpretative routines. He shows convincingly that, without being 'hyperadversarial', journalists are among the only actors able to question leaders deprived of the shield of their spin-doctors. His analysis clearly illustrates how the access given to ordinary citizens by the media creates situations of dialogue where politicians are condemned to abandon pre-prepared lines and where they have to answer questions linked to the daily experience of citizens. The strength of McNair's criticism comes basically from its ability to bring into full light the hidden presuppositions of some supporters of the 'critical paradigm'.

Weber used to describe a good scientific work as one which asks 'un-pleasant questions'. And McNair is not afraid to ask them. Are all critical interpretations based on strong data? Is the Enlightenment legacy the one and only possible way to understand contemporary political debate? Does any effort to adapt political debate to the interests of ordinary citizens and to give them media access threaten the ideal of democracy? Is it possible to argue that the only effect of commercial logic is the trivialisation of political news? All these questions are legitimate and stimulating. However, we shall suggest in our conclusions that they can also trigger other 'unpleasant questions'!

Call the witnesses!

The five contributors to Parts II and III of the book will not close the raging debate on political journalism and democracy. They will, however, make an input. Two of them highlight the importance assumed by scandal as a major press and media template in political information. Tiffen (Chapter 7) develops an in-depth study of a scandal involving two leading Australian radio journalists. He builds an interpretative framework explaining the rise of scandals in terms of three elements. First, the scandalous behaviour must be criticised in a central social forum which favours disclosure; second, the expansion of scandal is fuelled by a constellation of conflicts – in this case among journalists themselves, and between journalists and politicians and journalists and lobbies – which creates a process of escalation; finally, the nature of the scandalous facts must conform to criteria of newsworthiness.

Tiffen's attention to the details of the broadcasting scandal allows us to understand the complexity of the moves as if they are taking place in a slow-motion replay. His description never falls into the 'heroic illusion' of transforming journalists into fearless muckrakers, alone fighting for virtue. Against media-centric biases, Tiffen sees journalism as linked to multiple social fields. As Schudson showed in the case of Watergate, the scandal is always a nexus of relationships. It can take off only if it can mobilise clusters of actors and institutions interested in its development. The absence of a happy ending in the Laws–Jones scandals is also rich in questions. The careers of the two 'villains' were not significantly affected by the scandal. Far beyond this Australian case, such impunity questions the collective mechanisms of responsibility and ethics regulation of a profession whose members often behave as paradigmatic illustrations of the Beckerian moral entrepreneur. Which power will balance fairly that of the fourth estate?

The chapter by Pujas (Chapter 8) shares with Tiffen's the same interest in the development of scandals as an increasingly common and essential media template. Pujas' analytic strategy, however, is rather different. Her chapter is the only one in this book to develop a cross-national comparative analysis (France, Italy and Spain). While Tiffen's research focuses on the life-cycle of a scandal, Pujas is more interested in understanding its crystal-lisation. Why can similar events – the contamination of haemophiliacs by tainted blood – trigger a major political scandal in France yet fail to make the headlines in Spain? Pujas' inquiry identifies some significant differences. In France the victims of the scandal were organised and proactive on the judicial front, whilst the Spanish haemophiliacs were poorly organised and even suffered from a social stigma as many of them were gypsies. In addition, the management of blood and hemo-derived products in France was much more under the control of a state-operated institution than in Spain, a situation which opened up opportunities for politicising what was at stake. Yet another major difference was the behaviour of some major French daily newspapers and news magazines, which acted as advocates for the victims, whilst the prestigious *El País* never paid much attention to the problem of tainted blood in Spain. The silence of the most powerful and prestigious dailies and of other media blocked the chain reaction which usually develops from the centre of the journalistic field as soon as a major event hits the headlines.

Beyond this case-study, Pujas emphasises how scandals take off (or not) in the interactions both within and between three major social arenas. Journalism is, of course, one of those arenas where competing conceptions of political news – explainable in terms of political sympathies, commercial pressures or the rise of investigative reporting as opposed to a more deferential tradition – create opportunities for more critical coverage. Judges and courts – especially in countries where they have long been prisoners of a straitjacket of political control – are a second strategic actor. But Pujas also argues that one should not underrate the importance of cross-denunciations of dishonest behaviour among politicians themselves, since in a context of widespread mistrust of politicians, morality becomes a central resource in the (re)construction of their public images.

The chapter by Brants and van Kempen (Chapter 9) directly challenges the critical approach. The authors offer a clear reminder of its origins and main points, which they summarise in the 'spiral of cynicism thesis'. The adversarial and cynical coverage of politics amplifies an existing trend of disenchantment and mistrust which in turn leads to more cynical coverage. This Dutch case-study invites the reader to think in comparative terms.

The process of depillarisation of Dutch society and its media, followed by increased competition between less politically committed media, has similarities with the Italian situation studied by Roncarolo. The Netherlands confirms the Italian experience: the structuring of the relationship between political and media institutions is a key variable for understanding political journalism.

Yet the nexus of the debate here is also the linkage between the observation of a critical or cynical coverage of politics and the claim that this framing of politics triggers mistrust of politicians among citizens as voters. The patterns of coverage of recent Dutch elections reveal that the critical thesis has a real empirical basis. Issue-oriented news does decline while the amount of horse-race and 'hoopla' news increases. An emphasis on conflicts between and inside parties is also a central frame of the campaign coverage. Data analysis even suggests a correlation between media exposure and cynicism among the viewers of the network RTL4. So, does the misfortune of Dutch politicians exemplify the validity of the critical approach? The subtle analysis of media programming and statistical data by Brants and van Kempen offers a quite different conclusion. Changes in the style of coverage of political news does not hide the lasting weight of a journalistic tradition influenced by public service values. Dutch political journalists are more ironic than cynical and citizen trust in Dutch politicians has generally improved in the mid-1990s. Moreover, if the audience of RTL4 is more cynical than the average, the causal explanation does not derive principally from media consumption. Instead, it would appear that the viewers of this channel have a more cynical view of politics because they are less well educated. As our Dutch colleagues suggest in Chapter 9: 'It does not seem to matter what the news is about, but rather who watches what.' Education, generation and commitment to government parties are more important variables than media consumption. In short, the Netherlands does not support the thesis regarding the negative impact of political journalism on voter attitudes.

In their rich overview of American 'public journalism', Glasser and Lee (Chapter 11) examine another aspect of the debate on journalism and democracy. The shift can be simply expressed. The contributions by McNair and Brants/van Kempen demonstrate a concern to evaluate the civic impact of journalism. In contrast, Glasser and Lee are studying journalists whose reflexive attitude and overt goal are precisely how to improve democracy as a form and as a forum, and how to behave as a 'civic catalyst'. The chapter by Glasser and Lee is not a supporters' text. In fact, their conclusions clearly show the blind spots and intellectual weaknesses of 'civic journalism'. For instance, the emphasis put on 'community' by the practitioners of 'civic journalism' could be ambiguous. It may boost debate and problem-solving, but leaves unresolved the fate of outsiders and minorities when civic commitment is reduced to the invocation that 'everyone needs to pull in the same direction'. In short, 'civic journalism' is neither a panacea nor a magic wand for all the alleged ills of contemporary political journalism.

Yet one could also read their reflections as identifying a set of basic conditions or prerequisites for any substantial renewal of political journalism. One might mention in this context the process of redefinition of authoritative sources, the complete restructuring of specialisations and co-operation between newsbeats, the attention given to the lives of 'ordinary people' and the belief that 'conversation' more than 'dissertation' can trigger the participation of lay people in civic fora. American 'civic journalism' is based on a specific and debatable combination of these ingredients. However, they are also visible in many innovative experiences of political journalism in Europe.

How can we assess these contributions to the impassioned debate on journalism and democracy? Obviously, none of these studies lends support to the most radical expressions of the critical approach. This is quite clear in the case of McNair's contribution. Brants and van Kempen directly criticise the key assumption concerning media influence on political cynicism; and in her conclusion Pujas clearly articulates the view that the mobilisation of journalists in the denunciation of scandals can be regarded as more a contribution to a healthy system of checks and balances than a trivialisation of political debate. The Australian case developed by Tiffen can also be considered as an illustration of the (limited) power of control and criticism by journalists.

Should we conclude that the theoretical battle is won without serious resistance and that a paradigmatic shift is taking place? Such an interpretation would be precocious. The Dutch case invites caution concerning the impact of political journalism. It also shows that changes towards a more cynical, less issue-oriented coverage are taking place. At the same time, Tiffen and Pujas show that scandal is becoming an accepted format for the construction of narratives of political developments. The experience of 'civic journalism' clearly illustrates the will of some political journalists to invent new styles of political reporting.

Our own editorial interpretation of these contributions would be to reject any academic trench war, which reduces the debate to a repeat of Eco's great divide between the optimistic and the apocalyptic. Inventing a 'critical bloc' where Neil Postman, James Fallows and Jay Blumler are supposed to walk hand in hand is as simplistic as the reduction process of McNair and Norris from provocative questioning into a naive support for a panglossian democracy. As Neveu (2001: Chapter 6) suggests, the basic data of the current changes and crisis in the network of interdependencies explored in this book support the opening of windows of renewal for political journalism. The concept of 'windows of opportunity' could be borrowed to understand, like Glasser with civic journalism, how innovative formats of journalism appear in a changing balance of power and to perceive their limits. But the notion of 'windows of threat' may be useful too, in exploring situations where the changes are lived as constraints, as the compulsory submission to a market-driven journalism. The most difficult theoretical challenge for researchers is to make sense of the variety and contradictory trends in contemporary political journalism.

Research perspectives

Thinking political journalism 'globally'

Globalisation may have become a fashionable and overused concept. Nonetheless, we would argue that one of the most promising avenues for journalism studies is to 'globalise' its approach. Different levels of meaning can be attributed to this proposal. The first is closest to the dominant usage of 'global' and 'globalisation', where these terms are used as a shorthand to refer to the growing interconnection of economies, the transnationalisation of decision-making processes and the world-wide circulation of cultural goods, including news. In the realm of journalism these changes suppose three kinds of investigation. The first would explore – as Baisnée does in this book – how political (or other) journalists deal with the coverage of new institutions and fora of decision-making such as the European Union (EU) and the World Trade Organisation (WTO), as well as new movements such as the anti-globalisation protestors. Globalisation also invites us to investigate how the press and media invent new channels, new titles adapted to the emergence of a new political geography of transnational or diasporic audiences (Marchetti 2002). What does the 'Euro' of 'Euronews' signify? What framing of the relationship between business and politics does the *Financial Times* offer its international readership? Why did *The European* and the French news magazine *L'Européen* in the end fail to find a readership? Investigating global journalism also requires us to pay attention to the world and world-regional economics of press and media companies and to its impact on journalism.

Thinking political journalism globally can also be seen as a methodological and scientific strategy. Highly visible in the current multiplication of specialised journals which are both fora and prisons for micro-communities of specialists, one of the most worrying trends of contemporary social sciences is hyper-specialisation. This process creates the conditions for an increasingly in-depth knowledge of more and more dimensions of social life. Its costly consequence, however, is the Balkanisation of academia and an insufficient cross-fertilisation between researches whose confrontation could be highly productive. Specialists in cultural studies have their own journals and conferences, as do analysts of political communication. The two tribes do not mix that much. Sociologists who study journalism may have more affinities with sociologists of organisations or professions than with political scientists or scholars in media studies. The inflation of specialised micro-communities with their self-referential logic works like a tariff barrier to the circulation of theories. It leads to an endless re-invention of the wheel when a sub-field of research undergoes a paradigmatic shift already developed in the neighbouring provinces of academia.

If this diagnosis is correct, it suggests two research choices. The first concerns methods. The study of political journalism does not have to choose between the ethnography of the newsroom, the statistical analysis of news content or the role of journalists as narrative-makers. It should be more attentive to selecting among a broader range of methods, according to its questions and objects, and to combining rather than hierarchising its tools of investigation. It should also declare war on all the hidden academic protectionisms and frontier posts. This imperative should be evident inside the small world of academics studying journalism: how can we make sense of the changes in political journalism without mobilising the research on the new economics of media companies and without reading case-studies on the shifts in the balance of power between newsbeats and news sections?

Far beyond this first academic free trade, moreover, we need to cross borders and to buy 'abroad' concepts and data which enable us to highlight political journalism. Cultural studies have much to teach us about the reception of cultural goods. The enormous American literature on the rise and fall of 'social problems' can improve our knowledge of agenda building. Linguistics and semiotics could help us to explore press and media narratives. Far from working on another planet, the sociologists who study talk shows or entertainment media programmes can help us to understand the functioning of the most serious political news when they suggest what must be shown 'inside prime time'.

A last look at the current debate concerning the pro and cons of the 'critical paradigm' might help us to express more precisely what is at stake in this globalising approach. Putting aside for a few moments our editors' hats for those of simple researchers, we would agree that the new trend of 'counter-critical' research invites us to revisit research results and to explore new questions as the 'reception turn' in cultural studies did twenty years ago. But this comparison also allows us to make sense of the idea of the globalisation of methods and research. To express it perhaps too sharply, the real debate with the supporters of the idea of a democratic or virtuous action of the press or media should probably focus at least as much on what they do not speak of as on key elements of their analysis.

The 'Balkanisation' effect is visible here. How? Basically in an asymmetry. On the one hand, the challengers of the alleged 'critical orthodoxy' mobilise very rich data on questions such as the structure and categorisation of political information supply. They use sophisticated data treatment methods to understand from polls or Eurobarometers how this political information may influence (or not) global and specific audiences. On the other hand, the new trend does not seem to pay enough attention to significant results of the research on media developed since the 1980s. Which ones? First, there is the enormous and rich literature on reception produced by cultural studies. This lack of interest appears quite surprising as cultural studies have both directly investigated the question of what audiences are making out of messages and experimented with qualitative investigations (ethnography, focus groups) which are much subtler and inventive than the usual polls data. Second, the new trend of research appears to be basically interested in political news as data, as reports of politics which could be classified into categories (policies, horse race, interpretative reporting), capable of being measured according to positive or negative criteria. Let us state again that this methodological choice produces results which are worth debating. But the cost is also to consider many dimensions of the process of production of political news (in the newsroom, with other sources than politicians and spin-doctors) as black boxes, which remain closed. Nor does it use to a significant extent the rich legacy of studies about priming and framing effects (for example, Gamson and Modigliani 1989; Iyengar and Kinder 1987). It also considers the very different degrees of interest in politics among citizens more as a given than as something to explain sociologically (Bourdieu 1979; Eliasoph 1998).

The risk of such a selective mobilisation of data, methods and research results is nothing less than a transformation of exciting and challenging questions into a simple re-invention of the old 'uses and gratifications' research[4]. Putting our editors' hats back on, we would add to be fair that the difficulty of bridging an enormous variety of data, methods and research fields is visible in all quarters of academia. The challengers of the 'critical' tradition are absolutely convincing when they criticise a symmetric asymmetry: much more 'critical' literature has been dedicated to theorising the existence of the process of framing, cultivation or indexation by powerful sources than to demonstrating empirically the reality of their impact on citizens.

A plea for comparative research

Apart from the chapter by Pujas, the various contributors to this book have not directly undertaken comparative research. They have tried, however, to suggest connections between chapters and to look for yardsticks able to help comparisons between case-studies and countries. In their illuminating text on 'the extending frontier' of comparative research, Blumler and Gurevitch (1995: Chapter 6) have developed the most essential arguments to support the comparative project. As the new impulse of journalism studies substantially enriches the stock of data and case-studies available for researchers, the very increase in our knowledge is an invitation to compare.

Comparison clearly appears in this collection of chapters as a powerful key. It can first of all prevent the risks of naive generalisations or of a mere mosaic of case-studies without cumulative output. Through its focus on differences, comparison is able to direct attention to variables which are often unseen because they are too visible, as Pujas suggests when showing that the evident 'scandal' of the tainted blood requires more in-depth explanations when one discovers that the same tragic facts produced absolutely different press coverage in Spain and France.

A comparative approach is also the only way to overcome a theoretical gap in furthering a global theory on the production, framing, reception and uses of political news. The stakes are clearly visible in the chapters from the first part of this book. The dynamics of research offer from now on efficient tools to progress in this direction. Here again, as illustrated by Roncarolo's contribution, Blumler and Gurevitch offer a stimulating analytical framework. We should also mention the possible contribution of Bourdieu's field theory (Benson 1998) when it invites us to understand in each country the peculiar anatomy of the relationships between the economic, cultural, political and journalistic fields. Changes in the power balance inside and among these structured social spaces constantly reshape the context of journalistic activities. We might add that comparative research is finally an invitation to connect sociological approach and history. The work in progress of Hallin and Mancini (forthcoming) promises to offer researchers a fresh analytical framework which will emphasise the importance of a long-term historical approach and face up to the all too visible limits of the old-fashioned typologies of 'liberal' and 'Soviet' models.

In conclusion, let us freely admit that the project to bridge sub-fields of research, to fuse methods and to range across disciplinary borders is hugely ambitious. It is even probably beyond the reach of any single researcher. The same doubts can be expressed concerning comparative research. If comparison is not a flag of convenience masking some hasty data retrieved from the internet, its practice requires more than simple linguistic ability, but also the understanding of cultures and histories. These difficulties should not, however, push researchers into taking refuge in the routine of 'research business as usual'. They suggest a stimulating challenge: the growing need for collective research, boosting the development of new routes of theoretical import–export between social sciences. The memory of our Copenhagen workshop, which was a small-scale attempt to advance in some of these directions, is evidence that the challenge of interdisciplinary and cross-national confrontation can produce fascinating research results. We hope that whatever its imperfections this book demonstrates this.

Notes

1 Conversely the contributions of Esser (1999) on the notion of 'tabloidisation' and of Brants (1998) on 'infotainment' provide useful examples of studies which try to give an objective meaning to such concepts.
2 With the exception of the chapter written by Ted Glasser and Francis Lee, all the contributions to this book emerged from a workshop on the topic of political journalism which took place during the 28th joint sessions of the European Consortium for Political Research at the University of Copenhagen in April 2000.
3 Fallows (1996), however, shows that the incredible wages offered to some media

pundits and stars for giving public lectures in the USA may work as a kind of 'soft corruption', opening up opportunities for sources to exert influence.
4 A devastating criticism of this naively functionalist approach is to be found in Beaud (1984: Chapter 5)

References

Ang, I. (1985) *Watching Dallas*, London: Methuen.
Beaud, P. (1984) *La société de connivence*, Paris: Aubier.
Benson, R. (1998) 'Field theory in comparative context: a new paradigm for media studies', *Theory and Society* 28: 463–98.
Blumler, J.G. and Gurevitch, M. (1995) *The Crisis of Public Communication*, London: Routledge.
Bourdieu, P (1979) *La distinction*, Paris: Minuit.
Bourdieu, P. and Passeron, J.C. (1964) *Les Héritiers. Les Etudiants et la culture*, Paris: Minuit.
Brants, K. (1998) 'Who's afraid of infotainment?', *European Journal of Communication* 13/3: 315–35.
Chalaby, J. (1998) *The Invention of Journalism*, Basingstoke: Macmillan.
Eliasoph, N. (1998) *Avoiding Politics*, Cambridge: Cambridge University Press.
Entman, R. (1989) *Democracy without citizens. Media and the decay of American politics*, Oxford: Oxford University Press.
Esser, F. (1999) 'Tabloidisation of news. A comparative analysis of anglo-american and German press journalism', *European Journal of Communication* 14/3: 291–324.
Fallows, J. (1996) *Breaking the News. How the Media Undermine American Democracy*, New York: Vintage.
Gamson, W. and Modigliani, A. (1989) 'Media discourse and public opinion on nuclear power: a constructionist approach', *American Journal of Sociology* 95: 1–37.
Hallin, D. and Mancini, P. (forthcoming) *Media and Political Systems in Western Europe and North America; A Framework for Comparative Analysis*.
Iyengar, S. and Kinder, D. (1987) *News that Matters: Television and American Opinion*, Chicago: University of Chicago Press.
Katz, E. and Liebes, T. (1993) *The Export of Meaning. Cross Cultural Readings of Dallas*, London: Polity Press.
Lacroix, B. (1984) 'Ordre politique et ordre social', in M. Grawitz and J. Leca (eds) *Traité de Science politique*, vol 1, Paris: PUF.
Lijphart, A. (1984) *Democracies: Patterns of Majoritarian and Consensus Government in Twenty-one Countries*, New Haven: Yale University Press.
McNair, B. (2000) *Journalism and Democracy*, London: Routledge.
Marchetti, D. (2002) *Signifier L'Europe*, Rennes: PUR.
Mauss, M. (1950) *Sociologie et Anthropologie*, Paris: PUF.
Morley, D. (1992) *Television Audiences and Cultural Studies*, London: Routledge.
Negrine, R. (1996) *The Communication of Politics*, London: Sage.
Neveu, E. (2001) *Sociologie du journalisme*, Paris: La découverte.
Norris, P. (2000) *A Virtuous Circle. Political Communication in Post-Industrial Societies*, Cambridge: Cambridge University Press.
Padioleau, J.G. (1985) *Le 'Monde' et le 'Washington Post': précepteurs et mousquetaires*, Paris: PUF.
Pedelty, M. (1995) *War Stories*, London: Routledge.
Schlesinger, P. (1990) 'Rethinking the sociology of journalism: source strategies and the limits of media-centrism', in M. Ferguson (ed.) *Public Communication: The New Imperatives*, London: Sage.
Tunstall, J. (1971) *Journalists at Work*, London: Constable.

2 Four generations of political journalism

Erik Neveu

This chapter explores questions which are simple to express but complex to analyse. What is political journalism? How has it changed, especially since the 1960s? The chapter is divided into three sections which together seek to capture the changes in the networks of interdependencies which structure journalistic practice. The first section identifies the peculiarities and structural constraints of political journalism, so as to understand its basic logic, while the second and third sections describe ideal-types of 'generations' of political journalism.

For social scientists, the concept of generation usually refers to groups defined by both their age and the impact during their youth of a shared and powerful experience, such as war or crisis. By this traditional definition the concept can highlight changes in journalism, as Rieffel (1984) has convincingly shown in his study of contemporary French journalism. However, the use of the concept suggested in this chapter is rather different and probably less orthodox. The emphasis is no longer on the idea of a coherent age group, nor on a socialisation process shaped by the same events, as in the case of the 'generation' of New Journalism in the United States. What forms the 'generation' in this study is the common challenge that political journalists – old or new – must face every time that major changes result in new configurations of interdependencies between these journalists, on the one hand, and politicians, media companies, audiences and other actors in political communication, on the other. The great shifts in this complex web of relationships have triggered the rise of new repertoires of professional practices and of new 'generations' of political journalists. The second section outlines three of these ideal-type generations, from the 'publicist' of the early nineteenth century to the 'critical expert' of the 1960s. The third section examines in speculative fashion the possible rise of a fourth generation in recent years.

Since the empirical material in this chapter is drawn mainly from the cases of France, the United Kingdom and the United States, one of the risks of such an overview might be to lay oneself open to the charge of being too hasty in making wide-sweeping generalisations about political journalism. At one level the analysis developed here puts forward the principal trends visible in major Western democracies. However, it should also be read as an invitation to develop comparative research, which is the only way to identify both national peculiarities of current global changes and the underlying causes of such differences.

The peculiarities of political journalism

Three features of political journalism

Although different countries exhibit national variations, the particularity of Western political journalism may be identified in terms of three features. First, political journalism can be considered as enjoying a 'noble' status in the field. In the hierarchies of functions and newsbeats which structure the journalistic field, and especially in the press and media dedicated to general news, political journalists usually occupy leading positions. There are many reasons for this prominent status. Some are rooted in history. As Habermas (1976) shows, in numerous countries freedom of speech and political democracy have been won thanks to a substantial contribution from a politically oriented press. Broddason (1994) suggests the existence of a 'sacred side of journalism'. Parodying Bagehot, one might add that political journalism is the most 'sacred part' of journalism, since it speaks of power and makes sense of an activity which is considered capable of radically changing society. As Blumler and Gurevitch (1995) emphasise, political journalists often mobilise such references to sacrosanctity and develop a 'sacerdotal' vision of their activity when they invoke notions such as democracy, popular will, opinion and the 'right-to-know'. Edwy Plenel (1996), editor-in-chief of *Le Monde*, expresses such a belief when he writes: 'What political and intellectual powers have been constantly unable to admit is that it is the role of journalism to be an element of democratic conflict, a symbol of democratic responsibility, which cannot be identified with state responsibility. As citizens, to know and act in full conscience we need news which upsets the apple cart and those bringers of bad news which force us to think.' The prestige of the political newsbeat also contributes to the transformation of this specialisation into a fast track towards power in the newsroom. This dominant position is also visible in the process of 'promotion' of news. As soon as the raw material of news focuses on the public debate, it is caught in a process of transfer whereby it is taken from the hands of specialised journalists and is placed into those of political journalists who exercise a first right of refusal on the hottest news.

A second peculiarity of political journalism concerns the acuteness of the problems of transmission and intelligibility of the news that it has to deal with. Other specialisms (such as scientific and economic news) confront similar challenges. At least three reasons suggest that this difficulty is at its highest level for political coverage. First, the direct experience of political activities (especially elections) is more transient than the permanent experience of social roles such as consumer, television viewer or sports fan. Second, one of the most basic conclusions of research on political participation suggests that a majority of citizens do not pay much attention to politics (Gaxie 1978; Eliasoph 1998). The nature of institutional rules, the vocabulary of politics and the political significance of the differences between parties and candidates often remain blurred or mysterious for many citizens. Finally, there are the problems derived from the continuous process of professionalisation of political activities which locks practitioners into their 'small world' and reinforces the institutionalisation of politics, giving pride of place to esoteric 'insider' games above issues which have a stronger social claim for consideration (Bourdieu 2000). These factors strengthen the public perception of political news as often being indecipherable or boring, evidenced by the lack of audience interest in programmes with a political content on radio and television (Le Grignou and Neveu 1988). This situation poses a fundamental educational challenge for political journalism – a challenge which is not made any simpler by the nature of the relationship between journalists and their sources.

Third, the intensity and regularity of interactions between politicians and journalists, sharing the same timetables, agendas and space (party conventions, parliamentary sessions, buses and planes during campaigns), create an intimate relationship which has few equivalents, apart from the case of sports reporters. This situation induces a powerful integration of political journalists into a world that Linsky (1983: 6) depicts as a 'family' of 'political junkies' speaking in codes that only 'the politicians, their team, the consultants and political journalists can completely decipher'. In his study of parliamentary journalism in Quebec, Charron (1994) expresses this metaphorically in terms of an incestuous relationship or of the bond between nurse and patient. Such a situation exacerbates the problems created by the esoteric nature of politics. The peculiarity of political journalism is also linked to the nature of the competitor-colleague relationship between politicians and journalists.[1] The history of political journalism can be interpreted as an escape from a situation of journalists as supporters, rather early on in the case of the USA, later in that of France or Italy. Yet even the trend towards a real emancipation from party connections does not eliminate the structural ambiguity of political journalism. The temptation to behave like a political actor and to develop a normative discourse on politics can take subtler forms than visible political commitment, as the constant attempts by many journalists to behave like referees or pundits of the 'modern', 'moral' or 'serious' ways to practise politics shows.

The invariants of political journalism

The peculiarities of political journalism also suggest a framework of constraints in which journalists are caught. The interdependencies which structure it can profoundly change over time and space. However, the basic data remain. Three challenges, which are linked to the three peculiarities highlighted above, define the framework of political journalisms.

The first challenge is autonomy. In its simplest form, this refers to the choice between distance and political commitment. Autonomy, however, suggests many more questions. How can it be preserved in the face of the professionalisation of sources and the activities of spin-doctors with their ability to create media events and to anticipate journalists' practices and media templates? How can journalists resist the political linkages sometimes visible in the strategies of media companies (for example, Hersant in France, Murdoch in the UK and Berlusconi in Italy)? Even the most adversarial styles of reporting have to face up to this challenge: when they function as critics of politicians in the name of ideals such as democracy, morality or the struggle against populism, journalists can become independent political entrepreneurs and fully integrated actors in the political game through their capacity to bring about priming effects (Iyengar and Kinder 1987). The criticisms developed by political journalists against politicians can also be mobilised by political 'outsiders', such as Ross Perot in the USA or those politicians who claim to speak in the name of 'civil society' in France and Italy.

A second challenge concerns the blurred notion of the 'democratic role' of the press and media (Le Bohec 1997), its 'demopedic' function.[2] Schudson (1995) highlights the contradictory imperatives linked to the contribution of political journalism to democracy. Journalists are not only invited to act as public watchdogs in the face of rulers and to provide objective information, but also to make sense of politics and of the problems encountered by various social groups – to interpret politics by leaving out objectivity! Journalists must also give complete information, pay attention to the desires of different audiences and so take the risk of being accused both of being boring and of trivialising politics.

This ambiguity can be summarised in three basic questions. First, to whom will journalists speak about politics? To a universal and abstract audience of 'citizens' or to those sufficiently concerned with politics to understand its stakes and rituals? Second, how should journalists speak about politics? By taking for granted a certain degree of knowledge of this social field or by paying attention to the huge differences in the degrees of familiarity with and interest in politics? And if the latter, should they minimise the complexity of news coverage or try to improve the ability of the audience as receivers? Depending on the answers given to these first two questions, how should they then define the nature of the news which is allocated to a political news section? Should journalists focus on statements made by politicians and parties? Should they value less esoteric dimensions such as impressive characters or human interest stories? Should they value a kind of 'downstream' look at politics by covering the impact of policies and political choices on the everyday lives of citizens? The answers to these questions depend strongly on a network of interdependencies involving the market strategies of media companies, professional journalistic cultures and political structures and behaviour.

The answers to these first two sets of questions are themselves inseparable from a third factor: the situation of the political journalist on the newsdesk and in media organisations. Are political journalists the aristocracy of the newsroom? In competition with other news sections, do they have the power to exert a monopoly hold on a problem as soon as it comes on to the political agenda? Can they then frame it as a struggle between parties or candidates? Or do they have to bargain and share subjects and coverage with other specialist journalists? These questions are also linked to the power balance between commercial and managerial logic, on the one hand, and the imperative of news-gathering and news-processing on the other, analysed by Tunstall in terms of the dichotomy between 'media organisation' and 'news organisation' (1971: 25).

It is within this triangle of tensions and challenges – autonomy, 'demopedy' and position in the journalistic field – that the patterns and generations of political journalism have developed.

A tale of three generations

The aim of this section is to set out the analytic framework of the first three 'generations' of political journalism. Before doing so, we need to point out two limitations of this model. First, it conforms to the logic of the Weberian ideal-type as a 'utopian rationalisation', which substitutes stylised models for the complexity of reality. Our ideal-types of journalistic generations are not snapshots of the details of journalistic practices, but rather a tool to investigate them. Second, the notion of 'generation' does not refer to a rigid chronology. If generations follow one another, they also overlap. As their patterns and repertoires of professional practices are institutionalised, they may have a lasting influence, beyond a generational shift.

Political journalism before political journalism: the age of publicists

As Chalaby (1998) has shown in a seminal contribution – or Joana (1999) for the French case – to talk about political journalism before the middle of the nineteenth century would be a fallacy. The use of the press as an instrument of information and commentary on political activities was initially inseparable from political action itself. That is why, emulating Chalaby (1998: 9), we shall use the term 'publicist' to describe this proto-journalism. How does one define the publicist? Basically in a negative way compared to contemporary patterns of journalism. The publicist is a political actor: a politician, a supporter of a parliamentary group a representative of the rising working-class movement. Publicists write in order to take part in political debates and to mobilise support. Even if they earn their living through writing, publicists do not consider this activity as a career or profession. To write in the press is a temporary activity, a kind of activism which serves as a means to prepare oneself for an elected position.[3] The rhetoric of publicism – its order of discourse – has no autonomy in relation to political discourse. In mobilising, denouncing and lampooning, the publicist's speech is that of a militant using the press. As Chalaby shows, modern journalism has been institutionalised as a specific order of discourse. The bases of its rhetoric and patterns (objectivity, the rule of the five 'W's) have been established in contrast to the model of militant rhetoric.

Apart from these common features, publicism took various forms. One can identify a 'highbrow' publicism in France (Balzac 1965, first published in 1843) and in Britain, a press dedicated to social elites, and a popular publicism, often linked to working-class movements, expressed in the British 'unstamped' press or the revolutionary French press of 1848. One should also note that the social positioning of the publicist cannot be understood only in its relationship to the political field. In France, academic studies and the writing of novelists such as Balzac and Vallès show that this kind of participation in the press, in its elite variant, was also a means of gaining recognition in the literary field. The publicist era had an intimate relationship with the constitution of a public sphere from the eighteenth century onwards.[4] Publicism remained the basic pattern of journalism until the mid-nineteenth century, when it then became restricted (and hybridised) in a partisan press whose influence constantly weakened during the twentieth century.

The birth of political journalism

The appearance of political journalism required the institutionalisation of journalism as a true profession. Five sets of changes in the mid-nineteenth century press triggered a process of role redefinition.

The first change was the guarantee of freedom of the press. As Habermas (1976) shows, as long as this freedom was not organised by legislation, the very fact of printing a newspaper was a commitment to the struggle for rights and freedom. It is only when legal and fiscal restrictions on press distribution disappeared that its development could be managed in line with rational economic logic. Such a condition was realised in the USA in 1791 through the First Amendment, in Britain in the mid-nineteenth century with the abolition of the taxes on knowledge and in France in 1881 with the passing of the historic Press Act. Second, the new opportunity to build a press market required the input of entrepreneurs who considered the press as an economic and not just political venture. The Anglo-American 'press barons' (Pearson, Northcliffe, Hearst) could be classed as Schumpeterians, able to develop the press both through the constitution of powerful companies and the invention of goods and discourses tailored to win audiences (Chalaby 1997). The reference to audiences suggests a third central change: the constitution of readerships. The rise in literacy, and the extension of voting rights and of politicisation combined with the urban development of the industrial revolution to create and channel a potential readership interested in politics. Technical progress (including the railways and the rotary press) and the growth of advertising constituted another important change. These lowered the costs of production and distribution of newspapers and created the economic conditions for a broader circulation. These four changes triggered a fifth. The population of journalists began to grow and the social division of their jobs created specialisation. Journalism became a profession, clearly different from political or literary activities. Schudson (1978) sums up these changes as follows: 'Until 1830 newspapers were useful to politicians and to people who invested in trade; with the penny press a newspaper sells goods to the global audience and sells readers to advertisers.'

In this new situation, political journalism is first of all the simple application to political news of the rules and practices which structure the young profession of journalism: the importance of news-gathering and the institutionalisation of a specific order of discourse (Schudson 1978; Chalaby 1998). The shift also concerns the definition of newsworthiness, which from now on lies in the ability of the news to make sense to a large audience, whereas for publicists the importance of news lay in its contribution to political struggles. The dominant pattern of political journalism was now underpinned by a rhetoric of objectivity (Tuchman 1972), based on an emphasis on the accuracy of facts and distance from commitment and sensationalism. Political journalism developed by severing its links with publicism. The first development concerns autonomy. Journalists are no longer the herald of a party. They report facts and statements that they create through techniques such as the interview (Schudson 1995). They provide the readership with not only a verbatim account of parliamentary debates, but also the bargains and discussions happening backstage in the corridors of power, a speciality for parliamentary reporters. Second, if journalists work for an audience, it is no longer an audience defined in political terms, but an undifferentiated mass 'public opinion'. While the publicist was an actor in political struggles, the journalist is positioned 'above' politics. This panoptic position has been highlighted by Schudson's case-study on the coverage of the presidential speech on the 'State of the Union' (1995: Chapter 2), which suggests how the rise of an interpretative form of journalism is more a consequence rather than a betrayal of the search for a neutral reporting of facts. The higher the panoptic position, the more details it allows us to see and the more this complexity requires interpretation to make sense.

If the shift from publicist to political journalism is a clear international trend from the second half of the nineteenth century onwards, the process develops with strong differences both between and within specific countries.

For example, France and Italy appear as 'backward' countries in this process. The lasting strength of 'political parallelism' between the structures of the political and journalistic fields remained until the 1960s–1980s, providing publicism with an unusual longevity in these two countries (Mancini 1994). The economic weakness of press groups, the various links of collusion and corruption between politicians and the press, the strength of political rivalries and the late institutionalisation of journalism as a profession (Ruellan 1997; Delporte 1999), all combined to support the lasting survival of the publicist pattern. The launch of *Le Matin* in 1885 gives a superb illustration of this situation. Perceived as the Trojan horse of journalism *à l'Américaine*, the first issue of this newspaper announced: '*Le Matin* will be a newspaper without any political opinion, not tied to any bank – it will be a newspaper of telegraphic, universal and true news.' The proof of this political neutrality came in the recruitment of four famous columnists with notoriously different political opinions – a strange strategy of recruiting publicists to produce objective political journalism! Yet even in countries where political journalism succeeded in taking root, it took various forms. Schudson has studied the US coupling: information versus story. The *New York Times* symbolised the first approach, offering an educated readership the serious, verified and useful news which is the core of objective journalism. The *New York World* and the 'yellow press' expressed information through the story pattern, a more narrative approach, which paid greater attention to human interest as a strategy to seduce working-class readers. This emphasis on characters and scandals also posed an early challenge to the central position of political journalism, now in competition with crime, sport and society news. A similar opposition is visible as early as 1880 in Britain with the social polarisation of the press and its readership (Chalaby 1998)

The generation of 'critical expertise' and the widening of political news

From the 1960s – and even earlier in the USA – political journalism faced changes and challenges which modified the balance of social interdependencies that had contributed to its birth. The first change comes from the process of professionalisation of political communication. Despite the commonly held perception, this change is evident long before the 1960s. As early as the 1920s, American journalists such as Walter Lippmann recognised the growing power of public relations officers and of the weight of 'ready to publish' news produced by more and more efficient sources (Schudson 1978). In the UK, the public sector employed more than 200 PR officers by 1938 (Tulloch 1993), while in France, a real state propaganda had developed by the end of the 1930s (Georgakakis 1997). The changes of the 1960s and 1970s, including the systematic use of opinion polls and the increasing role of spin-doctors, represented a new stage in this evolution. They made the process of making politics a more rational and scientific endeavour clearly visible and underlined the importance of 'source professionalisation' (Schlesinger 1990).

A second change developed inside the journalistic field. Broadcasting journalists, and especially those from television channels, came to occupy a dominant position in this field. Considered by their colleagues from the press as mere readers of dispatches, unable to create the depth of analysis traditionally the domain of press journalists, they slowly began to reverse the power balance. Their rising strength came from the central position assumed by television in the political field. From the 1960s and 1970s onwards, it was now in front of the camera that leaders and candidates made their major statements. It was also the rule of 'live' news that gave the broadcasting media the power of speed. Finally, the weight of the audience gave the legitimacy of the ratings to broadcasting journalists and anchor-men, thus giving birth to a new regime of legitimacy based on audience size and instantaneous coverage.

Changes in the journalistic field must also be considered from the recruitment angle. Morphological changes are visible in the impact of more educated journalists, trained to practise a more thoughtful/analytic journalism, influenced by developments in the social sciences and especially the growth of opinion polls. This rationalisation of political journalism was visible during the Roosevelt presidency in the United States and thirty years later in France (Blondiaux 1998). It dramatically changes the relationship with politicians, allowing journalists also to mobilise a *vox populi* unerringly fresh thanks to the endless flow of polls. A fourth development assumes considerable importance in Western Europe, especially in those countries with a long tradition of public monopoly in broadcasting. This is the double process of the creation of private networks and the loosening of direct governmental control over radio and television. Combined with the growing weight of advertising in the funding of public networks, these changes reinforced the move towards greater competition for audiences, even in political news.

These developments created – albeit with a difference in timing between countries – a dramatic change in the practice of political journalism. Change did not catch journalism off guard as it also amplified older trends, such as the shift towards an interpretative journalism or the re-evaluation of commentary, both of which were already visible in the USA in the 1930s.[5] These changes have been analysed in a rich academic literature (Nimmo and Combs 1990; Poirmeur 1991; Hallin 1994; Kavanagh 1995; Kerbel 1995; Darras 1998; Barnett and Gaber 2001), the findings of which are globally convergent.

We do not intend to sum up this body of research here, but simply to examine certain particularities of this third generation by paying special attention to the French case. It should be noted that using France as a case-study involves a sudden shift from the first to the third generation. This situation makes the French case a kind of sociological *in vivo* experiment of the changes already outlined.

We will borrow from Padioleau (1976) the concept of 'critical expertise' to label and describe the main trend of political journalism in the period 1970–1980. This style of journalism retains from the 'objective' approach a distance from political commitment. However, it also values the claims of technical expertise and a reflexive knowledge of the social world covered by journalists. It is in the name of this expertise, not of political commitment, that journalists can develop a critical analysis. 'Critical expertise' allows judgement and comment on the basis of facts and data which are supposed to convince a rational reader, not to mobilise ideological commitment. This critical dimension – also visible in the American 'News Analysis' – assumes a special importance among political journalists, whose habitus has embodied a hyper-sensitivity to attempts at media manipulation by politicians and spin-doctors. It is expressed in a style of reporting whose practitioners are neither partisans, nor clerks of the court, but political analysts. With an in-depth knowledge of issues, they can spot blunders in strategy and mistakes in governing. They question politicians in the name of public opinion and its demands – identified 'objectively' by opinion polls – or in the name of supra-political values such as morality or modernity. The most visible expression of this 'critical expertise' is the use of a position above the political fray – adversarial or judicial – in dealing with politicians. The political journalist is both an insider, who knows the codes and secrets of the tribe, and a critic, whose point of honour is to decipher for the audience the secrets of their political competitor-colleagues.

Four dimensions of this behaviour can be outlined. The first is linked to an activity of selection and 'packaging' of news. This is a traditional ingredient of journalistic practice. However, in the case of political journalism it assumes a prominent importance due to the double-bind logic created, on the one hand, by the pressure for ever shorter formats of articles and soundbites and, on the other, by the growing flow of media events and institutional communication produced by political sources. An extreme case of this last trend is provided by the Japanese press-clubs (de Lange 1998) or by the EU Public Relations services. In these cases, political sources produce a veritable 'Niagara Falls' of official information, which just to read through would waste enough time to block any opportunity of investigative reporting. More than ever, political journalists must select and reselect political information and wrap it in attractive packaging (Hallin 1997).

The development of this know-how leads to a kind of 'meta-journalism'. The skills of political journalists are more and more concerned with the ability to decipher and divulge the tricks and hidden tactics of politicians. The interpretative evolution of journalism reaches a new stage, evident in the huge number of articles and reports whose goal is to decipher hidden agendas, moving beyond the evaluation of a leader or a parliamentary bill. For instance, the assessments made in Israel in February 2000 by the French Prime Minister, Lionel Jospin, about 'terrorists' from the Lebanese Hezbollah were covered by political journalists in terms of a tactical positioning in the light of the forthcoming presidential elections in 2002 rather than by correspondents in the Middle East reporting on the situation in south Lebanon.

A second dimension of these new skills can be compared to the know-how of the political bookmaker. Journalist's commentaries, even when they deal with policies, tend to function as an endless evaluation of the positions of competitors – both within and between parties – from the viewpoint of a popularity contest or competition for posts. Often interpreted as a form of professional cynicism, this trend must be understood as the result of the interdependencies in which journalists are trapped. The trend towards a multiplication of electoral contests – including primaries in the USA, European elections in the EU and referenda in Italy – combined with the opportunity given by polls for a continuous measurement of public opinion has broken the old tempo of politics. Yesterday's rhythm was characterised by prolonged cold periods between elections, punctuated by short, hot moments of the campaigns themselves. From now on, the tempo is dictated by a permanent competitive frenzy, which triggers a constraining media-activism on the part of politicians (Lacroix 1993). In such a context, the horse-race coverage of politics represents more reactive than proactive behaviour on the part of political journalists.

The new expertise of political journalism cannot be separated from a third trend: the use of polls by journalists. It has become difficult to read a newspaper or article without coming across a reference to an opinion poll. In a country like France, where politicians used to dominate in the relationship with journalists, the latter have found in polls a long-awaited tool to mobilise a *vox populi* legitimacy in the face of elected representatives. The ritual of the television programme *L'heure de vérité* on the public channel France 2 provided a wonderful example. The instant consultation of a 'representative' panel of French viewers allowed the journalist to quote several times in each broadcast the audience's verdict on the performance of its political guest. As the journalist-organiser of these debates admits: 'You need public opinion to become an active part of the debate, and it must be "live" mainly to give the journalists in the studio the popular legitimacy that they lack' (de Virieu 1989: 57).

A fourth trend – and distortion – of 'critical expertise' is a strained marriage between this expertise and entertainment in order to gain a larger audience. The framing of political competition as a horse race was an answer to this challenge. It perhaps requires an audience sufficiently interested in politics to pay attention to the race. Media journalists have thus invented repertoires of discussion designed to lower the 'reception costs' to audiences of political speeches through the use of less formal modes of interaction. For instance, an interview with politicians may focus on their characters. Politicians can be mixed in with other non-political guests. French television channels have shown politicians speaking about their favourite novels on literary programmes. When he was leader of the

Socialist Party, Lionel Jospin once sang *Les Feuilles Mortes* on a television show. During its final series the current affairs magazine programme *Sept sur Sept* on TF1 used to invite together on the same stage a politician and an artist or sportsperson. However, the most common answer to the challenge of making political journalism reach a large audience has been to widen the journalistic definition of politics to include elements linked to the private lives of politicians and the character of political actors, and to extend the topics on which it is legitimate to question a politician. Attention to the private lives of public leaders is not a recent invention. However, one could argue that new uses of this approach have developed recently. In the Anglo-American world this is expressed in a conservative reversal of the radical refrain 'the personal is political'. It has allowed the British tabloids to give rein to a highly profitable hubris of denunciation (Tunstall 1996), also triggered by careless moralising speeches evoking 'back to basics' (Jones 1998). In the USA this conversion of private behaviour into a criterion of political judgement derives to a large extent from its strategic use by the conservative fighters of the 'moral majority'. The French case suggests another side to these processes of redefinition of politics. In France, where a politician's private life remains protected by journalists' self-restraint, the redrawing of the boundaries of political news has taken other forms.[6] The first is the increasing importance devoted to the psychology of the political mind. Often promoted by female journalists, the investigation of politicians' psychology and character appears in reports and articles as the key to understanding their behaviour and tactics. Another manoeuvre – more specific to broadcasting journalists – has been to widen the nature of the questions asked politicians: comments on the week's current events in *Sept sur Sept*, biographical investigations in *Qu'avez-vous fait de vos vingt ans?* and questions on lifestyle and cultural tastes in *Questions à domicile*, broadcast live from the home of political leaders.[7]

Towards a fourth generation?

The whole range of compromises between the 'critical expertise' model and the quest for audience maximisation seemed to offer the right inter-pretative framework for the current developments and national variations in political journalism. In fact, the degree of stability and strength of this third generation model must be questioned. Any researcher facing a case-study today confronts facts that suggest new moves and changes in political journalism. The speed and variety of innovations, the turnover of political programmes on television, sometimes the gloomy mood of self-criticism among journalists themselves: all suggest a new situation of instability. The reflection developed in this section is thus twofold. First, it focuses on the limits of critical expertise. Second, it then argues that we are witnessing a crisis in political journalism, which is trying to invent new practices that may announce the arrival of a fourth generation.

Limits and crisis of 'critical expertise'

Various reasons suggest that, after having been a 'solution' to manage the interdependencies between journalists, the political field and commercial imperatives, 'critical expertise' is now becoming more of a problem than a response. This interpretation has important theoretical consequences for research. It clearly means that an analysis of contemporary political journalism can no longer be developed as a simple adaptation of the frameworks of interpretation dating back to the 1970s. Change in the structures of interdependencies between fields and between politicians and citizens, in what Blumler and Kavanagh (1999) have termed a 'third age of political communication', requires new approaches.

The first limitation of the 'critical expertise' approach concerns its practical results as evaluated both by audience ratings and professionals engaged in power struggles in the newsroom. The broadcasting of political programmes in France gives a remarkable illustration of this situation. The 1980s witnessed a phenomenon of renewal on all networks, evidenced in the emergence of a great variety of new styles of political programming. In the mid-1990s all these programmes were cancelled or exiled to late-night slots, most of the time because of ratings considered too low for prime time (Neveu 1995). In contrast, those programmes with political guests which achieve good ratings marginalise hard political news or put it in the hands of professional compères who are not political journalists. In the United States the success of Donahue and Larry King and the invitation given to election candidates by MTV in 1996 are symptomatic of the same trend (Cunningham 1995).

The position of the media's political journalists looks rather lugubrious. Either they play the entertainment card, in which case they stand a good chance of being outplayed by entertainment hosts or non-specialist journalists, or they stay in a position of 'critical expert' and must therefore wait for late-night broadcasting or the return of a major election campaign. The limits of 'critical expertise' are also visible in the press. As Padioleau (1976) notes, it often appears as 'an intellectuals' journalism for intellectuals' and seldom attracts huge readerships. Because it focuses on the dismantling of spin-doctoring and tactics, it is threatened by the risk of being 'a journalism of reports, interviews, comments and gloss. A journalism which is necessary, of course, but more and more caught up in the trap of communication, mirroring in real time, without distance or research, and seeing only what the powers that be are ready to let it see' (Plenel 1994: 98). One might even wonder if the very success of this journalism does not have a boomerang effect. Journalist's criticism – of corruption (Uriarte 1998) or of a 'crisis of representation' (Neveu 1993) – triggers a disenchanted perception of politics. Often perceived as members of the small world of politics, journalists rarely have to wait a long time to endure the same kind of disparaging evaluation as politicians.

The crisis also comes from the dramatic growth of the imperatives of audience and profit maximisation. These stimulate a market-driven journalism (Underwood 1993; McManus 1994) and an organised rational-isation of journalistic rhetoric and formats (Barbier-Bouvet 1994). As Champagne (2000) shows, even in prestige broadsheets like *Le Monde* a commercial logic means shorter articles and more space devoted to practical information (such as weather reports, cooking or television schedules) and soft news. All these trends contradict the pattern of 'critical expertise'. The impact of profit maximisation on the journalistic field is also visible in the growing percentage of insecure jobs and freelance 'journos' (Tunstall 1996; Accardo 1998). Political journalism is not the core of this evolution. But uncertainty over status and career prospects can hardly strengthen the ability of journalists to maintain their critical positions above the political field.

Changes are also apparent inside the journalistic field. Coming from television (and mainly from rolling news channels such as CNN, Euronews and BBC World), a pattern of professional achievement based on speed and 'live' coverage makes the distance and time for analysis required by 'critical expertise' increasingly difficult to achieve. Even in the press, one of the impacts of the race for audiences is to value in each and every news section the culture of scoops and scandals which allows for an original combination of investigative reporting and sensationalism. This new journalistic culture sharpens the competition for news slots to the detriment of political journalists. This has the additional consequence of opening up coverage of events which may have important political dimensions to journalists from other sections such as science, society or medicine, as illustrated in the case of the 'contaminated blood affair' in France and the 'mad cow' crisis across the EU. Paul Goupil, a leading member of the newsroom at the leading French daily *Ouest-France*, comments: 'Politics is losing ground. The weeklies give it less space. There is a move away from it. For a journalist, it's better to cover the contaminated blood affair than the Socialist Party conference . . . Today the "Society" news section is considered as more status enhancing. Politics has been brought back to its rightful position. It is still a noble field, but less valued than it was previously' (Interview, 8 July 1993).

The new landscape of interdependencies in contemporary political journalism is also modified by the presence of new actors. In France and Italy, judges investigating scandals and corruption affairs have established, through organised leaks or the action of barristers and lawyers, a tactical alliance with investigative journalists against politicians (Roussel 1998; Pujas and Rhodes 1999). The ability of American fundamentalist religious groups to introduce standards of private morality and behaviour into journalistic criteria regarding political coverage belongs to the same process whereby new actors enter the interdependency structure. Another recent significant change is the visible growth of a public which is disenchanted with or uninterested in politics. Well implanted in the USA, this trend is more and more visible in European countries, creating a stronger challenge for political journalism.

Finally, the flaws of 'critical expertise' also come from a journalistic *epistémé* concerning the definition of politics and ways of talking about it.[8] This *epistémé* of political journalism can be summarised in a few landmarks (Bennet 1997). The first comes from the basics of journalism: news is an event more than a problem, about dramas and spectacular happenings rather than incremental social changes. A second element of this hidden credo is the identification of politics as the cogs of representative democracy (elections, institutions). A third element is the reduction of politics to its most visible institutional figures and submission to its timetables and rites. The news-desks and news sections are often built on the basis of an homology with the institutions they cover. A French political journalist 'owns' a party or an institution. The nature of his/her 'ownership' is an indicator of his/her importance. 'If I consider my case, I have grown fatter and more important in shifting from coverage of the Communist Party to the Socialists' said a reporter from *Libération* (Reporters Sans Frontières 1991). The journalistic *epistémé* is also structured by an often naive vision of the democratic function of the press (Gans 1999). The line of reasoning is simple: political journalists contribute to the production of citizens; well-informed citizens are enlightened and active; they strengthen democracy. This line of reasoning prevents consideration of the possibility, even likelihood, that it is a preliminary interest in politics which brings the reader to the political pages in the first place. It dissuades a reflection on the social conditions required for the efficient circulation and reception of political information and leads away from a debate about whether being informed is enough to be active and influential in the face of organised social powers.

The *epistémé* of political journalists also consists of taken-for-granted interpretative frames. In the French case, for example, the powerful links of social and cultural proximity, epitomised in the shared education of the elite of politicians and journalists in the same 'power schools', have legitimised a neo-liberal vision (more or less blended with 'social' concerns) as an inescapable thought horizon (Halimi 1997). Any fundamental criticism of the rules of the political and economic system is then promptly labelled as belonging to the darkness of 'populism' or to a hidden nostalgia for the Soviet model. Over and above their strong contradictions – to value the private and the emotional versus covering 'serious' institutions and actors – the commercial pressures and the esoteric vision of political journalism paradoxically combine to create an invisible filter which eliminates a whole set of social facts from the very definition of politics and so from its coverage. As Cook suggests (1998: 93): 'We must look at the newsbeat system not only for the news it makes possible but for the news it discourages.' One might mention among the latter category, rarely considered as worthy of belonging to politics, the impact of policies on ordinary lives, the action of lobbies, the decision-making process in international organisations such as the EU and those social movements which do not shake the foundations of the state. Broadly speaking, all the slow changes of social life and their impact on political behaviour are ignored or exiled to other news sections.

The components of renewal

The failures of political journalism from the 'third generation' do not imply its rapid disappearance. Rather the space for its expression threatens to shrink or to limit itself to late-night slots on television. Conversely, the press dedicated to educated audiences manages to maintain such a space. On television and in the tabloids the various blends of 'critical expertise' and entertainment, which value the private dimensions of public characters, will also remain present. But do not even these elements of continuity pose a threat for political journalists? Does one really need journalists for an infotainment framing of politics?

Political journalism faces a major crisis concerning all the landmarks identified in the first section. Its 'demopedic' function is trapped between explanations for the happy few and the quest for audiences which threatens to transform it into a 'telenovelisation' of juicy affairs and picturesque characters. The crisis concerns autonomy as well. Journalists are facing increasing commercial pressures. They remain prisoners of the timetables and agendas of the political field and of the complex relationship with spin-doctors, a situation which condemns them to an endless game of dismantling the communication tricks of politicians. The crisis comes finally from their positioning in the journalistic field and the media world, as journalists face up to the invasion of their professionally guarded slots by television chat-show hosts, marketing services and journalists from other news sections. This nexus of uncertainty, however, has triggered various innovations on the part of journalists which suggest the blurred outlines of a 'fourth generation' of political journalism.

A first dimension of change is expressed in the attempts by part of political journalism to mobilise the intervention of laypersons – 'ordinary citizens' – in a less abstract, more active fashion than was allowed at the previous stage by the exclusive use of polls. The expressions of this move are varied. Their common element is to give journalists the function of the 'relay loudspeaker' for an approach to politics which tries to pay more attention to the ordinary worries and interests of the rank and file citizen. This style of journalism has at least three different forms of expression. The first is a kind of consumerist translation of political journalism strongly highlighted by Eide (1997; Eide and Knight 1999) in his case study of the Norwegian daily *Verdens Gang*. Eide points to

> an expansion of the service journalism into the domain of political journalism. The journalistic assessment is clear and simple: in the domain of politics, too, the reader is in need of guidance and clarity, in need of political consumer information, to be able to pursue his or her interests. The cultivated conception of the role of journalism is that the journalist is on your side, pushing the politicians to come up with clear arguments and effective solutions.
>
> (Eide 1997: 178)

In other cases the changes consist in making political journalism the medium of expression of a bottom-up political agenda, which values the assumed demands and problems of citizens. On radio and television this approach highlights the direct intervention of ordinary citizens. The goal here is to take control of the agenda of public debate away from politicians by challenging them with questions from laypersons. This change gives more weight to the everyday impact of political decisions (such as on unemployment, welfare and public health) and devotes less space to esoteric discussions (Coleman 1998; Blumler and Gurevitch 1997). In its final form, this approach tends towards the transformation of political journalists into spokespersons for the community. This trend is especially visible in the American 'civic journalism' movement (Charity 1998). Despite their frequent denials, this kind of journalism can give its practitioners a function of interest aggregation which was traditionally considered a feature of the behaviour of political parties. If one may question the threat of a journalistic 'populism' (Blumler and Kavanagh 1999), it is nonetheless true that the new relationship to audiences can trigger changes in the nature of the issues discussed, in that it can bring journalism closer to the way ordinary citizens experience politics (Neveu 1999a).

The importance given to the expression and 'demands' of ordinary citizens is linked to a second change, which concerns the very definition of political news. Citizens increasingly view politics in terms which are no longer restricted to the cogs of representative democracy. Three examples illustrate the nature of this change. First, the growing importance devoted to coverage of social movements should be noted (Neveu 1999b). Such reports can even, as happened at *Le Parisien* or *Le Monde* during the major strikes of December 1995 in France, be guided by the explicit desire to prevent a politically oriented coverage of the social movement and instead to value reports on the real-life experiences and claims of the people on strike (Lévèque 1999). The rise of what we can call 'ethnographic report-ing' also gives more importance to the publication of articles offering snapshots of ordinary lives as well as statements and reactions from 'real' citizens, regarded here as the beneficiaries and targets of policies and so experiencing the immediate effects of political decisions. These reports may concern civil servants experiencing a crisis in public services, lorry drivers on strike or disabled people talking about the welfare system. The common rationale is to rely on the experiences of ordinary people as related by themselves as they face the everyday impact of political decisions that were usually covered only through an analysis of the decision-making process and the positioning of party leaders. This style of journalism also widens the definition of 'politics' and reinforces a bottom-up approach. As a provisional remark, coming from our own research on the French case, we should mention that many of the new experiments in journalists' approach to political coverage come from journalists who do not belong to the politics newsbeat. The professional stakes are clear: if they want to maintain their central position in the power balance between services, political journalists must themselves integrate this new definition of politics and ways of covering it into their work.

The two previous trends of renewal are closely linked to the rise of new professional skills. Some of these are particular to television where the importance given to the participation of laypersons requires on the part of the organisers of debates an ability to manage a greater number of participants. Political journalists must therefore learn to pay attention to members of a studio audience less accustomed to speaking in public. This shift of professional skills is also evident in the press. To put together a good story after a discussion with nurses striking against cuts in hospital budgets requires different skills from those needed for an interview with a party leader. For all political journalists such changes imply a restructuring of their cognitive maps and frameworks. The shift of debate themes beyond the agenda of the 'small world' of insiders will require a more in-depth knowledge of issues, facts and figures concerning policies. The variety of knowledge needed to map and understand political stakes and the data of a broadened vision of politics may drive journalists toward a new kind of newsgathering, as they come to use the input of social scientists beyond the usual circle of pollsters and pundits. Such co-operation, where the new generation trained in social sciences will have a strong asset, can also promote new illustrations of what Meyer (1973) terms 'precision journalism'. Electoral sociology has for a long time allowed this precision journalism to develop within the political sphere. An increased amount of attention to the policy and behavioural dimensions of politics creates a window of opportunity for the renewal of this type of journalism and its combination with investigative reporting, as, for instance, a set of articles published in 1988 by the Spanish daily *El País* shows. In this instance the articles focused on the linkages between members of the Cortes and Spanish economic interests, using the results of a questionnaire sent to parliamentary deputies by journalists (Dader 1991).

Conclusion

Powerful influences can institutionalise a fourth generation of political journalism. Market logic is sufficiently ambiguous in both shrinking formats and producing enormous pressure for innovation so as to increase circulation and ratings. A framing of politics which emphasises its impact on everyday life, coupled with more attention to the demands of citizens and to new forms of political participation, can be a marketable strategy. In many countries, including the UK and France, the weight of new generations of more educated and more women journalists, combined with the struggle for jobs, pushes newcomers in the field towards subversive strategies of renewal of political journalism. The influence of actors coming from other fields (including intellectuals, researchers and judges) or of spokespersons such as community leaders willing to take part in public debates may also support these changes.

Conversely, the institutionalisation of a new style of political journalism also faces enormous resistance. The clearest lies in the tenacity of routines and professional habits. The older generation of fifty-something practitioners who still rule the journalistic fields has no strong incentive to support changes which threaten its legitimacy. In addition, most politicians have little to gain from changes which would give journalists (or citizens) more control of the agenda and allow them to demonstrate their experience or knowledge of the issues debated. Van Zoonen (1996) has developed an illuminating analysis of how the innovative potential of young Dutch female journalists was hijacked by the strength of marketing strategies and often directed towards emotional and even superficial coverage. Because new types of news-gathering from non-institutional partners require more investigative input, new forms of journalism are also costly and time-consuming, while the great goal of managers is to reduce costs. Finally, if the audience for political journalism can be increased, no sociological reason suggests that this kind of news could be as audience-seducing as sports, crime or consumer affairs. More than by a clear process of 'succession', it is probably by the invention and occupation of niches and slots among the traditional news sections that a fourth generation of political journalism will emerge.

Notes

1 Many books written by journalists can be read as an effort to produce what Goffman calls 'des-identifiers'. The critical style, the description of politicians as 'cut off from reality', sometimes the cruelty of their portrayals work as a claim for distance, the proof of an outsider status facing the small world of politics. (For France, see Alexandre 1988 and July 1989, and for the UK, see Coleman 1987).

2 The French utopian socialist, Proudhon, said that 'democracy is demopedy', i.e. is a pedagogy, a process of teaching politics.

3 In France, the age of eligibility was 30, sometimes 40 under the French Restoration. In such conditions, writing for a newspaper was a reasonable choice to make as one waited for electoral opportunities (see Joana 1999).

4 Recent historical studies suggest that the birth of publicism has to be located in the seventeenth century in England (see Zaret 1992). On the French case, see Popkin 1987.
5 Schudson shows in the American press the growing number of signed articles. He highlights the change with reference to the title of McDougall's classic textbook from *Reporting for beginners* (1932) to *Interpretative Reporting* (1938).
6 The top elite of French political journalists had known about the existence of Mazarine, Mitterrand's illegitimate daughter, for a long time. However, this information was kept out of the public domain for the first twelve years of his presidency.
7 One can find similar styles of coverage of politicians in the Dutch gossip press (van Zoonen 1996)
8 The concept of *epistémé* comes from Foucault. It refers to a way of thinking and reasoning, assumptions shared by a community which structure a common knowledge.

References

Accardo, A. (1998) *Journalistes précaires*, Bordeaux: Le Mascaret.

Alexandre, P. (1988) *Paysages de campagne*, Paris: Grasset.

Balzac, H. de (1965 [1843]) *Monographie de la presse parisienne*, Paris: J.J. Pauvert.

Barbier-Bouvet, J.F. (1994) 'Crise de la lecture ou lecture de crise?', *Médiaspouvoirs*, 34: 97–105.

Barnett, S. and Gaber, I. (2001) *Westminster Tales. The Twenty-first-century Crisis in Political Journalism*, London: Continuum.

Bennet, I. (1997) 'Cracking the news code: some rules that journalists live by', in S. Iyengar and R. Reeves (eds) *Do the Media Govern?*, London: Sage.

Blondiaux, L. (1998) *La fabrique de l'opinion*, Paris: Seuil.

Blumler, J.G. and Gurevitch, M. (1995) *The Crisis of Public Communication*, London: Routledge.

Blumler, J.G. and Gurevitch, M. (1997) 'Change in the air: campaign journalism at the BBC, 1997', in I. Crewe, B. Gosschalk and J. Bartle (eds), *Why Labour Won the General Election of 1997*, London: Frank Cass.

Blumler, J.G. and Kavanagh, D. (1999) 'The third age of political communication: influences and features', *Political Communication* 16: 209–30.

Bourdieu, P. (2000) *Propos sur le champ politique*, Lyon: Presses Universitaires de Lyon.

Broddason, T. (1994) 'The sacred side of professional journalism', *European Journal of Communication* 9: 227–48.

Chalaby, J. (1997) 'No ordinary press owners: press barons as a Weberian ideal type', *Media, Culture and Society* 19/4: 621–41.

Chalaby, J. (1998) *The Invention of Journalism*, Basingstoke: Macmillan.

Champagne, P. (2000) 'Le médiateur entre deux *Monde*', *Actes de la Recherche en Sciences Sociales* 131/132: 8–29.

Charity, A. (1998) *Doing Public Journalism*, New York: The Guilford Press.

Charron, J. (1994) *La production de l'actualité*, Quebec: Boréal.

Coleman, S. (1998) 'Interactive media and the UK General Election', *Media, Culture and Society* 20/4: 687–94.

Coleman, T. (1987) *Thatcher's Britain*, London: Corgi.

Cook, T. (1998) *Governing with the News*, Chicago: University of Chicago Press.

Cunningham, L. (1995) *Talking Politics: Choosing the President in the Television Age*, Westport: Praeger.

Dader, J.L. (1991) 'El periodismo de precision', *Telos* 36: 75–80.

Darras, E. (1998) 'L'institution d'une tribune politique: genèse et usages du magazine politique de télévision', unpublished PhD thesis, University of Paris 2.

Delporte, C. (1999) *Les journalistes en France 1880–1950*, Paris: Seuil.

Eide, M. (1997) 'A new kind of newspaper? Understanding a popularisation process', *Media, Culture and Society* 19/2: 173–82.

Eide, M. and Knight, G. (1999) 'Service journalism and the problems of everyday life', *European Journal of Communication* 14/4: 525–47.

Eliasoph, N. (1998) *Avoiding Politics*, Cambridge: Cambridge University Press.

Gans, H. (1999) 'What can journalists actually do for American democracy?', *Harvard International Journal of Press/Politics* 3/4: 6–12.

Gaxie, D. (1978) *Le Cens caché*, Paris: Seuil.

Georgakakis, D. (1997) 'Aux origines de la communication gouvernementale: socio-histoire d'un oubli', *Quaderni* 33: 131–44.

Habermas, J. (1976) *L'espace public*, Paris: Payot.

Halimi, S. (1997) *Les nouveaux chiens de garde*, Paris: Liber.

Hallin, D. (1994) *We Keep America on Top of the World*, London: Routledge.

Hallin, D. (1997) 'Sound bite news: television coverage of elections' in S. Iyengar and R. Reeves (eds) *Do the Media Govern?*, London: Sage.

Iyengar, S. and Kinder, D. (1987) *News that Matters: Television and American Opinion*, Chicago: University of Chicago Press.

Joana, J. (1999) *Pratiques politiques des députés français au XIXe siècle*, Paris: L'Harmattan.

Jones, N. (1998) *Campaign 1997*, London: Indigo.

July, S. (1989) *Le salon des artistes*, Paris: Grasset.

Kavanagh, D. (1995) *Election Campaigning: The New Marketing of Politics*, Oxford: Blackwell.

Kerbel, M. (1995) *Remote and Controlled: Media Polititcs in a Cynical Age*, Boulder: Westview Press.

Lacroix, B. (1993), 'A quoi servent les sondages?', in L. Sfez (ed.) *Dictionnaire critique de la Communication*, Paris: PUF, vol. 2: 1403–15.

Lange, W. de. (1998) *A History of Japanese Journalism*, London: Japan Library.

Le Bohec, J. (1997) *Les rapports presse-politique*, Paris: L'Harmattan.

Le Grignou, B. and Neveu, E. (1988) 'Emettre la réception: préméditations et réceptions de la politique télévisée', *Réseaux* 32: 67–107.

Lévèque, S. (1999) 'Crise sociale et traitement journalistique', *Réseaux* 98: 87–118.

Linsky, M. (ed.) (1983) *Television and the Presidential Election*, Lanham, Md.: Lexington Books.

McManus, J. (1994) *Market-Driven Journalism*, London: Sage.

Mancini, P. (1994) *Sussurri e grida dalle camere. L'informazione politico-parlamentare in Italia*, Milan: FrancoAngeli.

Meyer, P. (1973) *Precision Journalism*, Bloomington: Indiana University Press.

Neveu, E. (1993) 'Médias et construction de la crise de la représentation: le cas français', *Communication* 14/1: 11–54.

Neveu, E. (1995) 'Les impasses du spectacle politique', *Hermès* 17: 145–62.

Neveu, E. (1999a) 'Politics on French television. Towards a renewal of political journalism and debate frames?', *European Journal of Communication* 14/3: 379–409.

Neveu, E. (1999b) 'Medias, mouvements sociaux et espaces publics', *Réseaux* 98: 17–86.

Nimmo, D. and Combs, J. (1990) *Mediated Political Realities*, London: Longman.

Padioleau, J. (1976) 'Systèmes d'interaction et rhétoriques journalistiques', *Sociologie du travail* 3: 256–82.

Plenel, E. (1994) *Un temps de chien*, Paris: Stock.

Plenel, E. (1996) 'La plume dans la plaie', *Le Débat* 90: 169–92.

Poirmeur, Y. (1991) 'Marché de la communication politique et mutation de la vie politique', in CURAPP, *La communication politique*, Paris: PUF.

Popkin, J. (1987) 'The prerevolutionary origins of political journalism', in K.M. Baker (ed.) *The Political Culture of the Old Regime*, London: Pergamon Press.

Pujas, V. and Rhodes, M. (1999) 'Party finance and political scandals in Italy, France and Spain', *West European Politics*, 22/3: 41–63.

Reporters Sans Frontières (1991) *Les journalistes sont-ils crédibles?*, Montpellier: Editions RSF.

Rieffel, R. (1984) *L'élite des journalistes*, Paris: PUF.

Roussel, V. (1998) 'Les magistrats dans les scandales politiques', *Revue Française de Science Politique* 48/2: 245–73.

Ruellan, D. (1997) *Les pro de l'info*, Rennes: PUR.

Schlesinger, P. (1990) 'Rethinking the sociology of journalism: source strategies and the limits of media-centrism', in M. Ferguson (ed.) *Public Communication: The New Imperatives*, London: Sage.

Schudson, M. (1978) *Discovering the News: A Social History of American Newspapers*, New York: Basic Books.

Schudson, M. (1995) *The Power of News*, Harvard: Harvard University Press.

Tuchman, G. (1972) 'Objectivity as a strategic ritual', *American Journal of Sociology* 77/4: 660–79.

Tulloch, G. (1993) 'Policing the public sphere: the British machinery of news management', *Media, Culture and Society* 15/3: 363–84.

Tunstall, J. (1971) *Journalists at Work*, London: Constable.

Tunstall, J. (1996) *Newspaper Power*, Oxford: Clarendon Press.

Underwood, D. (1993) *When MBAs Rule the Newsroom*, New York: Columbia University Press.

Uriarte, E. (1998) 'Intelectuales y periodistas contra Politicos', *Claves* 86: 66–71.

Virieu, F.H. de (1989) *La médiacratie*, Paris: Flammarion.

Zaret, D. (1992) 'Religion, science and printing in the public spheres in 17th century England', in C. Calhoun (ed.) *Habermas and the Public Sphere*, Boston: MIT Press.

Zoonen, L. van (1996) 'One of the girls? Or the changing gender of journalism', unpublished keynote address to the conference on Gender and the Media, Oslo, 9 September.

Part I

The cross-management of the interdependencies between journalists and politicians

3   The first Blair government and political journalism

Raymond Kuhn

> Sadly, in Britain, the machinery of news management is allowed to operate with the often active collaboration of the press and broadcasters. . . . Too often the official managers of the political news have been allowed to dictate the agenda. . . . By these means, the agenda for political discussion in Britain is largely set by Whitehall.
>
> (Cockerell *et al.* 1984: 9 and 11)

> Their protestations notwithstanding, the powers and resources acquired by Blair and his media advisers have been unprecedented, and their ability to control events from Downing Street and to manipulate the political messages which they have sought to promote has been far greater than that of any previous government.
>
> (Jones 2001: 1)

These two evaluations of the practice of news management by the government in Britain were written seventeen years apart, during which time important developments occurred in the ownership, structures and functioning of media organisations, major innovations were introduced in communications technology, significant changes took place in the practices of political journalism and, not least, Labour replaced the Conservatives as the party in power. Yet both studies assess the nature of the interdependency between government and political journalists in broadly similar terms, bemoaning what they regard as the undesirable extent of government control over the media's news agenda, facilitated by the co-operation and compliance of many journalists. The authors ought to know what they are talking about, since both books were written by respected political journalists with considerable professional experience in the press and broadcasting.

There is no doubt that recent British governments have paid increasingly close attention to managing the news agenda, as part of a growing emphasis on communication activities by a range of political actors operating in a highly mediatised promotional culture (Wernick 1991). While in the past this concern was largely the preserve of political parties during the short periods of election campaigns, strategies of symbolic construction by elites are now commonplace in a political communication system characterised by a 'thoroughgoing professionalization of political advocacy' (Blumler and Gurevitch 1995: 207–10). Whether described in terms of 'packaging politics' (Franklin 1994), 'designer politics' (Scammell 1995) or 'the new marketing of politics' (Kavanagh 1995), the process whereby mainstream political actors in Britain have accommodated themselves to the demands of the media has been well documented in recent years.

Nowhere has this accommodation been more evident than in the case of the Labour Party since the mid-1980s. After its 1997 election victory Labour placed communication at the heart of its methodology for the formulation and implementation of governmental policy-making, taking the idea of the public relations state to new heights (Deacon and Golding 1994: 4–7). The first Blair government (1997–2001) regarded news management as an integral part of contemporary governance, not an optional extra (Scammell 2001). As a result, ministers and their special advisers tried to control or co-opt the media in the task of promoting Labour's achievements to the electorate. This approach had particular consequences for political journalists who were seduced, bullied, courted and criticised in an attempt to ensure that they were as 'on-message' as Labour ministers and MPs.

The professionalism of Labour's news management activities has been much commented on, not least by journalists themselves (Jones 1999 and 2001; Oborne 1999; Johnson 1999). Yet in seeking to harness the power of the media for its own political purposes, Labour had to recognise limitations on its agenda structuring capabilities. As a result, the interdependency between the first Blair government and the news media cannot be satisfactorily presented as a simple top-down process in which politicians and their advisers imposed their collective will on subordinate and supine political journalists. Rather, journalists have developed their own strategies and patterns of behaviour in response to the professionalisation of source activity by political elites.

Both sets of political communication actors, therefore, can be seen to be in a relationship of constant mutual adjustment in which their respective roles are normatively bounded within a shared culture which helps structure their interaction and allows for a certain level of predictability, even in the outbreak and management of conflict (Blumler and Gurevitch 1995: 32–44). This chapter argues that during the first Blair administration this interrelationship included elements of exchange as government engaged in strategic and tactical deals with media practitioners, including proprietors as well as journalists, and of adversarial contestation as spin-doctors and journalists mobilised their respective resources in their attempts to influence agenda construction and the framing of news coverage (Blumler and Gurevitch 1995: 27–32).

The chapter is organised in three main sections. The first examines the strategic approach to political communication taken by New Labour in government. The second has a source-centred focus, critically applying the concept of primary definer to the role of the first Blair government as an official source for the news media. The third section focuses on the interrelationship between the government and political journalists, analysing and evaluating the ways in which the two sets of political communication actors managed their interdependency.

The New Labour government's strategic approach to political communication

It is impossible to exaggerate the distance travelled by the Labour Party over the past twenty years in the professionalisation of its approach to political communication (Jones 1995; Esser *et al.* 2000). This formed part of a broader process of party reform which embraced an ideological repositioning, new policy proposals, a rebranding of Labour's electoral image and internal constitutional change to strengthen the power of the leadership (Hughes and Wintour 1990; Heffernan and Marqusee 1992; Shaw 1994). The modernisation of the party, symbolised by the rhetorical emphasis on 'New Labour' as an appropriate label to describe the reconciliation of Labour's core values with the needs of a modern society and economy, contributed to the spectacular general election victory of 1997 (Butler and Kavanagh 1997; Crewe *et al.* 1998).

On coming to power, Labour transferred to the task of government the political communications approach it had perfected in opposition. This consisted of four key elements. First, it was underpinned by clear goals. Labour wanted to ensure that it dominated the news agenda: to be in control as much as possible of the selection and construction of issues. The aim was to ensure that the desired positive focus on the so-called 'big picture' of Labour policy proposals and governmental achievements was not offset by events-driven media coverage of negative news and the froth of personality-dominated stories.

Second, the achievement of these goals required a coherent media management strategy, which included both proactive and reactive components (Heffernan and Stanyer 1998: 15). Proactive media management was accorded a central role in the functioning of the Blair government. By creating news stories, staging events for media coverage and controlling the release of information, the government might reasonably expect to have a major impact on the news agenda. However, Labour recognised that an effective media management strategy also required a reactive component. 'Essentially this involves a damage limitation exercise, its aim to kill off or otherwise reduce the life expectancy of the "issue attention cycle" of a news story that casts the party in a non-advantageous position' (Heffernan and Stanyer 1998: 16).

No government can control events in the real world, as Labour discovered with the Paddington rail disaster of October 1999, the fuel protest of September 2000 and the foot and mouth crisis of spring 2001 – all of which proved to be difficult media stories for ministers and their advisers. Yet a government has to be able to respond to unexpected events in a manner which limits potential damage. In opposition, for example, Labour had successfully employed techniques of rapid rebuttal in the face of political attacks from the Conservatives, thereby closing down the negative impact of the original critical story by immediately adopting an offensive position (Gaber 2000). In government too, speed of response was considered a vital element of a reactive media strategy, exemplified in October 1998 by the prompt resignation and public apology via a BBC television interview of the Secretary of State for Wales, Ron Davies, following an embarrassing incident with overtones of sexual scandal (Jones 1999: 244–52).

Third, the government's media management activities were well organised and resourced. Labour introduced several important changes in this respect. For example, the Prime Minister's Chief Press Secretary was given the joint status of civil servant and special adviser. This meant that he could adopt a more overtly partisan approach in his relationship with the media than had formally been the case with his predecessors. In addition, Labour established a Strategic Communications Unit in Downing Street to plan and co-ordinate the government's media management activities, assisted by a media monitoring unit of the type which the party had previously used in opposition. The Strategic Communications Unit contained ex-newspaper correspondents, such as Philip Bassett, former industrial editor of *The Times*, and David Bradshaw, a former political correspondent on the *Daily Mirror* (Jones 2001: 82). One of its tasks was to prepare a weekly diary, known as 'the grid', which 'was intended to integrate important initiatives so as to prevent a clash of events and ensure that positive developments were not blotted out by unwelcome news coverage for announcements that were known to have the potential to damage the government' (Jones 2001: 144).

Controversially, the government also reorganised the Government Information Services, modernising the provision of official information from ministerial departments and, in the eyes of some of its opponents, politicising the role of government information officers. Many of these either quit or were eased out as the task of professionalising the work of departmental press offices was carried out in the early months of the first Blair administration. Labour also increased the number of special advisers in government departments, several of whom fulfilled a proactive partisan media relations role which sometimes brought them into conflict with government information officers steeped in a civil service culture of political neutrality (Barnett and Gaber 2001: 116–24).

Overall, therefore, the government's communications strategy of command and control was reflected in a highly centralised organisation which sought to co-ordinate governmental communications and impose a single message from the top down. This formed an integral part of the Blair leadership style of 'command premiership' (Hennessy 2000: 476–523) which contained strong elements of a presidential model of governance (Foley 2000).

> The Government's overall strategy is set by the Prime Minister; he relies on the Chief Press Secretary and the No. 10 Press Office to ensure that the essential messages and key themes which underpin the Government's strategy are sustained and not lost in the clamour of events. . . . major interviews and media appearances have to be agreed in advance with the No. 10 Press Office, and policy statements have to be cleared with the No. 10 Private Office. The Chief Press Secretary and the No. 10 Press Office liaise with the departmental press offices to plan announcements in advance in order to secure a timely and well-ordered flow of significant government communications and they agree how best Departmental communications . . . can play into the broader Government messages and themes and, by fitting in with this bigger picture, signal the coherence of what the Government as a whole is doing.
>
> (House of Commons Select Committee
> on Public Administration 1998: xiii)

Finally, Labour's media management activities were run by highly professional personnel. The key figure in this context was the Prime Minister's Official Spokesman, Alastair Campbell. Campbell became Blair's press secretary in 1994 and the two then rose together in a symbiotic relationship. A former national newspaper journalist and editor, Campbell spoke to the media with the authority of the Prime Minister himself, just as Bernard Ingham had done as Number 10 Press Secretary during the Thatcher premiership (Harris 1990; Ingham 1991). However, whereas Ingham's role was confined to presentation and news management and lacked any policy influence, Campbell attended Cabinet meetings and acquired the reputation of having more influence in decision-making than some policy advisers (Oborne 1999: 161).

> It is not merely that Alastair is more political than Bernard [Ingham] and has carried further the imposition of a controlled output of government propaganda, but that he is higher in the Downing Street pecking order of determining how 'New Labour' wants to be seen. He is part of the inner circle of those who have given 'New Labour' its 'control freak' reputation.
>
> (Roth 1999: 22)

In short, fully integrated into the process of policy-making, the Labour government's approach to news management possessed in terms of goals, strategy, organisation and personnel all the characteristics of a highly efficient political communications machine.

The first Blair government as a primary definer for the news media?

The strategic emphasis placed on news management by Labour was underpinned by the structural resources of authority and legitimacy which any British government possesses in functioning as an official source for political journalists. One way of theorising the power of sources uses the concept of primary definer which places the media in a subordinate and secondary role to major power holders in society in the task of agenda construction (Hall *et al.* 1978). According to this account, the organisational demands and professional values of the news production process 'combine to produce a systematically structured *over-accessing* to the media of those in powerful and privileged institutional positions' (Hall *et al.* 1978: 58, emphasis in original). This 'permits the institutional definers to establish the initial definition or *primary interpretation* of the topic in question' (Hall *et al.* 1978: 58, emphasis in original). As a result,

> the media are frequently not the 'primary definers' of news events at all; but their structured relationship to power has the effect of making them play a crucial but secondary role in *reproducing* the definitions of those who have privileged access, as of right, to the media as 'accredited sources'.
>
> (Hall *et al.* 1978: 59, emphasis in original)

In the literature on government and the news media in Britain the system of mass institutionalised briefings of political journalists known as 'the lobby' has been widely regarded as one of the main links in this structured relationship (Tunstall 1970). Indeed, the lobby system has achieved a mythical status in the eyes of some commentators. Franklin, for example, contends that it has been 'appropriated by government as a conduit for information and, in this process, metamorphosed from an active and critical observer of political affairs into a passive purveyor of government messages' (Franklin 1994: 86). As a result, 'this rather furtive arrangement between politicians and journalists continues to offer governments of all political persuasions opportunities to influence the agenda of mainstream political discussion to a degree which must be considered unhealthy for a democracy' (Franklin 1994: 91). Franklin thus presents the lobby as an integral part of a process whereby those political journalists given accredited status effectively become part of the government's news machine.

The concept of primary definition has informed a considerable body of academic analysis on source–media relations. However, in so doing it has been subjected to important theoretical criticisms, most notably by

Schlesinger (1990). In addition, several empirical studies have called into question some of the key assumptions regarding the government's power as a primary definer, demonstrating that the capacity of ministers and their advisers to shape the news agenda is frequently highly constrained (Morrison and Tumber 1988; Miller 1993; Deacon and Golding 1994).

Three main weaknesses in the model are particularly relevant to the subject matter of this chapter. First, the notion of primary definer assumes that the government is not subject to internal division and so speaks to journalists with one voice. The model 'does not take account of contention between official sources in trying to influence the construction of a story' (Schlesinger and Tumber 1994: 18). Yet it is clear that no British government is a monolithic entity, acting with a unified will and a single sense of purpose. Rather, it is a divided and fragmented apparatus, where 'keenly fought rivalries between departments of government seeking to secure particular understandings of problems or particular "ways of thinking" . . . frequently stimulate new information flows, or "leaks", to the benefit of journalists operating within particular specialisms' (Manning 1999: 316).

Second, the model implies that 'the structure of access *necessarily* secures strategic advantages' for official sources and conversely that 'counter definitions can *never dislodge* the primary definition' (Schlesinger 1990: 66, emphasis in original). Yet the counter-definitional impact on the media of non-governmental sources needs to be borne in mind. The media regularly make use of other sources from a professional concern to cover an issue from different angles and, in the case of public service broadcasters, because they are also subject to regulations regarding impartiality and balance. Some sources may challenge the government's attempt to frame an issue in a particular way and may generate counter-definitions to try to displace the government's preferred primary definition. As a result, government actors often find themselves competing against other sources in their attempt to impose their perspective (McLaughlin and Miller 1996). The example of the Major premiership shows only too clearly the power that opposition spin-doctors can mobilise to undermine the government's version of events and impose their own agenda and news frames.

Finally, the notion of primary definition as put forward by Hall *et al.* tends 'to overstate the passivity of the media as recipients of information from news sources' (Schlesinger and Tumber 1994: 19). Yet the media may subject the government's definition of events to their own critical scrutiny, taking the initiative 'in the definitional process by challenging the so-called primary definers and forcing them to respond' (Schlesinger and Tumber 1994: 19). In addition, the primary definer thesis fails to take adequate account of variations not just between media sectors but also across genres within the same medium, as has been shown, for example, in the case of television coverage of 'terrorism' in Britain (Schlesinger *et al.* 1983).

An application of the primary definer model to the relationship between the first Blair government and the news media soon reveals its explanatory limitations. Two constraints on the power of the Blair government to dominate the news agenda from the centre are emphasised in the rest of this section. The first resulted from internal disunity at the very heart of the executive, which gave rise to confused and conflicting messages from the government's inner core. The second constraint was a product of the 'hollowing out' of the UK state, which resulted in an increased pluralism among official sources. To some extent both of these constraints on the primary defining power of the Blair government can be regarded as self-inflicted. This is clearly so in the case of the public manifestations of governmental division, but also, albeit to a lesser degree, in the case of greater source competition, since some of the new sources came into existence as a direct result of government policy. In certain respects, therefore, the Blair government was directly responsible for undermining its own command and control communications strategy.

First, the appearance of unity which characterised the public face of New Labour in opposition buckled when subjected to the stresses and strains of government. The fault-lines were rarely ideological. Sometimes they reflected the normal turf-war between ministerial departments; sometimes they were underpinned by divisions over policy, most notably on the issue of the single European currency; frequently they involved personality conflicts fuelled by ambition. Of course, division at the heart of government is scarcely a new phenomenon: during the Thatcher premiership there were significant disagreements between ministers on the question of state intervention in the economy, while under Major the European issue was a continual source of internecine strife. Both were running media stories during their respective premierships. The interesting element in the context of the first Blair government, however, was that examples of overt disunity as played out through the media frequently involved those at the very heart of the government's political communications machine leaking and briefing against each other. Paradoxically, those in charge of implementing the Labour government's communications strategy – the infamous spin-doctors – played leading roles in undermining one of its central rules: the maintenance of the semblance of unity in the public sphere. Two examples illustrate this point.

The first instance of a fall-out between Labour spin-doctors was the conflict between Peter Mandelson and Charlie Whelan, which culminated in the removal of both from their respective positions in late 1998/early 1999. Mandelson had been a key figure in the modernisation of the Labour Party following his appointment as the party's Director of Campaigns and Communications in the mid-1980s, acquiring the reputation of spin-doctor-in-chief of the New Labour project. A key figure in Blair's successful campaign for the party leadership in 1994, Mandelson was a close confidant of the Prime Minister in the early months of the Labour government, playing an important role in the formulation and implementation of the government's news management strategy. Whelan was special adviser in charge of media relations for the Chancellor of the Exchequer, Gordon Brown, who it was widely reported had no great fondness for Mandelson after the latter had allegedly betrayed him in the 1994 leadership contest (Macintyre 1999).

In the first eighteen months of the Labour government Whelan acted as a maverick in his relations with political journalists, effectively mocking the command and control organisation imposed by Number 10 on the communications activities of other government ministries. Instead, Whelan's briefings to the media were used to boost the popularity of his ministerial boss, with Brown consistently refusing to rein him in, despite obvious Downing Street irritation. The fractious relationship between Whelan and the Prime Minister's Office famously included a media story in January 1998 sourced from Number 10 that Brown had 'psychological flaws' which were increasingly irritating the Prime Minister (Rawnsley 2000: 143–66). While the relationship between Blair and Brown seemed to recover, the infighting between spin-doctors remained a feature of government throughout 1998. This culminated in a mutual letting of blood at the end of the year. From the Blair side Mandelson had to resign his ministerial post over media revelations of financial impropriety and conflict of interests. This was followed shortly by the enforced departure of Whelan, who was suspected by the Blair camp of having been implicated in the leaking of the news about Mandelson's financial dealings to a sympathetic journalist. The media had a field day in their news coverage of and commentary on this spectacular rift between leading courtiers in the Blair and Brown camps (Jones 1999: 259–80; Rawnsley 2000: 210–34).

The second example of public division involving leading Labour spin-doctors involved the two men who had masterminded Labour's communications strategy in opposition: Mandelson and Campbell. Again, the issue focused on Mandelson's probity in his ministerial conduct – in this case his alleged involvement in the granting of UK passports to three wealthy Indian brothers who had given money to the Millennium Dome project in which Mandelson had previously been closely involved. Media coverage of the Hinduja affair focused on both Mandelson's actions (what happened?) and his subsequent account of his behaviour to the media and the Prime Minister (had he told the truth?). Confusion on both counts led to Mandelson being forced to resign from government for a second time at the start of 2001 (Jones 2001: 265–302).

Following the resignation, a media briefing war immediately broke out between Campbell and Mandelson. Campbell tried to distance Number 10 from the activities of the now ex-minister, effectively giving him the political last rites when he described Mandelson as 'slightly detached' and wanting 'to get out of frontline politics' (*Independent on Sunday*, 28 January 2001). As Mandelson toured media newsrooms to put his version of events, former ministerial colleagues lined up to denigrate him in no uncertain terms: 'he has got problems telling the truth' said the Secretary of State for International Development, Clare Short (*The Guardian*, 29 January 2001).

Over the next few days the battlelines between government and ex-minister hardened, as scores were settled amid a blaze of media publicity. The fight to manage the news agenda was being lost by Number 10, as other stories which the government wanted to promote in this pre-election campaign period were submerged by the Mandelson affair. Ironically, in moving so quickly to try to kill off a possible story about alleged ministerial wrongdoing, Number 10 had unintentionally ensured that the Mandelson saga would dominate the news agenda for days. On this occasion the rapid reaction response – an integral feature of Labour's communications strategy – had disastrously backfired.

These two spectacular examples of conflict among Labour spin-doctors highlight three important points regarding the primary defining power of the first Blair government. First, and most obviously, they demonstrate how division at the heart of the executive sometimes made the transmission of a clear message impossible. This was especially the case because major figures in government were involved in competition and even antagonism as official sources for journalists. Second, they show how leading spin-doctors were active participants in the process of fomenting discord through briefings and leaks to the media. Correspondents did not have to engage in painstaking investigative journalism to uncover disagreement, nor did reporters merely observe the conflict from the sidelines as in coverage of a sporting contest. Instead, journalists were served up on a plate competing versions of events by professionals in political communication who as sources immersed in a culture of leaks and off-the-record briefings knew exactly the import of every comment they made down to the last detailed nuance. Third, the two examples reveal the dangers for government of high-profile spinning. When spin-doctors become the story, media attention inevitably focuses on public relations aspects of governmental activity. The risk for government is that this coverage will tend to be critical and run counter to its desire for the media to focus on positive achievements.

The second constraint on the agenda-setting and framing power of the Blair government as primary definer was a product of the 'hollowing out' of the UK state (Rhodes 1994). Alternative sites of power to the traditional Whitehall–Westminster axis, including the institutions of the European Union, a host of independent regulatory authorities, devolved assemblies in Scotland and Wales and the mayorship of London, have come to prominence in British politics in recent years, resulting in greater pluralism among official sources (Riddell 1998: 14). Of course, there has always been a degree of source competition, for instance between government and opposition in Parliament. However, the combination of the hollowing out process at the institutional level and the spread of the media-driven promotional culture has led to the growing involvement of non-governmental sources in professional news media relations, thereby increasing the supply to journalists of potential counter-definers to central government in the task of agenda construction (Manning 2001: 137–201. Parliamentary select commit-tees, single issue pressure groups and professional bodies among others have established themselves as routine sources for journalists because of their acknowledged expertise on an issue, for example the media input of hospital consultants and Health Service Trust managers on the question of NHS funding. This development has further ensured that 'every Lobby journalist develops sources against which he can test material from the centre' (Roth 1999: 24). While this does not mean that in general journalists actively seek out a large variety of alternative sources, evidence for which seems scant (Negrine 1996: 27), it does suggest that they routinely access information from a range of official sources, both within and outside government.

Moreover, ironically some of these new political communication actors were brought into existence as a result of the Blair government's programme of constitutional and institutional reform. Indeed, the establishment of devolved legislative institutions in Scotland and Wales and the introduction of a directly elected mayor for London did not just bring into existence new sites of political communication – locations for potential contestation in the definitional process of agenda construction – it also provided opposition actors with electoral legitimacy, public resources and a new institutional platform for their own news management activities. The inability of Labour to impose one-party control over the Scottish Parliament and Welsh Assembly undermined the Blair government's command and control communica-tions strategy in these parts of the United Kingdom. The failure of the official Labour candidate in the London mayoral contest, despite the personal endorsement of the Prime Minister, was also highly damaging. The process of the election campaign allowed internal party conflict to spill out into the public sphere, while the victory of the Labour rebel Ken Livingstone, standing as an Independent, provided those on the left of the party with a rare political communications base from which to criticise the New Labour project (Rawnsley 2000: 342–71).

The interdependency between government and political journalists

The previous section concentrated on two endogenous problems the first Blair government faced in acting effectively as a primary definer in agenda construction. Such a source-centred approach, however, focuses on only one set of political communication actors – the political elites of govern-ment ministers, special advisers and spin-doctors – and ignores the other group involved in the process of news production – media proprietors, editors and journalists. Rather than adopt an exclusively media-centred focus, however, this section concentrates on key aspects of the interdependent relationship between the government and political journalists.

This requires a more dynamic and nuanced approach than that provided by the primary definer model with its emphasis on the structural power of government as an official source. Instead we need to bring in elements of both the exchange and adversary models of source–journalist relations. We also need to recognise that important features in the organisation and functioning of the media affect the agenda-structuring strategies of sources, facilitating or impeding the access and coverage they crave. Some of these features are outside the control of sources and may have to be accepted by them as fixed elements in the political communications system, such as the norms of balance and impartiality imposed on public service broadcasters and to a large extent accepted by other broadcasting outlets. Other features are more amenable to being influenced by sources, such as the dominant system of news values and their application to a particular story (Blumler and Gurevitch 1995: 38), exemplified by the way in which political actors successfully stage pseudo events to grab media attention.

Even an apparently structural variable may in fact be open to change, with sources making a significant contribution to the process. Good examples in this context were the important modifications in national newspaper partisanship which occurred in Britain between the 1992 victory of John Major and Labour's general election triumph in 1997. In the light of the efforts made by Blair's Labour Party to neutralise traditional press opponents or, even better, bring them round to supporting the New Labour project, it is worth examining the impact of this aspect of interdependency between politicians and the media for political journalism during the first Blair government.

National newspapers have long been and remain powerful political communication actors in Britain. In part this is due to their high nationwide circulations, which make them important opinion-formers for their readers over time, even if their short-term electoral influence should not be overstated (Curtice 1997). Just as significantly, they are key agenda-setters for radio and television (Tunstall 1996), making a major contribution to setting the terms of political debate across the media as a whole (Hagerty 2000: 17). In contrast to broadcasters, newspapers adopt an overt editorial line, frequently functioning as a source of and platform for opposition to government – a role they performed quite devastatingly during the final years of the Major premiership (Jones 1995: 91–121; 189–219). Indeed, the intense partisanship of national newspapers in Britain distinguishes them from their counterparts in several other advanced liberal democracies.

For most of the postwar period this partisanship operated to the disadvantage of Labour, most cruelly during the Thatcher premiership in the 1980s (Seymour-Ure 1992). In the run-up to the 1997 general election, however, Labour was very successful in disarming the guns of the Tory press and even winning some national newspapers, most notably Rupert Murdoch's *Sun*, over to its cause (McNair 2000: 146–55). In the case of *The*

Sun it was the proprietor himself rather than the paper's chief editor or political editor who was held responsible for the change of political line (Scammell and Harrop 1997). Under Blair's leadership, Labour in opposition actively set out to curry favour with sections of the national press, especially the Murdoch papers (Neil 1997; Johnson 1998; Hagerty 2000: 15). As part of the charm offensive, Blair flew halfway around the world to give a speech to News International executives, giving rise to speculation that in return for support from Murdoch's newspapers an incoming Labour government would not introduce tough cross-media ownership legislation.

During the first Blair government national newspaper partisanship exhibited three notable traits: it was conditional, volatile and, especially among the broadsheets, multifaceted. First, while some national newspapers remained natural supporters of Labour (for example, the Mirror Group titles) and some committed opponents (for instance, the Telegraph titles), several newspapers were prepared to give support to the Blair government – but only on a conditional basis. *The Sun* was one of the best examples of this phenomenon. The support given by *The Sun* to the Blair government after 1997, evidenced by the paper again backing Labour in the 2001 general election, cannot be compared with the unconditional adulation the same newspaper accorded the Conservative government, and particularly Thatcher as Prime Minister, during the 1980s.

The European issue was the key factor in this respect. Murdoch is known to be opposed to Britain becoming more closely integrated within the European Union and in particular to British adoption of the single European currency. On this latter issue, *The Sun* remained wary of Labour, even portraying Blair in one headline as 'the most dangerous man in Britain' because of his stance on the Euro (*The Sun*, 24 June 1998). In its relationship with *The Sun*, therefore, Labour could not assume or command support. Rather, it had to bargain for it. On occasions, this caused some political disquiet, as when Blair was accused of intervening with the Italian Prime Minister, Romano Prodi, on behalf of a potential Murdoch media bid in Italy in 1998 (Jones 1999: 200–4). On a day-to-day basis, Trevor Kavanagh, the political editor of *The Sun*, was one of the lobby journalists selected by Campbell to receive preferential treatment as a conduit for stories. In return, the Murdoch press provided a good platform for the Labour government. For instance, Blair had numerous articles published under his byline, especially in *The Sun*: twenty-three in Murdoch newspapers overall and fifteen in *The Sun* alone between the election victory in May 1997 and January 1998, 'far more than the number of articles he has written for all other national newspapers' (Johnson 1998: 19).

Second, national newspaper partisanship during this period was volatile. A newspaper's proclaimed editorial partisanship did not determine the nature or tone of journalistic coverage on a daily basis. Newspapers generally supportive of Blair sometimes adopted a hostile attitude in their coverage on certain issues and at particular times in the electoral cycle. A leading media correspondent on *The Times*, for example, pointed to evidence of journalists turning on Labour at the start of 2000. 'What has been surprising as Blair marked his first thousand days has been *the criticism from the papers that are sympathetic to him*' (MacArthur 2000, my emphasis). Though such newspaper volatility was by no means a new development in British politics – witness the critical coverage given by the *Daily Mirror* to Labour Prime Minister Harold Wilson in the late 1960s (Pimlott 1992: 505–6) – for the media-sensitive Blair government it was a particularly worrying scenario.

Finally, newspaper partisanship, especially among the broadsheets, was increasingly becoming more multifaceted, demonstrated by 'the decline of the single editorial voice' (Seymour-Ure 1998: 43). Broadsheet newspapers magnified their tendency to incorporate different partisan viewpoints in their political coverage: 'Papers make a virtue out of a variety of opinion. Where they have a party tendency, they license some discordant voices' (Seymour-Ure 1998: 47). In providing commentary on events and inter-pretation of issues from a subjective viewpoint, political columnists were less restricted than lobby correspondents or leader writers by hierarchical controls or corporate constraints. The genre of columnist journalism lends itself both to a critical approach and a policy focus (Tunstall 1996: 281–96). Columnists could engage more easily in a highly personalised, opinionated and literary form of political journalism which did not necessarily conform with the editorial stance of the newspaper. According to one political journalist, during the first Blair government this was the case at *The Times* where

> readers of the top people's paper were presented with a schizophrenic menu. The political news pages endeavoured to place the best possible construction on [Labour] government policy, while on the comment pages Gove, Kaletsky, Rees-Mogg, Parris and others . . . were all capable of placing the worst.
>
> (Oborne 1999: 175)

Tabloid newspapers could also exhibit the same tendency. For example, Richard Littlejohn's forceful column in *The Sun* was often highly critical of Blair's premiership. While this form of internal pluralism is not synonymous with a simple rejection of party political endorsement, it is clear that editorial opinion as expressed in a paper's leader column no longer defines the framework for a newspaper's political coverage as a whole.

Within this context of weaker newspaper partisanship, government spin-doctors had to try to win over newspaper journalists and keep them 'onside'. The system of mass lobby briefings remained an integral institutional feature of government–journalist interdependency, with the Sunday lobby, for example, being used 'to trail forthcoming announcements on govern-ment decisions and policy proposals' (Jones 2001: 195). However, the effectiveness of lobby briefings as a tool of governmental news manage-ment has increasingly been called into question over recent years (Scammell 1995: 200). Peter Riddell, for example, the political columnist of *The Times* and former political editor of the *Financial Times*, describes the collective lobby briefing system as a 'minor source for any semi-competent political journalist' (Riddell 1999: 28). The sheer size of the lobby, now consisting of well over 200 journalists, militates against the notion of the all powerful Number 10 Press Secretary. In addition, the lobby lost much of its mystique after 1997. Though the televising of its proceedings continued to be rejected on the grounds that this would give too much publicity to the Prime Minister's Official Spokesman, briefings were carried out on an on-the-record basis, Campbell was frequently named in news reports and after March 2000 a selective summary of the briefing was made available on a government website.

With an unprecedented amount of mediated political information available to audiences – from traditional newspapers to rolling news channels (McNair 2000: 14–41) – the Blair government had to deal with a huge array of political journalists. While this made a command and control approach problematic, it provided the government with the opportunity to follow an alternative strategy of 'divide and rule'. Government spin-doctors exploited the highly competitive culture of lobby journalists by favouring some at the expense of others (Hagerty 2000: 13–14; Palmer 2000: 54). On a day-to-day basis certain lobby journalists were accorded information subsidies (Gandy 1982) in the form of advance notice of material that the government wished to bring into the public sphere. For instance, Campbell enjoyed good relations with Philip Webster, political editor of *The Times*, who was willing to provide generally sympathetic coverage of government initiatives in return for privileged access. Similarly, Whelan was renowned for having a close relationship with Paul Routledge, political columnist on *The Mirror* and a supporter of the Brown camp. Some, though by no means all, lobby journalists were willing to align themselves more or less overtly with a leading figure in the Labour government via the relevant spin-doctor.

In the broadcasting sector, the cultivation of the 'contextualising voices' of the political editors of British television news (McNair 2000: 73) was considered vitally important. At the same time the Blair spin-doctors were not slow to show disapproval of what they regarded as unfair broadcast coverage. For instance, Campbell went public on more than one occasion in criticising the political output of the BBC, especially its elite radio programmes such as *Today* and *The World at One*. One of the government's favourite means of refusing to engage with broadcasting journalists in the hope of killing off a story was to decline to provide a spokesperson for interview – a tactic employed, for example, on the elite late-evening television news programme, *Newsnight*. On one occasion the programme went so far as to display an empty chair in the studio, with presenter Jeremy Paxman complaining that 'no ministerial bottom' could be found to fill it (Rawnsley 2000: 101).

Yet in the interdependent relationship with government, journalists cannot simply be presented as either willing accomplices or passive victims. The news management operations of government spin-doctors necessarily involve journalists in an active process of selection, interpretation, evaluation and (re)construction of the information presented them. Referring to the work of Ericson, Baranek and Chan (1989), Negrine comments that while the information subsidy provided by the source 'lubricates the supply of, and demand for, information . . . it cannot guarantee that the information will be processed as desired by the source' (Negrine 1996: 28). Rather like the audience's relationship with media messages in Hall's encoding/decoding model (Hall 1992), journalists may accept, negotiate with or reject the proffered political spin.

Indeed, for the Prime Minister's Official Spokesman, it was the journalists who were the main spin-doctors during the first Blair government: from Campbell's perspective the government was more spinned against than spinning (Hagerty 2000: 7), a point he tried to put across to a wider public by giving unprecedented one-off access to a BBC camera team to film his relationship with lobby journalists for a documentary programme, *News from No. 10*. One example cited to support this view was coverage of the European issue by much of the British press (Anderson and Weymouth 1999), much of which the government regarded as unreasonably framed from a Eurosceptic perspective (see Chapter 6 by Baisnée). At the end of June 2000, for example, Campbell used the Number 10 website to launch an attack on the way in which much of the British press had covered a speech on the European Union given by Blair on a visit to Germany. He accused *The Sun* and *Daily Mail* of distortion and misrepresentation, while *The Times*, *The Independent* and *Daily Telegraph* were also lambasted. More serious, Campbell believed, was the way in which press bias and misrepresentation set the agenda for broadcasters 'who endlessly repeat the clichés of isolation, division and international conflict' (*The Guardian*, 1 July 2000).

While the Eurosceptic framing of the single currency issue was overwhelmingly shaped by the newspaper proprietors' self-interest, on other stories the government's approach to news management ran up against a 'media logic' (Altheide and Snow 1979) which may be regarded as part of what Blumler and Gurevitch call 'the journalistic fight-back' to the 'professionalization of political advocacy' (Blumler and Gurevitch 1995: 210–11). In a highly competitive media system, driven by the relentless pursuit of audiences and advertisers, the operationalisation of news values frequently pushed journalists into a critical or even adversarial stance with regard to the Blair government.

The revelation of scandal is an obvious case in point. Some of the toughest news management tests for the Blair government were in this area, hardly surprising in the light of Labour attacks on Conservative sleaze during the final years of the Major premiership. The Ecclestone affair, which concerned large secret donations to the Labour Party (Rawnsley 2000: 89–105), and allegations of impropriety made against a succession of ministers, including Geoffrey Robinson, Mandelson and Keith Vaz, revealed the capacity and willingness of the news media, particularly broadsheet newspaper journalists, to initiate and pursue stories highly critical of leading Labour figures. Coverage of both Mandelson resignations, for instance, had all the hallmarks of a media feeding frenzy as the journalist pack celebrated the kill (Rawnsley 2000: 210–34; Jones 2001: 265–302). *The Sun's* front page headline on the second occasion was particularly scathing: 'Goodbye and good riddance (This time don't come back)' (*The Sun*, 25 January 2001).

When in the case of his second resignation the official inquiry later cleared Mandelson of any wrongdoing, the Prime Minister's judgement in acting so hastily was called into question by the media, as journalists asked whether Blair had panicked (*The Times*, 9 February 2001; *The Guardian*, 10 March 2001). If true, this was cruelly ironic since the speed with which the resignation took place had apparently been driven by the need to give the lobby journalists a definitive statement so that they could meet deadlines. This example thus illustrated the importance of a point made by Tiffen with regard to the interaction of the media and politics in Australia: 'Prominent and extensive reporting, an urgent tone, and the presence of journalists *en masse* waiting expectantly, all escalate the pressure for an immediate, decisive resolution' (Tiffen 1989: 195).

Stories about internal splits, dissension and division also conform to news value criteria which are by no means unique to the British media (McCurry 1996: 5). As one leading political editor, Michael White of *The Guardian*, argued:

> I sometimes get a fear that it is impossible to have a civilised and reasonable debate about, let us say, the merits of the Euro within a political party . . . because people like us cry 'Split'. The reason we cry split is because it is one way of getting things into print in an adversarial media culture. The word 'split' will get you into a newspaper more quickly than the words 'total agreement', so it tends to feed a slightly vicious circle there which accentuates even mild disagreement between colleagues.
>
> (House of Commons Select Committee on Public Administration 1998: 19)

This media focus on internal disagreements encouraged the Blair government to intensify its command and control approach, since the journalistic imperative for a 'good story' conflicted with the government's desire for favourable coverage. This defensive response then evoked cries of 'control freakery' from the news media and ritualistic denials from government. As a result, increasingly during the first Blair government 'spin' itself became the story. Yet, despite their oft-proclaimed condemnation, political journalists have an ambivalent attitude towards the spinning activities of government. This is because to some extent journalists rely on spin and may even admire the sheer professionalism of the public relations activities of government as source. When Campbell announced in 2000 that he would be taking on a more strategic role in governmental communications and handing over the lobby briefings to his deputy, Godric Smith, many lobby journalists were disappointed since Smith lacked Campbell's insider relationship with Blair.

At the same time, political journalists need to emphasise their independence from government as part of their own professional self-legitimation in the eyes of audiences (McNair 2000: 136). One way of doing this is by unmasking and deconstructing the attempted political spin. Thus, as part of the increased media attention to political process as opposed to policy, government news management activities themselves became an integral part of media coverage as journalists unpacked the government's packaging for their audiences. For example, while stories about spending plans in the early years of the Blair government were spun reasonably successfully, journalists later became wise to the misrepresentation of figures by spin-doctors in their attempt to extract maximum partisan advantage from a story. As a result, subsequent news stories focused increasingly on the government's attempts to manipulate presentation.

Finally, on some issues journalists took upon themselves the mantle of advocates of public concern, holding the government (and relevant official bodies) to account. During the first Blair government such an approach was noticeable, for instance, in media coverage of the authorities' response to the Paddington and Hatfield rail disasters, when the issue of rail safety dominated the news agenda for several days and many sections of the media not only articulated but arguably fuelled high levels of public concern on this issue. Health was another issue where much media coverage reflected public disquiet, highlighted by the successive winter flu 'crises' which stretched the resources of the NHS to breaking point. In these instances the media fulfilled a critical social responsibility function. Sometimes the media appeared to agree the line on a story, framing it in a way unhelpful to the authorities. The almost universally critical coverage by newspapers of the Millennium Dome as a visitor attraction during 2000 had many elements of a good, critical story: ministers on the defensive, the wasteful use of lottery money, a Blair-backed project as a grandiose symbol of New Labour's populism, disappointing attendance figures. In this instance the news media were largely responsible for setting the agenda and framing the coverage of the Dome, in a way that in a self-fulfilling prophecy helped to determine its fate.

In short, in their interdependent relationship with the first Blair government, journalists frequently used their power to expose politicians, play up disagreements, demystify the political process and make a contribution to the agenda of public policy-making. Even the professional spin-doctors of Labour were increasingly driven to express their exasperation at their failure to shape news coverage as they would wish. In just one week in early March 2000, for example, Campbell berated journalists over their coverage of the genetically modified food issue for 'putting their own spin on the Prime Minister's words in pursuit of their own agendas'; criticised the coverage of the National Health Service issue by the London *Evening Standard* as 'exactly the kind of exaggerated, wilful misinterpretation that dogs not just health, but so many other serious policy issues'; wrote to the BBC to complain that a current affairs programme on the London mayoral election was nothing less than a 'poisonous piece of propaganda'; and argued that while it was once media fashion to be hugely pro-Blair, 'the current fashion is broadly to dump on him' (Ellis 2000).

Of course, these protestations of government helplessness in the face of an allegedly powerful news media might well themselves have been part of government spin. After all, it is in the government's interest to shape the news agenda without being seen to do so. They were certainly part of the ritual of exchange between government and media as the former negotiated a bad news trough. However, in all likelihood they also reflected genuine exasperation on the part of government as journalists exercised their relative autonomy and the resultant media coverage on a host of issues was rather different from what the government would have liked.

Conclusion

This chapter has argued that the interdependency between the first Blair government and political journalists is more usefully analysed with reference to the framework put forward by Blumler and Gurevitch, which incorporates ideas of exchange and adversarial contestation, rather than Hall's model based on the notion of primary definition (Blumler and Gurevitch 1995: 25–44; Hall *et al.* 1978).

Why then do journalists devote so much attention to the alleged 'spinning' power of politicians? Why the emphasis on Campbell and other spin-doctors as such omnipotent figures at the heart of the first Blair government? Various explanations suggest themselves. First, and most obviously, elite political actors in Britain do now pay more attention to communication strategies than in the past. It would be surprising if this development were not the object of considerable media coverage as it is a legitimate matter of public interest. Political journalists have learnt to live with this state of affairs, perhaps just as well since they are themselves implicated in its development. Spin can be functional to their work, helping them make sense of a story in an era of information overload and rolling deadlines. Moreover, journalists are ideally positioned to comment on the professionalism of some politicians and their advisers in this respect (for instance, Labour in opposition under Blair) as well as to show their contempt for those deemed to have failed (such as those involved in news management during the Major premiership after 1992).

Second, writing about process is easier than writing about policy. This is especially the case as journalists are intimately involved as 'insiders': they can write about a political game in which they are perfectly familiar with the players, rules, strategies and tactics and can communicate that 'insider information' to their audiences. Process journalism can focus on personalities and human interest stories – who's in and who's out of favour in the governmental entourage. This is information which audiences can easily assimilate. In contrast, a focus on policy may require the acquisition and deployment of different, and more specialist, skills: many parliamentary lobby journalists, for example, have little expertise in economics. In an age of increasingly technical debates and a more complex decision-making process involving supranational and global actors, it is more difficult both for journalists to explain the details of policy issues to audiences and for the latter to understand them.

Third, the focus on spin allows journalists to reassert their own power in the interdependent relationship with politicians and demonstrate this publicly to their audiences. In commenting on the political 'game' journalists seek to show that they cannot be fooled by the news management tricks of politicians. Building up the power of political spin helps in this self-legitimation exercise. The more powerful the spin-doctors are painted – 'the hidden world of the news manipulators' (Cockerell *et al.* 1984), the 'sultans of spin' (Jones 1995), 'control freaks' (Jones 2001) – the more significant is the role journalists ascribe to themselves in countering that power. By first demonising the power of spin, journalists can hope to create a positive image of themselves in the minds of their audiences when they then act subversively to reveal the machinations of the spin-doctors.

References

Altheide, D.L. and Snow, R.P. (1979) *Media Logic*, Beverly Hills, Calif.: Sage.

Anderson, P. J. and Weymouth, A. (1999) *Insulting the Public? The British Press and the European Union*, London: Longman.

Barnett, S. and Gaber, I. (2001) *Westminster Tales. The Twenty-first-century Crisis in Political Journalism*, London: Continuum.

Blumler, J.G. and Gurevitch, M. (1995) *The Crisis of Public Communication*, London: Routledge.

Butler, D. and Kavanagh, D. (1997) *The British General Election of 1997*, London: Macmillan.

Cockerell, M., Hennessy, P. and Walker, D. (1984) *Sources Close to the Prime Minister*, London: Macmillan.

Crewe, I., Gosschalk, B. and Bartle, J. (1998) *Political Communications: Why Labour Won the General Election of 1997*, London: Frank Cass.

Curtice, J. (1997) 'Is the *Sun* shining on Tony Blair? The electoral influence of British newspapers', *Harvard International Journal of Press/Politics* 2/2: 9–26.

Deacon, D. and Golding, P. (1994) *Taxation and Representation: The Media, Political Communication and the Poll Tax*, London: John Libbey.

Ellis, C. (2000) 'A week of spin', *Media Guardian*, 6 March 2000.

Ericson, R.V., Baranek, P.M. and Chan, J.B. (1989) *Negotiating Control: A Study of News Sources*, Milton Keynes: Open University Press.

Esser, F., Reinemann, C. and Fan, D. (2000) 'Spin doctoring in British and German election campaigns', *European Journal of Communication* 15/2: 209–39.

Foley, M. (2000) *The British Presidency*, Manchester: Manchester University Press.

Franklin, B. (1994) *Packaging Politics*, London: Edward Arnold.

Gaber, I. (2000) 'Lies, damn lies . . . and political spin', *British Journalism Review* 11/1: 60–70.

Gandy, O. (1982) *Beyond Agenda Setting: Information Subsidies and Public Policy*, Norwood, N.J.: Ablex.

Hagerty, B. (2000) 'Cap'n spin *does* lose his rag', *British Journalism Review* 11/2:7–20.

Hall, S. (1992) 'Encoding/decoding', in S. Hall, D. Hobson, A. Lowe and P. Willis (eds) *Culture, Media, Language*, London: Routledge.

Hall, S., Critcher, C., Jefferson, T., Clarke, J. and Roberts, B. (1978) *Policing the Crisis*, London: Macmillan.

Harris, R. (1990) *Good and Faithful Servant*, London: Faber and Faber.

Heffernan, R. and Marqusee, M. (1992) *Defeat from the Jaws of Victory*, London: Verso.

Heffernan, R. and Stanyer, J. (1998) 'The British Prime Minister and the Labour Government: political communication strategies and the formation of the news media agenda', paper presented at the workshop on Prime Ministers' and Presidents' Relations with the News Media at the 1998 ECPR joint sessions, University of Warwick.

Hennessy, P. (2000) *The Prime Minister*, London: Allen Lane.

House of Commons Select Committee on Public Administration (1998) *The Government Information and Communication Service*, HC 770, London: The Stationery Office.

Hughes, C. and Wintour, P. (1990) *Labour Rebuilt*, London: Fourth Estate.

Ingham, B. (1991) *Kill the Messenger*, London: Fontana.

Johnson, J. (1998) 'Rupert's grip?', *British Journalism Review* 9/1: 13–19.

Johnson, J. (1999) 'Second most powerful man in Britain?' *British Journalism Review* 10/4: 67–71.

Jones, N. (1995) *Soundbites & spin-doctors*, London: Cassell.

Jones, N. (1999) *Sultans of Spin*, London: Victor Gollancz.

Jones, N. (2001) *The Control Freaks*, London: Politico's.

Kavanagh, D. (1995) *Election Campaigning: The New Marketing of Politics*, Oxford: Blackwell.

MacArthur, B. (2000) 'Watch out Tony, the worm is turning', *The Times*, 28 January 2000.

McCurry, M. (1996) 'The background on background', *Harvard International Journal of Press/Politics* 1/4: 4–9.

Macintyre, D. (1999) *Mandelson*, London: HarperCollins.

McLaughlin, G. and Miller, D. (1996) 'The media politics of the Irish peace process', *Harvard International Journal of Press/Politics* 1/4: 116–34.

McNair, B. (2000) *Journalism and Democracy*, London: Routledge.

Manning, P. (1999) 'Categories of knowledge and information flows: reasons for the decline of the British Labour and Industrial Correspondents' Group', *Media, Culture and Society* 21: 313–36.

Manning, P. (2001) *News and News Sources*, London: Sage.

Miller, D. (1993) 'Official sources and "primary definition": the case of Northern Ireland, *Media, Culture and Society* 15: 385–406.

Morrison, D. and Tumber, H. (1988) *Journalists at War*, London: Sage.

Negrine, R. (1996) *The Communication of Politics*, London: Sage.

Neil, A. (1997) *Full Disclosure*, London: Pan.

Oborne, P. (1999) *Alastair Campbell*, London: Aurum.

Palmer, J. (2000) *Spinning into Control: News Values and Source Strategies*, London: Leicester University Press.

Pimlott, B. (1992) *Harold Wilson*, London: HarperCollins.

Rawnsley, A. (2000) *Servants of the People*, London: Hamish Hamilton.

Rhodes, R. (1994) 'The hollowing out of the state', *The Political Quarterly* 65/2: 138–51.

Riddell, P. (1998) 'Members and Millbank: the media and Parliament', in J. Seaton (ed.), *Politics and the Media: Harlots and Prerogatives at the Turn of the Millennium*, Oxford: Blackwell.

Riddell, P. (1999) 'A shift of power – and influence', *British Journalism Review* 10/3: 26–33.

Roth, A. (1999) 'The Lobby's "dying gasps"?', *British Journalism Review* 10/3: 21–5.

Scammell, M. (1995) *Designer Politics*, London: Macmillan.

Scammell, M. (2001) 'The media and media management', in A. Seldon (ed.) *The Blair Effect*, London: Little, Brown.

Scammell, M. and Harrop, M. (1997) 'The press', in D. Butler and D. Kavanagh, *The British General Election of 1997*, Basingstoke: Macmillan.

Schlesinger, P., Murdock, G. and Elliott, P. (1983) *Televising Terrorism*, London: Comedia.

Schlesinger, P. (1990) 'Rethinking the sociology of journalism: source strategies and the limits of media-centrism', in M. Ferguson (ed.) *Public Communication: The New Imperatives*, London: Sage.

Schlesinger, P. and Tumber, H. (1994) *Reporting Crime*, Oxford: Clarendon Press.

Seymour-Ure, C. (1992) 'Press partisanship: into the 1990s', in D. Kavanagh (ed.) *Electoral Politics*, Oxford: Clarendon Press.

Seymour-Ure, C. (1998) 'Are the broadsheets becoming unhinged?', in J. Seaton (ed.) *Politics and the Media: Harlots and Prerogatives at the Turn of the Millennium*, Oxford: Blackwell.

Shaw, E. (1994) *The Labour Party since 1979: Crisis and Transformation*, London: Routledge.

Tiffen, R. (1989) *News and Power*, Sydney: Allen & Unwin.

Tunstall, J. (1970) *The Westminster Lobby Correspondents*, London: Routledge & Kegan Paul.

Tunstall, J. (1996) *Newspaper Power*, Oxford: Clarendon Press.

Wernick, A. (1991) *Promotional Culture*, London: Sage.

4 A crisis in the mirror

Old and new elements in Italian political communication

Franca Roncarolo

The relationship between Italian journalists and politicians has recently gone through profound changes, from a paradigmatic example of parallelism (Seymour-Ure 1974) to what is now frequently open conflict. Prime ministers from very different political cultures, like the leader of the centre-right party Forza Italia, Silvio Berlusconi, or the former Communist Party leader, Massimo D'Alema, have shared a very similar antipathy to the press, which has stood accused of being more interested in controversies than in professional reporting. For their part, people who work in the information field complain about the effects of a growing 'assault on the media' by politicians who are accustomed to exploiting journalists' coverage while showing contempt towards its authors.

As is well known, the phenomenon is neither original nor unusual in Western democracies. Yet in the Italian case the emergence of tensions between politicians and journalists has causes – and follows dynamics – which merit close analysis so as to help explain the present situation and its possible evolution. More specifically, it is not clear whether the clashes between political leaders and reporters are signs of a conflict between different rationales, which usually results from the modernisation process (Swanson and Mancini 1996) and the emergence of a media logic (Altheide and Snow 1979), or whether the difficulties in Italian public communication must be explored with reference to a crisis that has broken the consociational logic and pushed the media to the centre of the political stage without freeing them from old ties.

Starting from the impression that – despite apparent changes – Italian political journalism has not yet found an appropriate role, the interpretative hypotheses suggested in this chapter is that it still suffers from a lack, rather than an excess, of autonomy as a link between politics and citizens; and, in the context of a more adversarial relationship with political actors, it is experiencing difficulty in finding new, less self-referential forms of political communication. If these hypotheses are valid, then in examining the Italian experience we must use the concept of crisis in a different way from that suggested by scholars with regard to other national cases

(Jamieson 1992; Raboy and Dagenais 1992; Blumler and Gurevitch 1995; Dahlgren 1995).

While the latter emphasise above all the negative effects on democracy deriving from the central role played by the media, and particularly from the capacity of television to frame political issues in line with a media-related rationale,[1] in the Italian case the main problem is a deficit in the structural and cultural autonomy of journalism. Of course, this does not mean that television has no influence, nor that it has not introduced into the Italian system the classic forms of personalisation and dramatisation typically shown by media politics (Arterton 1985; Patterson 1993; Bennet 1995; Jamieson 1996). But as the modernisation of the Italian media occurred in a system that was largely conditioned by political needs and party rationales, changes were only partial and were generally confined to a very superficial level. As a result, when the political system started to show problems, political journalism also entered an increasingly serious crisis.

In order to document this hypothesis, two complementary lines of argument are developed in this chapter. The first considers the phenomenon within a theoretical framework based on a systemic analysis which documents the main features of Italian political communication. The second reconstructs the most important changes in the relationship between journalists and politicians, focusing on continuities and discontinuities among the different phases and exploring the representation of the crisis proposed in the press and public debates.

Features of the Italian public communication system

Even if with regard to the Italian case we use the concept of crisis in a different way from that employed by Blumler and Gurevitch, their study still offers a very useful methodological perspective for two main reasons. First, there is no doubt that the 'roots of the crisis [regarding the relationships between politicians, citizens and journalists] are *systemic* – that is, they inhere in the very structures and functioning of present-day political communication systems' (1995: 4, italics in original). Second, the analytic schema for comparative research that Blumler and Gurevitch re-propose in *The Crisis of Public Communication* highlights interdependencies and interactions between the media and politics.[2] According to this schema, in each different national case the connection between media institutions and political institutions may vary along four dimensions (Blumler and Gurevitch 1995: 61–7). These are:

- the degree of state control over mass media organisations
- the degree of mass media partisanship
- the degree of media–political elite integration
- the nature of the legitimising creed of media institutions.

Degree of state control over mass media organisations

It is well documented that the Italian media have never been really independent of the political sphere (Marletti 1984, 1995b; Pasquino 1986; Castronovo and Tranfaglia 1994; Novelli 1995). Not surprisingly, in the 1970s Almond and Powell (1978) evaluated the freedom of Italian press and television to criticise national government and local administrations as a 'moderate' freedom. There is no doubt that for many years political parties have controlled the communication system.

The case of public television is well known and shows the long-term presence of a double level of control: one formal, exerted by the Supervisory Commission, and the other informal, but no less substantial, by parties through the appointment of their followers to top positions and executive boards. Even if the form and sources of political control of the RAI (the state broadcasting corporation) have changed over the years, the substance has remained almost the same.[3] Of course, modernisation of the communication apparatus has increased the autonomy of public television. And it is certainly true that 'the political system began to spiral out of control following the "*Mani pulite*" [Clean hands] affair' (Ricolfi 1997: 137). However, nobody can say that in Italy political control of public television has been totally eliminated. The simple fact that, even today, politicians appoint the board and top directors of the RAI shows that the autonomy of public television cannot be total. Moreover, the polemic that occurs after every election between majority and opposition over appointments to the RAI proves that the stakes are always considered to be politically significant.[4]

Albeit in a different way, not even the commercial television channels, have been truly free of political control. Indeed, while in 1976 Decision no. 202 of the Constitutional Court established the illegality of public monopolies, no regulation of private broadcasting was approved until 1990. As a result, private networks were obliged to operate without licences, facing the continual risk of being closed down by a member of the judiciary. Meanwhile, the entrepreneurs operating in this field needed political friends to bail them out in case of need, as clearly showed by Berlusconi's experience in 1984, when his television networks were twice blacked out by magistrates and twice saved by special decrees issued by Craxi's government. However, not even the first regulation introduced fourteen years later by the so-called Mammì law (no. 223/1990) overcame the problem completely.

Apart from the limits of this legislation[5] – some articles of which were the object of a referendum (Gobbo and Cazzola 1996) – other important changes were coming into play. In particular, the issue of the relationship between politics and the media became even more dramatic after Silvio Berlusconi entered the fray in the early 1990s, first becoming the leader of the centre-right wing and – for around seven months – Italian prime minister: a leader and prime minister who directly controlled television networks, which during the previous decade had become so dominant as to share control of television programmes with the RAI in a kind of duopoly.[6] The media magnate's decision to create a party so deeply integrated with his media empire as to be defined as a 'media party' (Calise 2000) and the fact that, after the victory of the centre-right coalition in the 2001 national election, Berlusconi again became prime minister without having resolved the conflict of interests between his private and public roles – together these give a clear idea of how the independence of political communication can work in Italy.

On the other hand, a structurally freer press never balanced the dependency of television on the political system for at least two reasons. First, Italian newspapers have always had a very low level of readership.[7] Second, as a result Italy has had very few true newspaper publishers. In the absence of a true market, people from the worlds of industry and finance have generally owned Italian newspapers and often used them as channels to influence policy-making.[8] Their influence, though, has not been one-way. Indeed, as Italian capitalism has always been weak and in need of state protection, political control has also often indirectly conditioned newspapers' editorial lines.

Degree of mass media partisanship

Since, until the crisis of the so-called First Republic, the Italian political system was such a total form of party government as to deserve the appellation of particracy (Calise 1994), state control over public television automatically implied a systematic partisanship of the broadcasting networks. Indeed, starting from the end of the 1970s, the system of *lottizzazione* [apportionment] within the RAI assured the representation of both majority and opposition parties, transforming the three public television networks into three partisan channels.[9] Moreover, the present situation is not as different as one might think: first, because Italian political culture has not changed that much and, second, because the cultural and material heritage derived from the long domination of the parties over television is not easily erasable. As some authors have noted (Marletti 1995b; Mancini 2000), instead of increasing journalists' autonomy, the modernisation of the Italian media has caused the emergence of a new model of partisanship that combines the new commercial logic of entertainment with the old rationale of party supremacy.

Of course, the crisis of the particracy system has partly reduced the degree of television partisanship, to the point that even among Berlusconi's networks there is one – Canale 5 – that is less aligned than the others.[10] But generally speaking we must say that the problem is far from being overcome. Incidentally, the very fact that the Italian political communication system requires an independent agency to control the political impartiality of public and private television channels is very telling. The data recently published by the Communication Authority confirm the continuing existence of the problems raised during the debate on Law no. 28/2000 – the so-called '*par condicio*' law – aimed at guaranteeing equal time and access on radio and television for all parties, affirming the tenets of impartiality and limiting the forms in which political communication may be broadcast.

It is interesting to note that, while the partisanship of television is one of the key issues in the debate, the lack of impartiality in the press is not a problem. To some extent it is expected – and legitimate – that the printed media be partisan. If television, which originated as a public medium, is supposed to be fair at least from a theoretical point of view, things are different in the case of newspapers, which have historically always been a tool and a channel for political conflict (Murialdi 1996, 1998).

The form of Italian press partisanship can be discussed starting from the criteria suggested by Seymour-Ure (1974).[11] As regards the editorial policies of the so-called 'independent' newspapers, it is perhaps relevant to recall that, for a long time, the pervasiveness of the parties' influence pushed journalists into giving some space to politicians' viewpoints or at least into taking into consideration their protesting telephone calls. Obviously this was particularly the case with the government parties, while opposition groups were forced to maintain their own networks for political communication, with the consequence that, in Italy, the party press was stronger and survived for longer than in many other Western democracies.[12]

Finally, a very interesting and peculiar phenomenon of press–party parallelism in Italy has been the case of the so-called '*giornale-partito*' (a newspaper that acts as a party). According to one of its major theorists, the former director of *la Repubblica*, Eugenio Scalfari, the '*giornale-partito*' has always been the kind of newspaper that 'makes itself the channel for structured opinion and tends naturally to broaden its influence'.[13] Actually, on the basis of Scalfari's experience alone, the notion of '*giornale-partito*' has a different meaning. It reminds us of the case of a newspaper born to increase pluralism in information (Murialdi 1983), but after a short time transformed into a covert political actor deeply engaged in the conflict between parties (Marletti 1984; Marletti and Roncarolo 2000) and affected by all the ambiguities implied in the model of advocacy journalism: a model that in the Italian case means a journalism seeking to oppose the absence of universalism by means of an over-politicised coverage.

Degree of media–political elite integration

One of the obvious consequences deriving from the tendency in politics and the media to develop a mutual and very close relationship is the deep integration between the two sets of professional elites. A keen observer like

Forcella highlighted this phenomenon in a paper written as long ago as 1959 and recently re-published.[14] He noted that:

> In Italy a political journalist can rely on about 1500 readers: ministers and under-secretaries (all of them), the deputies (some of them), party executives, trade-unionists, important prelates, and a few industrialists who want to look informed . . . The whole system is organised around the relationship between the political journalist and that group of privileged readers.
>
> Disregarding this element, one cannot understand the most typical feature of our political journalism, maybe of Italian politics as a whole: it is the atmosphere of a family performance . . . Of course, everybody performs just for pleasure, since there is no paying public. The relationship between the 1500 readers and the political journalist is so close that, in a sense, it is one of identification.
>
> (Forcella 1999: 177–8)

Many things have changed since Forcella wrote corrosively about the integration of the media–political elite, but the core of his analysis is still true (as the decision to re-publish the article demonstrates). The newspapers' readership is almost the same, both as regards numbers and in its composition.[15] Italian political journalists continue to share time and space with politicians who spend their lives in the *Transatlantico*, the lobby of Parliament where political news is informally leaked, discussed, interpreted and commented in a continual exchange between media and political actors. Moreover, even if the self-referential language shared by politicians and journalists – the so-called *politichese* – is now less usual in Italian political communication and takes less cryptic forms, the habit of communicating in code has not yet disappeared completely.

Incidentally, the very limited professionalisation of Italian politics is meaningful. While in most other democracies during the last few decades politicians have tried to control the media by engaging PR consultants, spin-doctors and similar figures (Kurtz 1998; Thurber *et al.* 1998), this has not happened in the Italian system, where structural and systemic control over the media still works well enough. This has the further consequence that, in the absence of filters imposed by professional media consultants, the interaction between journalists and politicians has gone on with more integration and fewer tensions than in many other systems.

The nature of the legitimising creed of media institutions

In line with the elements highlighted above, there is the fact that, having never been really independent of politics, Italian media institutions never developed a strong and consistent frame of legitimising creeds. According to Law no. 69/1963, journalism is not a 'profession' but just a 'typical liberal art with public interest functions' and even if it has now been organised like a profession, no symbolic identity has come with this process. Unlike the Anglo-Saxon model, the professionalisation of Italian journalism was not accomplished by introducing general rules and procedures (i.e. separation of fact from opinion) that were established independently in the media sphere, nor was it supported by the social acknowledgement of precise systemic functions.

While the formal institutionalisation of the profession of journalist is higher in Italy than in most other countries, the attention towards ethical problems and the practice of self-regulation have always been very weak, when not completely absent.[16] This is illustrated by the fact that in 1984 the Italian Supreme Court felt the need to issue a kind of journalists' 'handbook', thereby intervening in a field that should be the province of appropriate professional bodies (Mancini 2000). In addition, it is illuminating that almost half of those who work in the information field say they know the Charter of Journalists' Obligation only superficially and more than 20 per cent admit ignorance of it (Mancini 2000: 123). As a result, the percentage of people showing trust in journalists is very low (Abacus 1998).

With reference to the argument put forward here, it must be particularly emphasised that a highly institutionalised but poorly legitimised journalism, supported by few values or shared norms, easily develops into a cynical professional culture. This is a culture that, on the one hand, claims the right to work without limitations and, on the other, accepts severe political conditioning and simply hides it behind different masks. It is, however, interesting to note that – more than once, even if with little success – Italian journalists have tried to reformulate their subordination to politics, conceptualising it in a different way. The main strategy adopted to achieve this aim began with the typical criticism of the concept of objectivity and evolved until it claimed a right: the right – but also the duty – to hold a position in the political debate, openly siding with one side (not necessarily a party), one way of thinking, one mood.

The first controversial debate about journalistic objectivity was started by *L'Espresso* in 1969 and rapidly spread among journalists and intellectuals (Eco 1979) on the wave of the same critical culture that was changing American journalism (Schudson 1978). The problem was that unlike the American media, the Italian press was not facing the epistemological ambiguity of a myth practised daily, nor challenges from a power that was learning to exploit this myth by news management strategies.[17] On the contrary, its problems were a deficit of objectivity deriving from the direct and indirect pressure from politicians, a difficulty in representing all aspects of reality and a lack of autonomy from institutional sources. Criticising the tenet of objectivity without enjoying the conditions to practise it in full, Italian journalism did not help the emancipation of political information, nor did it make the general public more aware of the problem. Moreover, although the polemic was soon stopped by the brusque impact of the communication strategies of terrorists, who were replacing words with weapons, its negative influence continued during the following years, up until the beginning of the 1990s, when arguments against objectivity re-entered the framework of the growing political crisis.

Types of democracies and models of political communication

Having explored the relationship between the Italian media and politics by means of Blumler and Gurevitch's analytic schema, we now have to explain its underlying causal factors. In order to achieve this, a useful starting point is offered by Lijphart's classic distinction between majoritarian and consensus – or consociational – systems (Lijphart 1984, 1989).[18]

It is well known that consociational and majoritarian democracies differ significantly not only from the political point of view, but also with regard to the relationship between politics and the media (Marletti 1995a). Using the Italian case, we suggest that the distinctive features of a consociational political communication system are the need to control the media and to keep controversial issues as far as possible out of the public domain. While in majoritarian systems the clear demarcation between majority and opposition favours the strategy of going public via the media (Kernell 1986) whenever a controversial issue requires it, in a consociational democracy things work very differently. Here the complex search for political consensus among the many interests and voices that are represented by the multi-party system discourages the typical strategies of mediated politics, instead imposing the need for a more protected arena (Marletti and Roncarolo 2000). As a result, a certain subordination of the media to politics seems to be a functional imperative, especially with regard to the most influential and pervasive medium, television. Of course, each model of political communication involves some risks, which in majoritarian systems are above all the inclination to develop populism and change it into anti-politics (Schedler 1997), while in consociational democracies there is the specific tendency towards excessive enclosure of the system and true self-referentiality (see Table 3.1).

The question is: to what extent does the political communication model of consociational systems maintain its typical features when entering the phase of mediated politics? And what conditions affect this process? Even if we need to analyse more fully what generally happens when the media rationale rushes into the political set-up of a plural society, some elements can first be highlighted.

More specifically, looking at the Italian case we could suggest that as the modernisation of society stimulates the development of the communication system, not even consociational democracies can keep the spotlights of television away from politics for very long. Thus, for instance, while at first it was possible to control Italian television by occupying key positions and limiting its role to the spheres of education and entertainment, things

Table 3.1 Political communication systems in majoritarian and consociational democracies

Political system	Position of media towards politics	Political culture	Function of media	Risks
Majoritarian	Autonomous	Focuses on the role of public opinion and the search for popular consensus	Checking the actions of political actors and acting as a link between political and public systems	Trivialising politics, hyper-dramatisation inclination to develop anti-politics and cynicism
Consociational	Subordinate	Focuses on the role of parties and the search for political consensus	Communication channels for political actors	Self-referentiality, detachment from public, increased withdrawal from politics

changed when television became a differentiated apparatus with greater social influence.[19] As is well known, the turning point was the emergence of a mixed television system which – after the abolition of public television's monopoly in 1976 – created a new environment for politics and offered new platforms for politicians. The first signs of change were already visible during the 1979 national campaign, and became more evident in 1983 when the rationale of commercial television made the style of electoral communication more popular and appealing, introducing new genres like talk shows and political advertising into election campaigns.[20] In any event, election campaigns were not an exception in the field of political communication: as the chronicles of the late 1970s brightly remind us, by then politicians were starting to include television among their usual channels of communication (Novelli 1995). Accompanied by a significant phase in the development of television provision, these changes meant a huge increase in the visibility of political issues and actors.[21]

From our point of view, it is interesting to note that in the highly fragmented Italian consociational democracy, the growing space given to politics by television from the second half of the 1970s onwards – and the increasing use that politicians made of it – shifted the forms of political control from a logic of defence to strategies of occupation of the electronic media. These strategies were designed to guarantee the presence of all politicians and to neutralise the effects of media logic. In short, during the 1970s and 1980s, Italian democracy progressively included the media among the arenas of political confrontation, without changing the systemic relationship between politics and communication (see Table 3.2).

Table 3.2 The Italian political communication system: continuities and changes

Historical period/type of political system	Television system	Forms of relationship between television and politics	Mediated political communication strategies
1954–1974 Consociational	Public television monopoly	Political control and occupation of RAI top management by majority parties	Omission and removal of politics from television
1975–1992 Consociational with strong particracy	Deregulated mixed system with public and commercial television	*Lottizzazione* (apportionment) of top RAI posts among majority and opposition parties, weak commercial television that needs informal political protection	Television as showroom for politics, development of widespread, but weak media logic
1993 – Partially oriented towards majoritarian model	Regulated mixed television system, duopoly of RAI and Fininvest (Mediaset)	Direct and indirect forms of political control over RAI and Fininvest (Mediaset)	Start of political marketing and booming propaganda, political journalism taking sides

Two main factors particularly affected this process. On the one hand, in the second half of the 1970s, the need to involve – at least partially and informally – the most important opposition party (the Communist Party) in the running of public affairs[22] brought about the *lottizzazione* system, which slowed down the transformation of Italian television into a truly autonomous apparatus and limited the effects of the media rationale, protecting the world of politics from it for a little longer. On the other hand, the social and political complexity that was growing during the 1970s increased the political instability of alliances and produced the need for new channels of internal political communication. Encountering supply from a journalism that was looking for a more influential role, this demand enabled the impact of media development to be absorbed, by assigning a showroom role to television and transforming newspapers into the privileged site of an indirect interaction among continuously competing, but necessarily always allied, party leaders. Of course, the media logic that framed the relationship between journalists and politicians after the years of political control over the media was actually very 'poor' (Mazzoleni 1987). However, it was certainly functional for the most important needs of a consociational system that was facing deep changes and tough challenges, like the attack from terrorism (Marletti 1984). As is well known, the negative price of this phase was the self-referentiality produced by the close integration of media and political elites in a framework of continual interaction between the two apparatuses (Marletti 1985).

This dominant feature of Italian political communication was an important factor in the crisis of the late 1980s and early 1990s. In part, this was because day after day the virtual closure of political communication was becoming less acceptable to a neo-television (Eco 1983; Casetti 1988) that in contrast had been introducing practices aimed at increasing the involvement of the public in programmes since the early 1980s. In part it was because while the crisis of Italian politics was growing due to both internal factors and international events, the political system found itself unable to lead the mood of its citizens and lacking in appropriate forms of communication.

What must be stressed here is that the consociational political communication rationale seems to work well as long as (direct or indirect) control over the media is possible. However, control becomes weaker and more difficult when politics enters the symbolic environment of the media. Moreover, the Italian case suggests that when a political communication system is too oriented towards control of the media and closure to the public, it is exposed to a high risk of crisis. This is a risk that is almost bound to become reality if new challengers break the self-referential logic of the consociational political communication system and exploit the media as a resource in order to appeal to the public. As the following section shows, this is exactly what happened.

Phases and images of the crisis between Italian journalists and politicians

Up to now we have considered the relationship between media and politics from the general perspective of a macro-level analysis. It is now time to focus on the crisis that has assailed journalism and its relations with the political sphere over recent years, starting from a more precise definition of what we mean when we talk about 'crisis'. In line with Dobry's analysis (1992), we consider crisis as a 'fluid juncture', which breaks the usual systemic routines and is characterised by high 'structural uncertainty'. Though the anomalies of Italian democracy have induced analysts to speak of a system in 'permanent crisis' (Bobbio 1981), this analytic category acquires a more precise meaning when applied to the present situation. Indeed, both the concepts of 'fluidity' and of 'structural uncertainty' are particularly suitable to describe the still unsolved transition of a country where during the last ten years much of the old system of rules and relationships has gradually disappeared, even if no new configuration has yet fully emerged. Moreover, there is a further element that supports the use of this analytic category. As Dobry reminds us, besides the objective dimension, one of the key factors in the emergence of crises is the process conceptualised by Thompson and Merton as the 'definition of the situation' (Merton 1949). Now, we can certainly debate whether the difficulties faced by the Italian system at the beginning of the 1990s were or were not signs of a true crisis, but there is no doubt that many social and political actors defined the situation in this way (Mastropaolo 2000), operating as true political 'crisis entrepreneurs'.[23]

This inclination was particularly evident in the case of journalists, whose analyses structured the general perception of the relationship between media and politics in the most negative light. As illustrated in the remainder of this chapter, since the end of the 1980s journalists have represented their relationship with politicians – and more generally their attitudes towards the health of the political system – in terms of an increasingly critical configuration. In doing so, they contributed to the mobilisation of social dissatisfaction and the delegitimation of the political system, favouring the emergence of the crisis that, in the end, broke the consociational model. Whether by feeding this crisis journalists made a significant contribution to the democratic process is questionable. The main point, however, is that their protest failed to address the true imbalance affecting the media system and its relationship with the political system. Thus, even if the crisis offered various symbolic identities to journalists who were looking for a new profile, in the final analysis it helped Italy to go through changes without truly changing.

The emergence of crisis in the declining consociational system

As previously mentioned, according to Dobry's indications, in the concept of crisis there are two analytic dimensions: the first concerns the objective level of the critical juncture and the second the subjective perceptions of this. It is noteworthy that both these dimensions are present and interconnect during the recent phases of Italian political communication.

A good starting point to illustrate the emergence of journalists' subjective perception of crisis is the meeting organised by the Parliamentary Commission to guide and supervise radio and television services in 1989. Indeed, in the year that was to be marked by the fall of the Berlin Wall, the Italian political system started to face the issue of public communication, with an emphasis on its critical features. The debate confirmed that the self-referentiality of the political system was the central problem, revealed difficulties in giving the public more accessible information and highlighted the 'obscurity' of politicians who – in the words of one authoritative commentator – were 'simply the most visible terminals of a crisis that involves everyone and particularly professional communicators' (Jacobelli 1989: 92).

Yet, paradoxically, nobody noticed that things were already changing. The fact was that change was not coming from the noble world of the press, nor from high-profile political television programmes, but from 'infotainment'. While leading personalities in traditional journalism were complaining about the crisis, other journalists including anchormen and women – each with his or her own style – were introducing profound changes into the rationale of political communication.[24] For the first time, starting from the late 1980s, their programmes used direct (and sometimes even coarse) language. Politicians were asked to explain their positions clearly, public opinion was explored through opinion polls and people's voices were broadcast 'live' from town squares or by telephone from their homes. If the tendency of consociational systems to lose control over political communication had required any proof, this was it.

Of course, given the Italian experience of continuity, up until 1992 the influence of these programmes was severely limited by the widespread view that very little would ever truly change in the political system. Nevertheless, they succeeded in producing a marked effect in the public arena. This was accomplished by favouring the formation of a new anti-political mood, fed by the electronic populism of adversarial information,[25] by appealing to the people against parties and by theorising the need for a 'factious journalism' directly involved in the political fight and finally free from the old myth of objectivity.

Without entering the debate about the democratic pretensions of populism (Canovan 1999; Mény 2000), one might ask how different things might have been if a more autonomous and balanced information system had proposed critical political analyses instead of leaving the field to those journalists and anchorpersons who liked to stage protest in their programmes. What is certain is that the populist approach of political 'infotainment' created the climate – and prepared the models – for the break in the relationships between journalists and politicians that would have occurred sooner or later and which began with the *Tangentopoli* scandal. By dismantling the old party system, the inquiries into political corruption offered the media the unexpected chance finally to exert true political influence by performing the unusual function of a 'watchdog'. This was a role the effects of which were amplified by the increased number of television news bulletins[26] and which, in the end, transformed the coverage of scandals into collective 'rituals of degradation' (Giglioli 1996), showing representatives of traditional journalism shoulder to shoulder with those of political 'infotainment' in the trial of the 'old politics'. Not surprisingly, the second meeting promoted by the Parliamentary Commission focused on a twofold crisis: the crisis caused by the objective difficulties in the political system and that stressed by the media, tired of simply being a mirror for politics. Even the most critical commentators argued that this was a crisis fed by the media, which deformed problems by looking at them through the lens of adversarial and dramatising coverage (Jacobelli 1993).

Finally, it must be remembered that, if the emergence of the *Tangentopoli* scandal had offered journalists a new social legitimisation, another circumstance gave them the occasion to share a stable political agenda. This was the entry on to the national scene of the referendum-wing, a composite movement that brought together widespread demands for change and was strongly supported by the press and television networks (Warner and Gambetta 1994). Until then, the information system had neither expressed a widely shared political agenda, nor mobilised itself in a united front. The campaign, aimed at affirming majoritarian principles, was linked to the various media, both with regard to content (all of them were favourable to the majoritarian solution) and in terms of the referendum issue's relevance (Calise 1998). So, in the summer of 1993, all the premises for a radical change were in place in a scenario where a new politics was anticipated and where the media seemed to be ready to play the unusual role of key political actors.

From a supposed videocracy to clashes between politicians and journalists in the incomplete transition towards a majoritarian democracy

While the subjective perception of crisis had been growing, the objective level was also changing, mainly because the owner of the three most important commercial networks was preparing himself to begin an unusual political career. As is well known, the characteristics of Berlusconi's election campaign induced many observers to talk of 'videocracy' (Mazzoleni 1995a) and to complain about the effects of the media, especially the power of television. The truth, however, was very different. First, Berlusconi used television as a stage to launch a new product in a de-structured political market (Marletti 1997), a market where almost all the old parties had collapsed and where a wide range of substantial interests were looking for political representation. In this context, far from being the decisive tool for 'virtual politics', television was reduced – once again – to a channel for a new political organisation. Secondly, the hypothesis of 'videocracy' underestimates the key role played by the 'multimedia corporation' (Calise 1998) on which Forza Italia relied: a corporation comprising the nationwide organisational networks offered by Publitalia (Fininvest's marketing agency) and Mediolanum (the insurance company controlled by Berlusconi). In short, this was an extraordinary machine connecting interests, marketing services and organisational structures in a highly powerful mix. Moreover, in order to understand the reasons for Berlusconi's apparently easy success, other factors need to be taken into account: his influence and reputation as a leading industrialist and the aura derived from his ownership of an important football team, supported by a great number of fans organised in various clubs.

Of course, there is no doubt that, however influential it finally might have been in determining 'the people's choice' (Ricolfi 1994), television was an important factor in Berlusconi's success. However, the point is that television was not the winner. Paradoxically, just when media professionals were experiencing a more autonomous and influential role due to the collapse of the old party system, the creation of a 'media-mediated party' forced them to return to the ranks. As the owner of Italy's biggest commercial television networks entered the political game with the aim of representing his own interests and those of the centre-right, the media also took up position (Mazzoleni 1996), resulting in two important outcomes. First, many journalists and anchorpersons openly sided with him or opposed him, while others waited for the election results more out of prudence than a concern for objectivity. Second, for many people, showing a preference for the Fininvest or the RAI networks became a kind of political act, a sign of belonging to one or other wing.[27]

No less important were the effects that the centrality of television in the 1994 campaign produced in the press sector. It both forced newspapers and political magazines to actively engage in the political battle[28] and, by interpreting Berlusconi's success as a television victory, led to the generalised idea that printed information was in a deep and perhaps final crisis. The key argument had the appeal of simplicity: (a) Berlusconi's victory was mainly based on the intensive political advertising campaign broadcast by his networks and on the televisual culture created over the years; (b) the press had been able neither to offer antidotes to this culture nor to impose any model of popular journalism that could act as a contrast to the dominant position of television; (c) as a consequence, while Berlusconi controlled both public and commercial television, the press was in a serious crisis. The six issues that the left-wing political review *Reset* devoted to this crisis between autumn 1994 and spring 1995 demonstrated the pessimism of the debate. This emphasised the limits of a type of journalism that was neither adequate for the elite nor for the general public (Bosetti 1994), induced journalists to self-critical reflection, disregarded the structural dimension of problems and ended up by increasing the entropy of the system, raising the confusion between structural and contingent problems without really facing the challenges implied by the passage of Italian democracy from the consociational to the majoritarian model.

The direct attacks by politicians, which started during the first Berlusconi government, should have made it clear that the crisis of Italian political communication was systemic. Until then there had been pressure and polemic, but seldom real clashes. Even the tension between Craxi and the press – which had anticipated the eventual developments of the relationship between leaders and journalists – was different, less systematic and explicit, because it occurred in the softer context of the consociational system. The central point, however, was that the framework of the relationship between leaders and journalists was changing (Jacobelli 1995). After the electoral reform, many processes accelerated while others began to take shape. As in other systems, so in Italy the majoritarian rationale increased the prime minister's need to communicate more directly with the general public, seeking popularity as an additional political resource (Roncarolo 1994; Marletti and Roncarolo 2000).

Berlusconi's intolerance of journalistic mediation was both the most direct consequence and the most visible proof of this change, even if many regarded it as the result of personal dislike, made stronger by the centre-right culture. In reality, the fact that the clashes between Forza Italia's leader and journalists could not be explained simply on the basis of personal idiosyncrasies or cultural factors soon became evident. As a matter of fact, at the end of Berlusconi's first government, tensions between the political and information apparatuses did not stop. On the contrary, they continued – if possible more vigorously – when D'Alema entered government and went on during the following years with greater or less punch according to the moment and the leading characters on the stage.

This tension exhibited a particular feature that distinguishes the Italian crisis. Since the dual role of Berlusconi as politician and television magnate is one of the main objective elements at the basis of this crisis – and since this has not yet been resolved – the tensions between leaders and journalists increased the partisan habits of political journalism. So, while some journalists declared themselves to be public critics of a politics reduced to 'virtual politics'[29] – often clashing both with the centre-right and the centre-left – many others sided against one or the other coalition. As a result, in the 2001 election campaign one of the central themes in the debate was the argument about the factiousness of public television and Berlusconi's networks (Roncarolo, forthcoming).

Finally, besides the tendency towards an openly partisan style of journalism and the difficulty of reconciling two systems that are profoundly different but not yet reciprocally autonomous, a more general problem must be emphasised. This is the paradox of an institutional context that is not fully oriented towards the majoritarian model but keeps various elements of consensual democracies,[30] and that consequently imposes two opposite strategies of political communication, one driven by the rationale of going public and the other inspired by the logic of political mediation among the parties. In order to increase their popularity with the general public, politicians must indeed make direct appeals to public opinion, going if necessary over the heads of journalists. However, in order to manage their relations with competitive partners in what are frequently unstable coalitions, they must resort to the old style of communication, made up of declarations, denials and allusive messages, which requires more inclusive forms of relationship with the integrated elite of journalists. On the whole, the result is that journalists, who generally lack both the cultural habit and the structural resources to play a truly autonomous role, often fluctuate between the temptation to surrender to the sirens of power and the ambition to become influential political actors (Marini and Roncarolo 1997).

Conclusion

The set of relationships between journalists and politicians described above confirms the systemic nature of the crisis occurring in Italian political communication and highlights the need to consider it within the frame-work of the unresolved institutional transition.

As we have seen, the first signs of crisis became visible during the 1980s when the modernisation of the media sphere partly reformed the former system of political control, thus revealing the contradictions of a journalism pushed to the centre of political communication, but prevented from working autonomously by the dominance of the parties. Yet the true crisis arrived in the first half of the 1990s when the political system collapsed. Just when Italian political journalism seemed finally to have found new democratic functions by denouncing the inner crisis of the majority parties, it discovered the depth of its weakness – a weakness that is still in existence and that rests on two main problems. The first is the permanence of the structural and cultural ties that keep both the public and the commercial media subordinate to politics. The second is the fact that as the political system has not yet found its final configuration, neither has the communication system been able to develop an appropriate role. Indeed, since the transition towards the majoritarian model remains incomplete, the rationale of a more public-oriented political communication model has to coexist with the self-referential habits which are typical of consociational systems.

Beyond any preference for the majoritarian or the consensual system, there is no doubt that with regard to political communication both present advantages and, at the same time, the risk of serious drawbacks. The majoritarian model seems to be more able to guarantee the autonomy of the media from politics and journalism's watchdog function, but risks shifting towards an electronic populism that often prefers the appeal of scandal over the complexity of problems, uses forms of negative com-munication and feeds the 'spiral of cynicism' among the general public. In contrast, the consensual model can perhaps be more protected against 'media malaise', but it easily shifts towards autistic forms of self-referentiality, making politics less transparent and keeping people away from it. The core point, however, is that without a clear choice of one or other model, the Italian system of political communication risks being overwhelmed by both sets of difficulties, with no possibility of guiding the process. In a context where the media are highly modernised, but affected by a serious deficit of structural autonomy, these risks are more than probable.

Finally, we can say that both the common elements and the contrasts between the majoritarian and consociational models of communication – together with those problems deriving from the media logic that the Italian system shares with other Western democracies – are at the core of the recent crisis. With specific regard to the role played by journalists, the problems deriving from the unresolved institutional transition have favoured the continuation of bad habits and old faults. On the one hand, this is because the coexistence of majoritarian and consociational elements makes it hard to redefine the journalistic role in the direction of a more auto-nomous model. On the other hand, this coexistence makes the real nature of problems less apparent. As a result, journalists risk being easily trapped between the communication strategies that try to keep them in the magic circle of self-referentiality with politicians and those adopted by leaders who use the media as personal channels to seek public support. Of course, this risk could be reduced – even if not fully avoided – by a more reflective and conscious approach on the part of journalists to the systemic relationship between media and politics in Italian democracy. However, as the Italian experience shows, when you come from a long history of being in a subordinate relationship, such a reflective and conscious approach does not come easily.

Notes

1 A different point of view is in Norris 2000.
2 The essay 'Towards a comparative framework for political communication' was first published in Chaffee 1975: 165–93.
3 The control of public broadcasting was in the government's hands until 1975 when the reforming law charged the Supervisory Parliamentary Commission with the task of overseeing the contents of televised programmes and appointing the board of directors (Mazzoleni 1995b). During the turbulent days of the inquiries into the widespread corruption in the political system, Law no. 210/1993 took the power of appointing the RAI's general board out of the hands of the Parliamentary Commission and gave it to the Presidents of the Senate and Chamber of Deputies (Chimenti 2000; Mancini 2000).
4 In order to compare the present problems regarding appointments at RAI and those of the past, see Marletti 1988.
5 Among other reasons, the 'Mammì law' (from the name of its proposer) was criticised as it merely confirmed the market status quo (according to it, a company is limited to owning no more than three national broadcasting channels, which is by chance just the number of Berlusconi's networks). Moreover, the law failed to establish a plan for the allocation of frequencies (which – at the national level – was realised just at the end of the 1990s by the new Authority for Communications, while work for the local plan is not yet finished).
6 In 1992, only nine private networks had the frequencies concession stated by the Mammì law. Six of them were controlled by Silvio or his brother Paolo Berlusconi. The average audience was distributed as follows: RAI 47.3 per cent, Fininvest 43.4 per cent and other networks 9.3 per cent.
7 We must remember that Italy has a different history from most Western countries. There, the creation of large television audiences was preceded and prepared for by the existence of a general public used to reading newspapers, magazines and books. In Italy, however, long-lasting illiteracy confined the habit of reading to the elite and was really overcome only after the Second World War when the first television programmes were broadcast. Not surprisingly, given the absence of a generalised reading habit, television has become more than the main information source: for many people it has been the sole medium since the beginning.
8 A chronicle of the period of the 1970s, during which newspapers were continually being bought and sold in a general frame of political and financial manoeuvres aimed at gaining control of the Italian press industry, is provided by Pansa (1977). For a more comprehensive history of the Italian press, see Murialdi 1978 and 1996.
9 The 1975 reform law stated that each public network would be managed by parties of different political complexions, firstly by appointing the director

general. So RAI-1 openly became a Roman Catholic network, controlled by the Christian Democratic party; RAI-2 became a Socialist network and – from 1979 onwards – the newly created RAI-3 was the television channel influenced by the Communist party (Monteleone 1992).

10 According to the Authority, during the first days of the 2000 regional election campaign, the news programme Tg-5 devoted 49.1 per cent of time to the centre-left (73 per cent if one includes the time devoted to the government). One year later, though, things looked different. During the month before the 2001 national election campaign Tg-5 devoted 19 minutes to Berlusconi and just 9 minutes to Rutelli.

11 Seymour-Ure (1974) suggests three criteria for the degree of 'press-party parallelism': (a) party involvement in mass media ownership and management; (b) the editorial policies of newspapers; (c) the party affiliations of readers.

12 The most important example was the PCI's newspaper *L'Unità*, which was both sold with other newspapers and distributed by activists (Bechelloni and Buonanno 1981). Albeit with growing signs of crisis, *L'Unità* remained an important channel of political communication until the end of the 1980s.

13 See the summary of the lesson presented during the ceremony for his *laurea honoris causa* by the former director of *la Repubblica*, Eugenio Scalfari, about *L'ascolto come elemento propulsivo della comunicazione* [Listening as a driving element of communication] in *la Repubblica*, 28 March 2000.

14 The article was originally published in the review *Tempo presente*.

15 According to the FIEG (Italian Federation of Newspaper Publishers) the estimated 1999 daily newspaper circulation averaged 5.9 million copies, which was 0.3 per cent up compared with 1998. On the recent crisis of the Italian press see Lenzi 1999.

16 While the Order of Journalists strictly controls intake as well as any undue interference with the journalistic profession, it has often been less sensitive to cases of misrepresentation and deceptive practice by journalists. On the characteristics of Italian journalists, see Mancini 1999.

17 In order to have a comparative view of the different positions about this point in US, British and German television news, see Semetko 1996b. The issue of objectivity in American journalism is considered by Schudson (1995).

18 According to Lijphart (1989: 39) the consensus and consociational models of democracy are 'similar but not identical', having been differently defined. As the distinction is not relevant with regard to the analysis proposed here, I am using the label more appropriate for the Italian case: that is the consociational model of democracies. The concept of consociationalism was originally proposed by Lijphart (1968, 1977) in order to show how culturally and politically fragmented societies can enjoy a high degree of stability adopting political practices (grand coalition, segmental autonomy, proportionality and mutual veto) that are far from the majoritarian principles and based on the search for consensus more than for alternation. A different comparative perspective which focuses more on the role of media than on the features of political systems is in Semetko (1996a).

19 Until 1960 politics was almost completely absent from Italian television and even when it entered on to the electronic stage through electoral programmes, its space was strictly rationed (Novelli 1995).

20 It should be noted that – given the absence of any regulation for commercial television – private networks did not have to respect the rules deliberated by the Supervisory Commission for RAI and could consequently innovate formats of political communication in a freer way.

21 While in 1968 the weekly amount of programmes broadcast by RAI was around 6,600 minutes, fifteen years later – in 1983 – every week public television

broadcast for more than 14,200 minutes and the main commercial television channels – Rete 4, Canale 5 and Italia1 – broadcast for almost 21,900 minutes (Natale 1985: 207).

22 It is important to remember that although international vetoes and the Cold War rationale prevented the PCI from entering government, it remained a very strong party to the extent that in 1976 it obtained 34.4 per cent of votes.

23 As Briquet (1996) emphasises, the break of routines that causes political crisis is not simply the natural effect or the inevitable consequence of a system's autonomous development. To a large extent it results from the choices and activities of social and political actors who are involved in it and who – more or less consciously – operate in order to bring about radical changes. The definition of political 'crisis entrepreneur' comes from Diamanti (1993).

24 Examples included journalists like Santoro, whose first political talk show was broadcast in 1987 on public television, or anchormen like Funari, who had arrived from showbusiness and, after 1991, hosted on Fininvest popular programmes which included in their mix music, quizzes and very polemical interviews with politicians. See Grasso 1996.

25 I use the concept of populism in order to highlight the (more or less implicit) ideology of those journalists and anchorpersons who were stressing the centrality of common sense in public discourse and theorising the virtue of the people in contrast to the frequent corruption of politicians.

26 It must be remembered that as a consequence of the Mammì law, the private networks also started to broadcast national and local news in 1992, thus breaking the last public monopoly and enlarging the general supply of information.

27 Some empirical evidence of the connection between preferred network (RAI or Fininvest) and vote is in Grossi (2000).

28 Most newspapers and political magazines devoted a great deal of their coverage to either representing Berlusconi as a dangerous devil or ridiculing him.

29 See, for example, Curzio Maltese in *la Repubblica*, 15 June 1999.

30 After much controversy, the 1993 electoral reform finally achieved a compromise solution which reconciled the majoritarian system with proportional elements. The law is a hybrid that provides for the election of three-quarters of the deputies on a simple majority constituency basis and one quarter on a proportional basis (Parker 1996).

References

Abacus (1998) *Italia al macroscopio*, Milan: Feltrinelli.

Almond, G.A. and Powell, P.J. Jr. (1978, 2nd edition) *Comparative Politics. System, Process and Policy*, Boston: Little, Brown and Company.

Altheide, D.L. and Snow, R.P. (1979) *Media Logic*, Beverly Hills, Calif.: Sage.

Arterton, C. (1985) *Media Politics: The News Strategies of Presidential Campaigns*, Lexington, D.C.: Heath.

Bechelloni, G. and Buonanno, M. (1981) 'Un quotidiano di partito sui generis: L'Unità', *Problemi dell'informazione* 6/2: 219–42.

Bennet, L. (1995, 3rd edition) *News. The Politics of Illusion*, New York: Longman.

Blumler, J.G. and Gurevitch, M. (1995) *The Crisis of Public Communication*, London and New York: Routledge.

Bobbio, N. (1981) 'La crisi permanente', *Pouvoirs* 18: 5–19.

Bosetti, G. (ed.) (1994) 'Stampa melassa, né élite, né massa', *Reset* 10.

Briquet, J.-L. (1996) 'Mobilitazioni politiche e congiuntura critica. Ipotesi per l'analisi della crisi politica in Italia', *Teoria politica* XII/1: 15–30.

Calise, M. (1994) 'The Italian particracy: beyond president and parliament', *Political Science Quarterly* 109/3: 441–79.

Calise, M. (1998) *La costituzione silenziosa. Geografia dei nuovi poteri*, Rome–Bari: Laterza.

Calise, M. (2000) *Il partito personale*, Rome–Bari: Laterza.

Canovan, M. (1999) 'Trust the people! Populism and the two faces of democracy', *Political Studies* 47/1: 2–16.

Casetti, F. (1988) *Strategie di coinvolgimento dello spettatore nella neotelevisione*, Rome: Rai/Eri.

Castronovo, V. and Tranfaglia, N. (eds.) (1994) *La stampa italiana nell'età della tv. 1975–1994*, Rome–Bari: Laterza.

Chaffee, S.H. (ed.) (1975) *Political Communication: Issues and Strategies for Research*, Beverly Hills: Sage.

Chimenti, A. (2000) *Informazione e televisione. La libertà vigilata*, Rome–Bari: Laterza.

Dahlgren, P. (1995) *Television and the Public Sphere*, London: Sage.

Diamanti, I. (1993) 'La Lega, imprenditore politico della crisi', *Meridiana* 16: 99–133.

Dobry, M. (1992) *Sociologie des crises politiques*, Paris: Presses de la Fondation Nationale des Sciences Politiques.

Eco, U. (1979) 'Obiettività dell'informazione: il dibattito teorico e le trasformazioni della società italiana', in U. Eco, M. Livolsi and G. Panozzo (eds) *Informazione: consenso e dissenso*, Milan: il Saggiatore.

Eco, U. (1983) 'Tv: la trasparenza perduta', in U. Eco, *Sette anni di desiderio*, Milan: Bompiani.

Forcella, E. (1999) 'Millecinquecento lettori', '1999. Giornalismo e politica in Italia', *Problemi dell'informazione*, 24/ 2, dossier tematico: 177–90.

Giglioli, P.P. (1996) 'Political corruption and the media: the Tangentopoli Affair', *International Social Science Journal* 149: 381–94.

Gobbo, F. and Cazzola, C. (1996) *Il sistema televisivo dopo i referendum e di fronte alla rivoluzione multimediale*, in M. Caciagli and D.I. Kertzer (eds.) *Politica in Italia. I fatti dell'anno e le interpretazioni*, Bologna: il Mulino.

Grasso, A. (1996) (ed.) *Enciclopedia della televisione*, Milano: Garzanti.

Grossi, G. (2000) 'La televisione a tre dimensioni. Comunicazione mediale e intenzioni di voto nella campagna delle elezioni europee 1999', *Comunicazione politica* 1/2: 205–29.

Jacobelli, J. (ed.) (1989) *La comunicazione politica in Italia*, Rome–Bari: Laterza.

Jacobelli, J. (ed.) (1993) *Lo specchio e la lente. Crisi e informazione*, Rome–Bari: Laterza.

Jacobelli, J. (ed.) (1995) *Check up del giornalismo italiano*, Rome–Bari: Laterza.

Jamieson, K.H. (1992) *Dirty Politics. Deception, Distraction and Democracy*, Oxford and New York: Oxford University Press.

Jamieson, K.H. (ed.) (1996) 'The media and politics', *The Annals of the American Academy of Political and Social Science* 546.

Kernell, S. (1986) *Going Public: New Strategies of Presidential Leadership*, Washington, D.C.: C.Q. Press.

Kurtz, H. (1998) *Spin Cycle. Inside the Clinton Propaganda Machine*, New York: The Free Press.

Lenzi, C. (1999) 'Giornali, lettori e promozioni: le ragioni della crisi. È chiara l'immagine che viene dalle ricerche: l'Italia è cambiata, i quotidiani no', *Problemi dell'informazione* 24/1: 79–91.

Lijphart, A. (1968) 'Typologies of Democratic Systems', *Comparative Political Studies* 1/1: 3–44.

Lijphart, A. (1977) *Democracy in Plural Societies: A Comparative Exploration*, New Haven: Yale University Press.

Lijphart, A. (1984) *Democracies: Patterns of Majoritarian and Consensus Government in Twenty-One Countries*, New Haven: Yale University Press.

Lijphart, A. (1989) 'Democratic political systems. Types, cases, causes and consequences', *Journal of Theoretical Politics* 1/1: 33–48.

Mancini, P. (1999) 'Giornalisti in Italia. Indagine socio-demografica sui professionisti dell'informazione', *Problemi dell'informazione* 24/1: 92–108.

Mancini, P. (2000) *Il sistema fragile. I mass media in Italia tra politica e mercato*, Rome: Carocci.

Marini, R. and Roncarolo, F. (1997) *I media come arena elettorale. Le elezioni politiche 1996 in Tv e nei giornali*, Rome: Rai-Eri.

Marletti, C. (1984) *Media e politica*, Milan: Franco Angeli.

Marletti, C. (1985) *Prima e dopo. Tematizzazione e comunicazione politica*, Turin: Rai/Vpt.

Marletti, C. (1988) 'Parties and mass communication: the RAI controversy', in R. Nanetti, R. Leonardi and P. Corbetta (eds) *Italian Politics: A Review*, London: Pinter.

Marletti, C. (1995a) 'Media e comunicazione politica nelle democrazie', *Quaderni di scienza politica* II/2: 285–312.

Marletti, C. (1995b) 'I media e la politica', in G. Pasquino (ed.), *La politica italiana. Dizionario critico 1945–95*, Rome–Bari: Laterza.

Marletti, C. (1997) 'Perché non siamo ancora un paese "normale"', in I. Diamanti and M. Lazar (eds.) *Stanchi di miracoli. Il sistema politico italiano in cerca di normalità*, Milan: Guerini e associati.

Marletti, C. and Roncarolo, F. (2000) 'Media influence in the Italian transition from a consensual to a majoritarian democracy', in R. Gunther and A. Mughan (eds) *Democracy and the Media: A Comparative Perspective*, New York: Cambridge University Press.

Mastropaolo, A. (2000) *Antipolitica. All'origine della crisi italiana*, Naples: L'ancora.

Mazzoleni, G. (1987), 'Media logic and party logic in campaign coverage: the Italian general election of 1983', *European Journal of Communication* 2/1: 81–103.

Mazzoleni, G. (1995a) 'Towards a "videocracy"? Italian political communication at a turning point', *European Journal of Communication* 10: 291–319.

Mazzoleni, G. (1995b) 'The Rai: restructuring and reform', in C. Mershon and G. Pasquino (eds) *Italian Politics: Ending the First Republic*, Boulder, Colo.: Westview Press.

Mazzoleni, G. (1996) 'Patterns and Effects of Recent Changes in Electoral Campaigning in Italy', in D.L. Swanson and P. Mancini (eds) *Politics, Media, and Modern Democracy: An International Study of Innovations in Electoral Campaigning and Their Consequences*, Westport, Conn.: Praeger.

Mény, Y. (2000) *Par le peuple, pour le peuple: le populisme et les démocraties*, Paris: Fayard.

Merton, R.K. (1949) *Social Theory and Social Structure*, New York: The Free Press.

Monteleone, F. (1992) *Storia della radio e della televisione in Italia*, Venice: Marsilio.

Murialdi, P. (1978) *La stampa italiana del dopoguerra*, 2 vols, Bari: Laterza.

Murialdi, P. (1983) 'Contributo alla storia di *Repubblica*, il quotidiano diverso', *Problemi dell'informazione* 8/4: 605–17.

Murialdi, P. (1996) *Storia del giornalismo italiano*, Bologna: il Mulino.

Murialdi, P. (1998) 'Giornali e giornalismo in crisi', *Problemi dell'informazione* 23/1: 3–8.

Natale, A.L. (1985) 'Cultura di massa, giornalismo e servizio nei palinsesti televisivi della Rai e dei networks' *Problemi dell'informazione* 10/2: 205–43.

Norris, P. (2000) *A Virtuous Circle. Political Communication in Post Industrial Societies*, Cambridge: Cambridge University Press.

Novelli, E. (1995) *Dalla tv di partito al partito della tv. Televisione e politica in Italia: 1960–1995*, Florence: La Nuova Italia.

Pansa, G. (1977) *Comprati e venduti*, Milan: Bompiani.

Parker, S. (1996) 'Electoral Reform and Political Change in Italy. 1991–1994', in S. Gundle and S. Parker (eds) *The New Italian Republic. From the Fall of the Berlin Wall to Berlusconi*, London and New York: Routledge.

Pasquino, G. (ed.) (1986) *Mass media e sistema politico*, Milan: Franco Angeli.

Patterson, T. (1993) *Out of Order*, New York: Vintage Press.

Raboy, M. and Dagenais, B. (eds) (1992) *Media, Crisis and Democracy. Mass Communication and the Disruption of Social Order*, London: Sage.

Ricolfi, L. (1994) 'Elezioni e mass media. Quanti voti ha spostato la tv', *Il Mulino* 13: 1031–46.

Ricolfi, L. (1997) 'Politics and the mass media in Italy', in M. Bull and M. Rhodes (eds) 'Crisis and transition in Italian politics', *West European Politics* 20/1: 135–56.

Roncarolo, F. (1994) *Controllare i media. Il presidente americano e gli apparati nelle campagne di comunicazione permanente*, Milan: Franco Angeli.

Roncarolo, F. (forthcoming) 'Virtual clashes. The 2001 Campaign in Print and Broadcast media', in J. Newell (ed.) *The Italian General Election of 2001*, Manchester: Manchester University Press.

Schedler, A. (1997) *The End of Politics? Explorations into Modern Antipolitics*, New York: St. Martin's Press.

Schudson, M. (1978) *Discovering the News. A Social History of American Newspapers*, New York: Basic Books.

Schudson, M. (1995) *The Power of News*, Cambridge, Mass., and London: Harvard University Press.

Semetko, H.A. (1996a), 'The Media', in L. LeDuc, R. Neimi and P. Norris (eds) *Comparing Democracies*, Thousand Oaks, Calif.: Sage.

Semetko, H.A. (1996b), 'Journalistic culture in comparative perspective: the concept of "balance" in U.S. British and German TV news', *Harvard International Journal of Press/Politics* 1/1: 51–71.

Seymour-Ure, C. (1974) *The Political Impact of Mass Media*, London: Constable.

Swanson, D.L. and Mancini, P. (1996) *Politics, Media, and Modern Democracy: an International Study of Innovations in Electoral Campaigning and Their Consequences*, Westport, Conn.: Praeger.

Thurber, J.A., Nelson, C.J. and Dulio, D.A. (1998) 'Political consulting: a portrait of the industry', paper presented at the Annual Meeting of American Political Science Association, Boston, September 3–6.

Warner, S. and Gambetta, D. (1994) *La retorica della riforma. Fine del sistema proporzionale in Italia*, Turin: Einaudi.

5 Political journalists and their sources in Thailand

Duncan McCargo

Thailand is one of the major nations of Southeast Asia, with a population of over sixty million. Traditionally a rice-growing and agricultural economy, since the 1960s it has experienced rapid economic growth and industrial-isation. During the late 1980s Thailand was the world's fastest growing economy, but the Asian financial crisis which began in Bangkok in 1997 raised questions about the sustainability of the country's success.

Thailand has a lively print media, with a constantly changing range of daily and weekly news publications. Top-selling newspapers are charac-terised by 'yellow journalism' and feature front pages festooned with gory pictures of accident and murder victims. Nevertheless, even the down-market newspapers have surprisingly extensive political coverage, and politicians are particularly concerned about the way their activities are written up in top-selling publications such as *Thai Rath*. Circulation figures are often inflated; the total daily sales of newspapers are probably less than two million. At the same time, each copy of a newspaper generally passes through many hands – especially in rural areas, where the main dailies are often centrally available in village 'reading shelters'.

Prominent newspaper columnists who write highly opinionated critical pieces are often very influential. Close personal connections, sometimes financial ones, exist between newspaper owners, editors, columnists and reporters, on the one hand, and their counterparts in the political world, on the other. Historically, newspapers have rarely functioned as conventional businesses in Thailand. Those who established or purchased newspapers typically did so in order to secure power and influence for themselves: the Thai press has generally been partisan to the core. While the leading newspapers *Thai Rath* and *Daily News* remain family concerns, other press outlets are typically owned by companies in which their founders retain a significant or controlling interest. Even a loss-making newspaper may bring financial or personal benefits to its owners in Thailand. Some owners have used the business pages of their newspapers to talk up companies in which they held shares, while others have backed particular politicians or pro-minent figures and been rewarded in other spheres. There is considerable pluralism in the Thai media system, and a fair diversity of views. At the same time, the lack of clear ideological debates and party platforms in the Thai context limits much of the quality of discourse in the public sphere.

Television is undoubtedly the most important source of political news in Thailand. Yet because the state has always been able to undermine the integrity of the broadcast media in times of crisis, people are mistrustful of the quality of political information they receive from television. The government directly controls Channels 9 and 11, Channel 5 belongs to the military, and the notionally private Channels 3 and 7 have always emphasised profitability above journalistic principles. During the mass demonstrations of May 1992, which culminated in the fatal shooting of an estimated 100 protesters by the military and the resignation of the military-backed government, television stations produced disgracefully distorted accounts of political developments. Yet the more outspoken iTV, a news-based television station founded in the wake of widespread post-1992 criticism of the existing channels, was acquired in 2000 by Thai Rak Thai party leader, and now Prime Minister, Thaksin Shinawatra. His company has fired outspoken journalists and appears to be turning the station into a pro-Thaksin outlet. Radio also flowered after the 1992 events, with the launch of several independent news-based stations, most of which relied heavily on phone-in formats. The 1997 economic crisis unfortunately forced some of these off the air.

The Thai political system is difficult to characterise. Though not fully democratic in practice – institutions such as the monarchy, the bureaucracy and the military still play significant roles – Thailand has a liberal demo-cratic political order which was most recently re-enshrined in the 1997 constitution (the country's sixteenth constitution since the end of the absolute monarchy in 1932). Thai politics is highly pluralistic, and the last two decades of the twentieth century saw elected politicians and political parties assume a dominant role in the political order. There are numerous political parties – typically around eight to ten, with four to six forming a coalition administration. Governments come and go pretty regularly: there were eight different governments during the decade from 1991 to 2001. Despite recent moves towards political reform, the electoral system is characterised by vote-buying and fraudulent manipulation, especially in rural areas. Non-governmental organisations, intellectuals and various interest groups play a vocal role in the public sphere, contributing to one of the most vibrant and open political orders in Asia.

Conceptualising the role of the Thai media

Understanding the role of media in conceptual and comparative terms poses some challenges. A great deal of the literature dealing with media in developing countries emphasises the dominance of state power and the role of censorship. Media are seen as serving the needs of the state. While appropriate in some cases, in countries such as Thailand (and comparable neighbours like Indonesia and the Philippines) this kind of emphasis is too state-centric; it does not do justice to the diverse and plural character of the media in Thailand, and especially the inventive way the print media cover politics.

The media are also often described as a 'watchdog', guarding the public interest. *The Nation*'s founder-editor, Suthichai Yoon – a consistent advocate of public interest journalism – has propounded this view in Thailand, even publishing a book of his articles entitled *Watchdog* (Suthichai 1995). It is a view shared by Thitinan Pongsudhirak, who argues that the Thai press has gradually changed from 'servant' to 'watchdog' (Thitinan 1997: 218). By monitoring abuses of power and pushing for greater openness, a watchdog media could contribute to political liberalisation and even democratisation. Views such as those of Suthichai reflect calls by some journalists for a more 'Western', professional form of journalism. At the same time, these calls must be understood partly as operating at the level of lip-service. While energetically campaigning for the reform of political institutions and other aspects of Thai society, the Thai media have been singularly ineffective at reforming themselves; the existing ownership structure offers little incentive for reform, and few journalists have articulated coherent calls for change.

Yet the watchdog analogy immediately raises questions of ownership: who owns the dog? A watchdog normally belongs to the owner of a house and is loyal to the hand that feeds it. If a newspaper is a watchdog for its owner, then its actions may not always be in the wider public interest. And where ownership can be viewed as plural and contested – including the multiple owners of a business listed on the stock exchange, as well as the influence of advertisers who buy their own stakes in a publication – the idea of a watchdog animated purely by journalistic principles of independence and fairness becomes more difficult to sustain. Those who argue for a watchdog model must be understood as trying to advocate and promote an alternative reality, rather then describing current realities in Thailand. Not even self-proclaimed 'quality' publications such as *Matichon* or *The Nation* are immune from political pressures. Although sometimes functioning as watchdogs, such newspapers are inherently partisan.

Another common view of the media as a 'mirror' of society, passively reflecting information and passing it on to the reading and viewing public, seems particularly far-fetched in the Thai case. Rhetoric about media 'neutrality' bears little relation to Thai realities. A more persuasive view of the Thai media is the 'agenda-setting' model. Agenda-setting media are assumed to be positive actors, raising salient policy issues and ferreting out corruption. Yet in the Thai context, agenda-setting may be a mixed blessing: agendas can be driven by partisan motives, and newspapers can run political campaigns on behalf of anonymous stakeholders or patrons. If the idea of agenda-setting is applied to the Thai case, it must be accompanied by critical questions concerning precisely who sets the media's agenda. Where the media themselves (or individual editors or influential columnists) have a partisan agenda which is driven by personal connections with politicians, crime bosses or military officers, then the 'agenda-setting' of the media may be simply another version of elite power-play. Political stories often find their way into Thai newspapers for political reasons, reflecting attempts to attack or discredit rivals, or to counter such attacks by others. Sources are given to the selective leaking of stories and information, while newspapers – always eager to break new stories – are willing collaborators in all kinds of political machinations. Calling this 'agenda-setting' only dignifies a pretty grubby business. Veteran journalist Wasant Paileeklee cites various instances when the media asserted its political role; some of his examples illustrate the potential of the media to set agendas counter to the public interest (Wasant 1992).

An interesting attempt to conceptualise the media in another Asian country is Susan Pharr's depiction of the Japanese media as a 'trickster' (Pharr 1996: 24–36). While Pharr sees the trickiness of the media as a potential virtue, building *communitas*, in the Thai context this trickiness appears more problematic. Pharr's trickster media are loyal to no one, but the Thai media are typically enmeshed in multiple loyalties and plural obligations to a diverse range of stakeholders. Whereas Western analysts have tended to portray 'partisanship' in terms of formal and informal links between media organisations and political parties (Blumler and Gurevitch 1995: 64–5), such a definition is woefully inadequate in Thailand's free-wheeling multi-party system, where party coalitions rarely last more than a couple of years. It is argued here that the Thai media are indeed a trickster, but not the benevolent trickster depicted by Pharr. Rather, they are an unreliable trickster, capable of acting in the public interest, but also capable of thoroughly anti-social behaviour. It could well be argued that newspapers (and indeed, their reporters, columnists and editors) are partisan political actors who are driven mainly by the pursuit of their own interests (this is the core argument of Cook 1998). Such a view applies with considerable force to the Thai case.

Conceptualising the Thai media involves questioning standard views of ideas such as ownership and partisanship. Instead of one owner supporting one political party, Thai newspapers have numerous owners and stake-holders, with plural loyalties and obligations to a range of other political actors. This makes neutrality unthinkable except as a lofty aspiration, and makes agenda-setting rather an ambiguous term. To illustrate these issues, two cases will be examined here: first, relationships between parliamentary reporters and their sources and, second, the relationships between the leading Thai daily *Matichon* and political power-holders.

Reporters and their sources

Thai parliamentary reporters will be used as a case-study for political reporters generally. This section draws upon an extended period of fieldwork based at the Thai parliament in May and June 1995, including seventeen in-depth interviews with reporters. On a typical day, there might be as many as 100 reporters stationed at the Thai parliament. Most of these were aged 20 to 25, had less than two years' work experience and did not see themselves making a career as journalists. Most were graduates, but many not from journalism programmes (for more details, see Korakot 1997). They were generally poorly trained, picking up reporting skills on the job, with minimal supervision from remote desk editors. Most of their work consisted of gathering 'routine' quotations from politicians, which were phoned or faxed back to their organisations, and attending press conferences. Only a small proportion of reporters made serious efforts to find exclusive stories: these came mainly from leading Thai language dailies, and the English language newspapers *Bangkok Post* and *The Nation*. For the most part, reporters hunted in packs, waylaying politicians and plying them with questions. After a group interview in a parliamentary corridor, the five or ten reporters who had taken part compared notes to cross-check their versions of what had been said. Some reporters expressed frustration that they were unable to write in-depth stories analysing developments. This was due to the structure of news-gathering in the Thai context; information sent in by reporters was edited by 'rewriters' at the newspaper office according to a formalised system. Only editors and columnists were allowed to write pieces that went beyond the presentation of facts and quotations.

For the great majority of more junior reporters, their main sources were a relatively small number of members of parliament (MPs) and ministers who appeared regularly at parliament. In the Thai context, parliament tended to be a focal point of activity for the opposition; most senior figures in the government parties served as ministers, with offices at Government House (for the Prime Minister and the numerous deputy premiers and PM's office ministers) or the relevant ministry. Parliament was one of the sites from which the opposition sought to undermine or topple the government during no-confidence debates, which became virtually a twice-annual event. Opposition MPs seeking to make a name for themselves would appear regularly at parliament and cultivate reporters there. In May 1995, a group of young MPs known as the 'Group of 16' were among the most regular attenders at parliament; they were the main force behind the no-confidence debate that month which successfully toppled the Chuan government. A small group of government MPs also called in regularly at the reporters' room, seeking to counterbalance the arguments of the Group of 16. Yet the great majority of MPs were conspicuous only by their absence from parliament until the debate itself.

More experienced reporters sought to set up individual appointments with sources, conscious that they might learn more by establishing a closer personal rapport with politicians. In practice, it was only longer-serving reporters – particularly those from major dailies – who regularly gained individual access to sources. Some such reporters claimed to have close regular contact with up to forty politicians. For the most part, politicians much preferred to give an important piece of information to a leading newspaper (*Thai Rath* or *Matichon* in particular); lesser newspapers and radio stations were lower down the pecking-order. One radio reporter complained that sources would sometimes ask her to hold back on a particular story until the next day, so that it could first appear in the newspapers. In effect, Thai parliamentary reporters could be divided into two groups based on their news-gathering strategies. Much as Baisnée found evidence that journalists at the European Commission adopted two different news-gathering strategies, one 'institutional' and the other more 'investigative' (see Chapter 6 by Baisnée), so most Thai parliamentary reporters were content to accept a narrow definition of their role as simple gatherers of political quotations. Only a critical minority (perhaps half a dozen out of eighty or ninety reporters) sought to find their own exclusive stories, which rocked the boat of parliamentarians. This minority found their working style regularly criticised by other reporters, who saw them as 'selfish' (McCargo 2000: 73–5).

Length of service was also important. The longer a reporter was stationed at a particular beat, the more she or he was likely to build up personal connections with sources. However, most Thai newspapers operated a rotation system which meant that capable reporters who stayed in the job more than three years were likely to be transferred to desk positions within the editorial offices, so that there were relatively few experienced reporters even at key news sites such as parliament. This tendency to transfer experienced reporters to editorial offices reflected the shortages of personnel faced by the media industry in the expansionary period of the late 1980s and early 1990s.

Reporters normally hoped to have at least one good news source in each of the ten or so parties; some claimed to have three or four in each. They typically valued information from senior politicians more than that of more acessible 'no name' MPs, since senior figures were regarded as closer to the centres of power and hence more authoritative. The ideal source was a member of the party executive or someone close to the leadership, but not himself a minister or party leader. In a study of Japanese parliamentary reporters, Ofer Feldman discovered that they all cited the same twenty-five politicians as their main sources (Feldman 1993: 65). A story from a more elite source was deemed more newsworthy. Exactly the same principle applied in the Thai case, though the larger number of parties meant that perhaps fifty individuals were the sources for the great bulk of political news. Some media organisations made use of reporters from the same part of the country as the politicians they were covering. For example, several publications assigned reporters from the south of Thailand to cover Government House during the two administrations led by southerner Chuan Leekpai.

While politicians were important and useful sources, reporters were always wary of placing too much trust in them. More experienced reporters were always conscious that politicians tended to use the media to disseminate leaks (sometimes little more than rumours) for their own purposes. Although they were supposed to cross-check important information, many reporters would file a story based on a single source. Some of these stories were later disputed or denied by those who had originated them, placing the publications involved in a difficult position.

Whereas parliamentary reporters in most countries could approach MPs by visiting their offices, Thai MPs had no offices provided at parliament. Offices assigned to the chairs of parliamentary committees were often used as gathering places for MPs from the same party or faction as the committee chair, but the rudimentary level of office and catering facilities at parliament meant that many MPs attended parliament only occasionally. While MPs were allowed to have three assistants paid for by public funds, in practice many of these sidekicks were bag-carriers and business associates rather than political secretaries in any true sense. Thus reporters could rarely access MPs by liaising with their assistants. Those relatively few MPs who made themselves accessible to reporters could easily become the main conduits of information between political parties and the media.

The problem of relying on a limited number of sources was exacerbated at many of the other beats. Foreign Ministry reporters, for example, relied almost entirely on briefings from officials and comments from ministers, with little sense of alternative sources of information. Asked whether he had other news sources, one of the most experienced reporters there could only cite USIS and the American Embassy (field notes, 9 October 1995). Reporters stationed at a particular beat had a tendency to regard the outpost of the bureaucracy where they worked as their sole focus, to the exclusion of other sources; they often began to identify too closely with the relevant government officials. At the military headquarters, matters were even worse – reporters were not free to leave the press room without an appointment to see a specific officer, and reporters who adopted a critical perspective were likely to be cold-shouldered by the top brass (field notes, 22 April 1995). Similar conditions applied at the Interior Ministry, where one reporter estimated that only a couple of the thirty or forty reporters based there were capable of obtaining exclusive stories in the face of mistrustful and conservative officials (field notes, 13 April 1995).

Reporters as news sources

Reporters interviewed all agreed that communication between themselves and politicians was a two-way process – as one put it: 'We are news sources for them just as they are for us.' This view supports Blumler and Gurevitch's 'exchange model' of relations between media and politicians (Blumler and Gurevitch 1995: 29–31). Feldman has similarly argued that one of the main incentives for Japanese politicians to talk to reporters was to obtain information from them (Feldman 1993: 52); this often took the form of asking reporters for advice (Feldman 1993: 145). It was common for Thai politicians to ask reporters what others had been saying before offering their own responses to questions; in the words of one reporter: 'So it's like you are the bridge between two groups of people.' Sometimes this extended to asking reporters how particular incidents or conflicts had damaged their public image.

Nor was this two-way exchange limited to simple chats in the corridor. Thai politicians, who lacked proper research resources and had little detailed knowledge of policy issues, might also ask reporters to provide detailed information for them on particular subjects. Newspaper offices maintained large clippings libraries, and a clippings file prepared by a helpful reporter could be an invaluable tool for a politician. Sometimes these materials were used as the basis for speeches in important debates, such as a no-confidence debate or budget debate. One newspaper, *Phujatkan*, even provided briefing sessions for Muanchon Party leader Chalerm Yubamrung to prepare him for no-confidence debates. In some circumstances, reporters became confidantes of politicians, offering them detailed policy advice. When the then finance minister, Surakiart Sathirathai, took part in a dinner with around twenty journalists and company executives at the offices of the *Matichon* newspaper group in July 1995, he asked those around the table whom he ought to choose for important posts such as central bank governor.

Meeting sources

Most meetings between parliamentary reporters and sources took place at parliament itself, but there were some occasions when meetings were held in other locations. This practice was encouraged by some news organisations in the belief that their reporters would gain more useful information in informal settings or in small gatherings. Certain politicians favoured invited groups of reporters to attend dinners or parties with them; typically, they would be the main reporters assigned to cover his (the great majority of senior Thai politicians are male) ministry or party. Reporters typically had mixed feelings about these invitations, seeing them as a potential attempt at co-optation, but also fearing that, if they failed to attend, they would miss out on important information or fail to build up strong relationships with their sources. Meals of this kind were a rare event for junior reporters, unless they were travelling with a politician in the provinces, when such hospitality was almost *de rigueur*. Some reporters, however, did flatly refuse to eat anything paid for by a politician.

Certain newspapers preferred to organise their own meals, at which politicians would be guests of the company. *Matichon* even had its own executive dining room, expressly designed for hosting such events, on an upper floor of its office building; *Matichon* also owned a riverside restaurant in the old part of the city (*Ton Po*, on Phra Athit Road) that was regularly used for similar gatherings. Other publications such as *Thai Rath* held smaller dinners on a much more ad hoc basis; *The Nation* had previously followed a *Matichon*-style policy of regular dinners, but these were greatly reduced in 1995 following budget cuts. Individual reporters were often told that they could invite politicians for meals when necessary, but in practice it was usually difficult to prevent them from paying the bill: in the Thai context, bills are almost always paid by one person, usually either the inviter or the most senior person present. Since politicians were invariably senior to the reporters covering them, they would generally insist that they be allowed to pay the bill as a matter of custom.

Unprofessional relationships between reporters and sources

Maintaining professional integrity in their relationships with sources placed constant burdens on Thai reporters. Numerous grey areas existed in these relationships, ranging from simple matters such as whether or not to accept a politician's offer of a meal, or whether to provide a source with potentially useful political information, to more difficult decisions about handling offers of bribes or valuable favours. Not all of the impropriety lay with the politicians: some reporters actively solicited cash or other benefits from their sources.

In interviews, reporters all acknowledged the existence of improprieties, but (unsurprisingly) all denied having committed any themselves, and some even denied having witnessed anything improper. One form of borderline impropriety was a kind of group partisanship, the identification of reporters on a particular beat with the sources they covered. Military reporters, for example, generally liked the navy and were sympathetic to its needs. When naval commanders requested the purchase of submarines in 1995, most military reporters were very much in favour of the idea despite the fact that the strategic case for these purchases was extremely questionable. On a trip back from Sattahip naval base, one such reporter exclaimed 'If only we could get them just one submarine!' (field notes, April 1995). In May 1995, many reporters were sympathetic to the outspoken criticisms of the young 'Group of 16' MPs; one reporter interviewed repeatedly used kinship terms for these MPs, implying that they were her 'elder brothers'. Some politicians sought to turn the circle of reporters assigned to cover them into an informal support group, or singled out particular reporters as favourites. Because Thai reporters had relatively little contact with their newspaper offices (given Bangkok's traffic problems, many went to their offices only once a week or less), they often felt outsiders both in their own news organisations and in the organisations they were assigned to cover. By offering selected reporters 'insider' status, politicians made them feel more highly valued.

Yet relationships of this kind, where reporters derived part of their standing from their privileged proximity to sources, were vulnerable to commercialisation from either side. On trips to the provinces or even abroad (Thai ministries often provided a budget for reporters to escort ministers on foreign trips), reporters were exposed to greater temptations than in Bangkok. For example, on one 'fact-finding' trip to Chantaburi province on the eastern seaboard, organised by opposition politicians in May 1995, the politicians concerned laid on free transport for press reporters (television reporters and crews were flown by helicopter, making excellent footage for normally quiet Sunday night news programmes) and provided them with lunch at a luxury hotel. However, the bus transport was chartered simply to meet up with the politicians and allow the reporters to cover their side of the story, an 'investigation' into allegedly corrupt land transactions involving a government MP. Reporters were unable to interview other sources unless they took their own cars on a long drive through a flood-bound area. The hospitality provided by the politicians had been so constructed as to distort news coverage of the issues involved.

Greater complications arose when an overnight stay was required. An extended trip to Phuket and other southern provinces in April 1995, on which a group of opposition politicians had been accompanied by a sizeable contingent of reporters, had generated significant controversy. The MPs involved had constantly sought to pay the hotel and meal bills for all the reporters. Since many of the hotels at which they stayed were quite expensive, it was inconvenient for reporters to use their own funds to cover all the costs; many of them found recouping expenses from their organisations troublesome and long-winded. Yet to stay at cheaper hotels was not an easy option; many Bangkok-based reporters, especially women, were uncomfortable about checking into downmarket hotels in unfamiliar places; and if they did so, they ran the risk of missing out on their stories. Some reporters managed to make discreet arrangements with hotel staff to settle their own bills.

When I accompanied a group of reporters to Suphanburi province on 4–5 June 1995, where they would be covering the beginning of the election campaign, we arrived at the main hotel in town but nobody checked in. It emerged that the reporters were expecting a local MP to cover the costs of the hotel, but needed to establish this for certain. When we visited this MP's house later in the afternoon, he confirmed (in response to a direct question) that he would be paying everyone's hotel bill. One reporter told me that she planned to obtain a receipt from the hotel, and claim these 'expenses' (then equivalent to 700 or 800 baht, or roughly £13 to £14) back from her company. She described this as a common practice on provincial trips: reporters were not simply accepting hospitality, but exploiting it to cheat on their expenses. However, many other reporters who arrived in Suphanburi later in the day did pay their own expenses, often sharing rooms to keep down costs: these 'common' practices were far from universal.

The giving of cash or gifts to reporters was another common practice. When I attended a military ceremony on 10 April 1995, all the media representatives present (myself included) were given a white envelope containing a Buddha amulet and a 100 baht note (then about £1.60), which my reporter colleagues described as 'bus fare money' or 'coffee money'. This practice facetiously known in Indonesia as the 'envelope culture' (Hanazaki 1996: 127–30) was quite common at press conferences, and was even more widespread in business circles. Similar practices were widespread in the Philippines (Florentino-Hofilena 1998). Public relations firms sent a regular supply of small gifts out to the business editors of newspapers, and at New Year newspapers were bombarded with corporate-sponsored goodies. One leading politician facing intense media scrutiny over his alleged involvement in the drugs trade was accused of having handed out gold amulets to a large number of news photographers at the end of a press conference; this incident took place after all the reporters present had left the room in protest. In another controversial episode, the then foreign minister (later Prime Minister), Thaksin Shinawatra, gave out free mobile phones to a group of reporters at a 'thank you' party; these were all later returned.

However, these acts of collective gift-giving were less significant than more discreet and more substantial transactions between sources and individual reporters. One reporter assigned to cover the Chat Pattana Party explained how one of its ministers had offered him and a colleague a thousand baht after a controversial move by the party in December 1994. Another experienced reporter recalled several offers of small sums (all under a thousand baht) by politicians. Common ploys included offering reporters who were going on trips abroad cash for 'shopping' (this could be ambiguous, since politicians challenged on this might respond that they wanted the reporters to buy something for them with the money), or giving reporters donations which were ostensibly for charity. Most Thai newspapers were associated with charitable foundations, or engaged in fund raising for good causes; a 'donation' given to a reporter might find its way to the 'intended' cause, or could be discreetly pocketed by the reporter, as was probably intended by the donor.

Many of these cases may appear trivial, and indeed they are not very significant within the wider context of relations between the press and politics in Thailand. It is well understood that the more serious corruption that characterises these relationships is at a much more senior level: the close ties between newspaper owners, editors and columnists, and their counterparts in the parallel universe of politics. Many Thai newspaper columnists enjoy comfortable lifestyles far beyond the purchasing power of their salaries, and it is an open secret that some have engaged in the practice of providing sympathetic coverage of politicians in exchange for material rewards. Former Prime Minister Banharn Silpa-archa was said once to have had a retinue of newspaper columnists in his pay known as the '18 knights' (18 *orahan*); more recently, most such columnists have probably served as freelance operators rather than salaried employees (Bunlert 1996: 180–93; McCargo 2000: 137–8). By the boom period of the 1990s, most columnists were believed to prefer payment in stocks and shares to straight cash. A senior editor at *Thai Rath* admitted in a 1993 newspaper interview that some columnists at the newspaper took bribes. Because columnists were entitled (and were expected) to express strong political opinions in their writings, paying a columnist was much more effective than paying a lowly reporter.

Nevertheless, examples of political reporters receiving substantial favours from politicians did exist. Somchai Meesaen, a Government House reporter for the normally squeaky-clean *Bangkok Post*, had to resign in 1999 after evidence emerged that he had accepted 150,000 baht (by then around £3,750) from a government minister as a down-payment on a new car (see McCargo 2000: 172–5). He claimed that the minister had simply done him a favour by booking the car in his own name, thereby enabling him to short-circuit the waiting list. The story caused an uproar, and was referred to the newly established Press Council for adjudication. However, despite leaving the *Bangkok Post* under a cloud, Somchai was immediately rehired by a Thai language daily, *Naeo Na*, and continued to work as a Government House reporter. This was a rare example of a corruption case involving a political reporter coming to light, but it must be assumed that many similar deals went undetected.

Matichon's relationship with politicians

The leading political daily *Matichon*, which prides itself on being a 'quality' newspaper, faced some interesting dilemmas in its relationships with politicians. During several weeks of participant-observation fieldwork at the newspaper in July and August 1995, it became clear that *Matichon* staff sought to characterise their own relationships with politicians as 'professional', in implicit contrast to the 'beneficial' relationships between journalists and sources alleged to prevail at rival newspapers such as *Thai Rath*. While a couple of members of the editorial team had good ties with particular senior politicians, *Matichon* was generally weaker in finding out important information about current political developments. *Matichon* staff believed that it was much easier for their counterparts at *Thai Rath* to get hold of the Prime Minister or other senior politicians (say, by telephone) than for themselves to do so. In mid-1995, only one of *Matichon*'s six front-page editors had close personal ties to a minister. While *Matichon* attempted to redress this by inviting politicians over for combined interview and dinner sessions in the executive dining suite, the resulting sessions tended to be unwieldy, with numerous company executives in attendance and the key front-line reporters given little opportunity to talk freely to the guests in the face of so many big shots.

A significant obstacle to the creation of close ties between politicians and *Matichon* staff lay in the characters of senior figures at the newspaper. Many Thai politicians had a background in shady provincial business; some were implicated in activities such as smuggling, illegal logging, underground lotteries and even drug-dealing. This included some of the most senior figures in the main political parties, who were nicknamed 'godfathers' or 'influential people' (see McVey 2000). These politicians spent much of their leisure time in bars, massage parlours and illegal gambling dens, places where certain columnists from *Thai Rath* and other downmarket newspapers were alleged to be very much at ease. However, the senior editors of *Matichon* were mostly highly respectable figures of an intellectual or academic bent, who never (or hardly ever) drank, and would not be able to move in the social circles favoured by such politicians. As the political editor Pakpom Pongbhai argued:

> Most of our reporters don't have the right personal characteristics to fit in with Thai politicians, so they won't be able to get involved in taking money, drinking and gambling. If they knew how to carry it off, they might be able to do it, but it would go against their natural behaviour. This means we can't reach the highest level.
>
> (Interview, 6 August 1995)

Pakpoom linked 'taking money' directly with drinking and gambling, suggesting that the three activities were inextricably interrelated. *Matichon* was in a tricky dilemma, since its image and reputation were based on the idea that it was a quality publication that did not engage in dubious connections with sources, yet this very same stance impeded it from access to important information. As deputy political editor Sanchai Chantrawatanakul explained concerning his contacts with sources:

> I always tell them clearly before getting close to them that if I find out they are doing something bad, I will try to find out more information and expose it. So they know, but they may still be open with us. This may be an obstacle to getting close to them, and sometimes it's uncomfortable for me: should I present this or that story? But once it gets to a certain point, when there is a trend in that direction or it becomes an issue, then I publish it. Sometimes in publishing something, I do wonder whether I am putting my life in danger. I've been in some situations when money has been given out and I've sat there thinking, should I publish this? They can understand this. It might mean that they won't take us to see certain people in the future, but they know what job we do.
>
> (Interview, 4 August 1995)

This kind of understanding between political reporter and source was a Faustian one: the source provides information, but the more useful the information, the more limited the reporter is in his/her capacity to publish it, and the more he/she becomes involved in a form of complicity with the source that prevents him/her from writing the full story. Sanchai admitted that he sometimes had to be satisfied with publishing some inside details of stories only after the issue had reached the public domain, rather than breaking new ground on the basis of his inside knowledge.

One obvious example of *Matichon*'s failure to obtain scoops from inside sources was the publication of the Banharn Silpa-archa government's policy statement in July 1995. *Thai Rath* procured the whole document before it was officially announced, publishing it in its entirety (*Thai Rath*, 24 July 1995). Despite having invested considerable efforts in trying to obtain the document, *Matichon* had drawn a blank. While *Matichon* had requested a copy directly from those who had prepared the policy document, *Thai Rath* had apparently asked deputy Chart Thai Party leader Vattana Assavahame to request a copy for himself and pass it on to them. This method drew on their strong personal ties with Vattana, a controversial politician who might later call in the favour by soliciting *Thai Rath*'s help in his efforts to defend himself against allegations that he was engaged in illegal business activities. As Pakpoom explained: 'This is our problem; all the key men in Chart Thai are godfathers, but the personal characteristics of the senior people in the newspaper aren't suitable for getting close to them' (interview, 6 August 1995). *Matichon* lacked good connections with senior party figures, seeking instead to cultivate links with 'Young Turk' politicians; this strategy, though good in the long term, failed to pay immediate dividends at crucial junctures.

Even when *Matichon* did achieve some success in building a rapport with leading politicans, matters did not always work out as the newspaper intended. Recognising that Chart Thai Party leader Banharn Silpa-archa was likely to become the next prime minister (as he did in July 1995), *Matichon* had carefully nurtured good relations with him during meals and informal meetings. But when he became Prime Minister, he began phoning *Matichon* to complain that stories critical of his administration were appearing for three or four days in a row, in spite of the fact that he and *Matichon* were members of 'the same group'. As Sanchai explained:

> His idea of 'being in the same group' and *Matichon*'s are different. We don't think of ourselves as 'being in the same group' in the sense that we have to help him. But we do think that we are 'in the same group' if he does something good. Banharn thinks of *Matichon* as well-disposed to him, because we have had meetings and meals with him, and expects that we will help him and support him all the time. It's not like that.
>
> (Interview, 4 August 1995)

Thai politicians sought to secure unconditional support from allies in the press, rather than the highly conditional approbation that *Matichon* was willing to offer. *Matichon*'s inability to accept the rules of the game as understood by the likes of Banharn was an obstacle to securing the benefits that could accrue from a close rapport with leading politicians.

Conclusion

This chapter has argued that political journalists are in fact political actors. Using the examples of a particular site of political news (the Thai parliament) and a particular newspaper (*Matichon*), it has explored the elaborate interdependencies between political journalists and politicians in a culture characterised by patron–client relations. It has examined issues such as gift-giving, hospitality and bribery as they influence journalist–source relationships in Thailand, and has drawn on recent cases of apparent corruption among political reporters to illustrate the dilemmas and options facing journalists and news sources alike. Relationships between individual reporters and their sources on a beat such as parliament were intimately linked to the relationships between a reporter's own publication and the politicians concerned. Where politicians enjoyed close personal ties to columnists, editors or owners of a given publication, they were likely to offer more assistance to that publication's reporters. Yet sometimes personal ties of this nature were not even known to reporters on the ground, who often had relatively little face-to-face contact with senior figures in their own publications. Relationships between media practitioners and their sources reflected a Byzantine web of connections, some perfectly respectable and others highly questionable.

Challenging Western-centric models of the way the media operate, this chapter has sought to show that there are deeply symbiotic ties between Thai journalists and politicians which undermine conventional notions of balance and objectivity. Power-holders provide a range of services (including financial incentives and political protection) for journalists, who in turn reciprocate with favourable coverage. The linkages that exist between Thai journalists and power-holders have been shown to be multifaceted and ambiguous. Two key concepts have been problematised: ownership and partisanship. Media ownership is an important factor in shaping political news coverage, yet ownership is much more complex than it appears. Newspapers have numerous stakeholders; columnists and editors may themselves hold shares in the company they work for, and they may also be in a position to sell their services to outside bidders, thereby sub-letting or franchising space within publications. Similarly, in a multi-party system of constantly shifting political alliances, no newspaper can tie itself to supporting a single party. Partisanship must be multi-directional; instead of simple relationships between particular politicians and particular political parties, partisan connections are far more complex and confusing networks of linkages.

While these arguments apply with particular force to Thailand, they also have considerable validity in relation to the media in other Southeast Asian countries such as Indonesia and the Philippines, and there is every reason to believe that they may have comparative relevance to an understanding of how politics and media interact in many other developing countries.

References

Blumler, J.G. and Gurevitch, M. (1995) *The Crisis of Public Communication*, London: Routledge.

Bunlert Changyai (1996) *Song Khao Nangsuephim* [White Envelopes and Newspapers], Bangkok: Matichon Publishing.

Cook, T. (1998) *Governing with the News: The News Media as a Political Institution*, Chicago: University of Chicago Press.

Feldman, O. (1993) *Politics and the News Media in Japan*, Ann Arbor: University of Michigan Press.

Florentino-Hofilena, C. (1998) *News for Sale: The Corruption of the Philippine Media*, Quezon City: Philippine Center for Investigative Journalism.

Hanazaki, Y. (1996) 'The Indonesian press in the era of *Keterbukaan*: a force for democratisation', unpublished PhD thesis, Monash University.

Korakot Surakul (1997) 'Kanpeutpradenkhao lae Krabuankanthamkhao Phusuekhao Kanmuang' [News Issue Opening and the news-making process of political reporters], unpublished MA dissertation, Chulalongkorn University.

McCargo, D. (2000) *Politics and the Press in Thailand: Media Machinations*, London: Routledge.

McVey, R. (ed.) (2000) *Money and Power in Provincial Thailand*, Copenhagen: NIAS.

Pharr, S.J. (1996) 'Media as trickster in Japan: a comparative perspective', in S.J. Pharr and E.S. Krauss (eds) *Media and Politics in Japan*, Honolulu: University of Hawaii.

Suthichai Yoon (1995) *Ma Fao Ban* [Watchdog], Bangok: Nation Publishing.

Thitinan Pongsudhirak (1997) 'Thailand's media: whose watchdog?', in K. Hewison (ed.) *Political Change in Thailand: Democracy and Participation*, London: Routledge.

Wasant Paileeklee (1992) 'Interactions between the press and politics in Thailand from 14 October 1973 to 23 February 1991', unpublished MA dissertation, School of Oriental and African Studies, University of London.

Acknowledgements

This research was made possible by an ESRC research fellowship (H52427002694), a grant from the British Academy Committee for South-East Asian Studies, and generous support from the Department of Politics, University of Leeds. This funding allowed me to spend twelve months undertaking fieldwork in Bangkok from February 1995 to February 1996. I am extremely grateful to Sombat Chantornvong and to all those who assisted me in my research, especially those media practitioners who allowed me to interview them.

6 Can political journalism exist at the EU level?

Olivier Baisnée

Obscure decisions taken by unknown politicians or technocrats in a political and institutional system nobody can understand might be a good way to summarise the impression that EU public affairs frequently give. Some writers criticise the EU's lack of a co-ordinated communications strategy for this state of affairs (Meyer 1999). A more common complaint focuses on the EU's so-called 'democratic deficit', with most writers insisting on the legal and procedural aspects of this legitimisation problem: the unelected Commissioners, the weakness of Parliament and the complicated decision-making process.[1] From this point of view, legitimacy would be solely a technical problem, adequately resolved by institutional reform. However, the question of legitimisation might be rather more complex. The issue of the 'democratic deficit' has probably been badly presented since very few studies have questioned the representations given of the original political system: its processes, issues and actors. Indeed, most of the time, European decisions seem to come out of nowhere because the political process they have been through has a very low public profile.

Yet, there are about 800 people in Brussels whose job it is to scrutinise the EU, to interpret it and to make their findings public; 800 journalists who know perfectly well the political dimension of any decision. They are the filter through which institutions that have no natural audiences – except geographically, culturally and politically divided publics – are given publicity. Yet even though it is one of the biggest press corps in the world and despite the increasingly crucial role it plays for EU citizens, it remains an anonymous body which has been studied very little (Morgan 1995; Schickel 1995). This is somewhat surprising, since a study of EU correspondents is a unique occasion to compare journalists from different countries in a context which is not comparable with the work of traditional foreign correspondents. In our opinion, the study of this journalistic community, and especially its ability to politicise EU news, is of crucial importance (Padioleau 1976; Tunstall 1970). Until the EU political system has been given social visibility, it will probably remain a 'cold monster' in the opinion of European citizens.

In general terms, three main attitudes toward the politicisation of EU news can be observed among EU correspondents. These can also be regarded as three conflicting or competing definitions of the job of an EU correspondent. The first, which we call 'institutional journalism', produces coverage more concerned with 'policies' than 'politics': a technical and expert-like coverage of European current affairs. As this chapter shows, an older generation of French journalists exemplify this approach. In contrast, a newer generation of French journalists have developed a definition of their role which is closer to the most legitimate forms of journalism – investigative reporting and political journalism. Finally, and this approach is particularly relevant to the British correspondents, coverage of EU matters may be framed through the prism of national political debates. In this case the politicisation of events is related to the national issue agenda and the resultant coverage does not treat the EU as an independent political system.

This chapter is divided into two main sections. In depicting the 'small world' of Brussels journalism, the first section argues that the organisation, rules and rituals of the press corps strongly influence the way in which EU matters are covered in national media. The second section focuses on three approaches to the politicisation of EU news, using French and British journalistic practice to exemplify the argument's central analytic points.

The microcosm and the way it works

The group of about 800 official EU journalists constitutes a particular microcosm: a specific and limited social group with its own history, practices and customs. In studying media coverage of the EU we need to understand how this community of journalists functions. Given that the vast majority of these journalists are working abroad, they organise themselves in a very specific manner which is quite unlike that of any national press corps.

A small world

The rhythm of an EU press correspondent's life is governed by visits to unchanging places and events in which they experience a real feeling of community that gives the press corps the appearance of a 'travelling cocktail' going from lobby to lobby. The most ritualised moment is the Commission's daily press briefing. This encounter between the central institution of the EU and the journalists demonstrates a powerful paradox: while journalists are given very little new information at these events, most of them are anxious to attend what appears to be more of a social ritual than a press conference. Nevertheless, these rituals are very important for the press corps in Brussels because it is through them that they are socially incorporated into the institutional and political system of the EU. Indeed, after a few years, these journalists become members of what can be called the 'first public of Europe'. By this term we mean an over-informed social group which is aware of every single (political) fact that happens in the EU political world. Yet while they all know what is going on behind the scenes, as well as being familiar with the official discourse, very few will openly discuss this political reality.

Every day, at a few minutes before noon, between 200 and 300 journalists flock to the Commission's presidency building. Most of them arrive at the Breydel on foot from nearby offices. Their destination? The ritual *rendez-vous de midi* to which they are invited by the Commission's spokesman. With their official credentials in hand (which they will not even be asked to present if they are considered 'regulars'), they reach the underground press centre where they meet their colleagues over a drink in the nearby lobby bar. At precisely 12 o'clock, press information in the form of Commissioners' speeches and various documents from Commission services (such as reports, economic data and surveys) are arranged on display stands. While the most scrupulous will get all the papers, the more relaxed will grab only the ones that seem interesting to them. At this moment, the quickest off the mark are the agency journalists who, while still queuing, will phone through the most urgent news to their offices – for example, on merger authorisations.

The formal press conference takes place after the correspondents have obtained their documents. It is then that they enter the press room: a semicircle with barely room for 200 people. This crowd is remarkable in that a third of EU journalists spend at least an hour of their precious time attending a press conference at which they will learn scarcely anything that they do not already know. In fact, the press conference merely consists of a presentation of the current subjects and the latest developments concerning particular problems. The whole is presented in a very civilised way by the spokespersons who tend to soften all problems and disguise conflicts.

The most striking point about this somewhat sanitised presentation is that most of the journalists are aware of the conflicts and problems that the spokespersons refuse to talk about. Indeed, they have their own sources: their 'off the record' declarations collected from civil servants and sometimes directly from the spokesperson, which enable them to know what is going on behind the scenes. Most of the time at these press briefings, information comes from the room, not from the speaker. It is often the questions asked, rather than the answers given, that underline the problems that a particular decision might imply for the various countries involved. Given that these journalists cannot be aware of all the national particularities and situations concerning the numerous subjects dealt with by the Commission, the press conference enables them to anticipate the debates that certain questions will raise.

A fascinating feature of this *rendez-vous de midi* (the name itself is significant) is the regularity with which the journalists and the European

Commission spokespersons attend. When asked about their activities, journalists spontaneously mention this ritual moment as the fixed point of their working day. They have even adopted a religious vocabulary: the spokespersons are referred to as 'high priests' saying a 'mass', while 'our daily bread' is used to qualify the documents given to the journalists. Some of them even doubt the meeting's professional interest: 'the press room to me, it's a place where I have fun. No, it's absolutely not a working tool . . . the press room never provided me with information' (interview with a French broadsheet journalist).

In fact, it is above all a social event; an occasion to meet colleagues in a relaxed atmosphere, to discuss daily matters of interest and to encounter spokespersons in an informal way in order to get off the record reactions or information. The most important feature of the 'briefing' is certainly not the press conference itself, but the daily meeting it generates among all the journalists. Deprived of editorial offices and of their habitual colleagues, they recreate (in the same way as they do in the press centres provided by all the European institutions) a professional environment through which they can break out of their isolation. In the Commission's press bar, as in the Council's, they can share views and sometimes information and contacts. Thus they can compensate for the fact that they are often the only representatives of their national media.

> It looks like a mass. These people are isolated. They work all day long in their office. For some of them at home, in their flat . . . it's quite a useful contact.
>
> (Interview with a French press agency journalist)

This ritualised encounter is, therefore, extremely important to the internal functioning of the microcosm: it is the place where affinities and feelings of animosity are most obvious and where the existence of distinct journalistic cultures is most apparent (in the way questions are asked, for example). However, it is also a way for newcomers to find out the opinions of their more experienced colleagues: it reduces the uncertainty concerning the interpretation of information. When we use the term 'ritualised encounter' we mean that this daily *rendez-vous* has quite an invariable structure: every day new subjects appear in the press conference but the interaction between the institution and 'its' journalists remains broadly the same, hence, conferring on it the dimension of a ritual.

Some journalists have pointed out that the atmosphere inside the official Brussels press corps has changed and they highlight the fact that the growing number of journalists tend to establish more formal and professional relationships. At the same time, others underline the shock they felt when discovering this microcosm and the rules that govern it. The most striking factor seems to be the interpenetration of the journalistic circle by other social actors such as the civil servants, politicians and lobbyists who populate Brussels. When mentioning his very first days in the Belgian capital, this journalist speaks of:

> the absolute horror: a technocratic world that was obeying incomprehensible rules for the outsider . . . a world where I would say journalists, civil servants and diplomats were sleeping together. There was no distance at all, no objectivity. A European militants' world of people persuaded that they are working for the good of humanity. In short, I couldn't distinguish between who was a journalist, who was a civil servant and who was a diplomat. It's a bit strange, isn't it?
>
> (Interview with a French broadsheet journalist)

Thus, these journalists form part of a wider microcosm that includes all those with a professional occupation linked to the EU. This 'European people' (Shore 2000), as we might call them, is perhaps this political Europe's only public: constantly looking for news, rumours and gossip.

Journalists often mention this phenomenon of a closed environment because this 'European people' lives shut off from the rest of the world in very specific districts. What is more, they frequent the same places which they alone are able to afford. This promiscuity has an enormous effect on the journalistic work of people who are in Brussels for more than twenty years and who become prominent personalities of this small European world.

> All these people live within an area of about two square kilometres . . . they send their children to the same schools, obviously go to the same expensive restaurants because only the expatriates and the civil servants can afford them. So they meet in the same bars, in the same schools, in the same stores, . . . So it's very difficult not to get into this network. You meet a young civil servant: he's pleasant, he's your age and little by little he moves up the hierarchy . . . .
>
> (Interview with a French broadsheet journalist)

It is surprising to see how the geography of the European institutions significantly diminishes the journalists' working perimeter: Breydel (home of the European Commission Presidency), Justus Lipsius (European Council) and the European Parliament are just a few hundred metres from each other. Within this triangle (or close by), one can find numerous bars and restaurants and most of the correspondents' offices (de la Guérivière 1992). Consequently, these people are in constant contact with each other: at work, in bars, in restaurants, in the street and inside the buildings of the European institutions. This enables the establishment of a real *esprit de corps*.

This rather friendly and fraternal atmosphere is further strengthened by a low degree of rivalry among journalists – very few scoops appear at the

EU level that are considered as such by the national editorial offices. Barely concerned with competing against each other, journalists can more easily develop collaborative relationships: when several events take place at the same time, they share information and, sometimes, the workload. Whenever someone has an exclusive the others are not embarrassed because they do not have to justify themselves to their editorial offices.[2]

Training and socialisation

The microcosm represents more than these rituals and places. It is also a regulatory system where journalists gain experience of a political reality that most of them discovered only on arrival in Brussels. Besides the lack of information concerning what European political life entails, the EU suffers from a deficit of recognisable political imagery which, practically speaking, prevents an effective widespread understanding of European politics and current affairs. In fact, there are very few symbolic 'common places' and no immediately recognisable reference points, both of which would facilitate coverage of the EU's activities.

During their first weeks in Brussels, most journalists confess that they believed they had 'landed on the planet Mars' since the 'Euro-speak', the technicalities and the complexity of EU processes corresponded little with what they were previously accustomed to. Nevertheless, daily contact with the European political and institutional system has meant that these EU correspondents, and all those whose professional activity is linked to Europe, have since gained an intimate knowledge of its processes, the political staff, the places and the issues.

The technicalities and political complexities mentioned above appear to be a popular point of contention. In fact, most of the journalists interviewed spontaneously mentioned how tough it was at first to understand the decision-making processes. Indeed, most affirmed that they needed a one-year period in order to adapt themselves. One particular press agency journalist recalls the 'humility' one needs when beginning as an EU correspondent, even after a long and prestigious career as a foreign correspondent, such as he had enjoyed. The intricacies of the work and the institutions with which these journalists deal are such that journalists must completely rethink their methods.

The harshness of the situation, the existence of this microcosm where everybody knows each other and where there is very little competition, partly explains the phenomenon of mutual aid and the welcome given to newcomers. As one journalist puts it:

> When I first arrived here, I was an absolute layperson on these subjects but, in fact, things soon went well. I met some journalists who helped me, who showed me the way, who explained how things work . . . As the Brussels world is rather small, when you know two or three people, you

soon know ten then twenty then fifty. So finally, from this point of view, it went well.

(Interview with a French regional newspaper journalist)

This mutual aid and friendliness are clearly visible. As we have already said, the absence of an editorial office is compensated for by help from colleagues from other newspapers. Indeed, the Brussels 'old boy network' is extremely active: it possesses a kind of moral authority on the younger members since its members have an intricate knowledge of the issues and workings of 'the European machine'. Additionally, they are Brussels' 'best address books' and can therefore help the newcomers establish a network of acquaintances.

Moreover, once the training period has ended, the posting appears much more rewarding than other 'foreign' journalist posts. Press agency journalists often recall how much the EU post is different from a traditional foreign correspondent's post where access to sources is much tougher, most of the work is limited to following the national press and where there is little direct contact with current affairs. Thus, several journalists evoke a certain fascination with the EU system and a growing satisfaction which results from an impression that in Brussels they are finally 'at the very heart of things'.

Indeed, unlike most citizens, the journalists whose job it is to cover current affairs within the EU follow a kind of self-imposed political 'crash-course' in order to grasp the workings of the European political system. Of course, they confess that initially they had only a very superficial knowledge. However, given their obligation to write articles, they are rapidly forced to become familiar with the specific EU political processes, issues and institutions. They develop a kind of formula which enables them to decode European issues and, once they have gained the necessary experience, they can even anticipate events rather than merely react to them. While for most Europeans decisions seem to crop up from nowhere or from 'Brussels', once their training period has ended, these journalists are able to understand what is at stake as well as spot all the actors and problems involved:

> When a directive comes out, we know perfectly well the reasons for its ambition or on the contrary for its modesty and almost all the obstacles it will have to go through and we could almost anticipate the end result: that Italy will remove that because . . . That the French will moan about it because of the sovereignty thing, that the Germans . . . the trade unions and the Danish . . . will respond in a particular way . . . .
>
> (Interview with a French economic broadsheet journalist)

Therefore, the press corps has become a privileged observer of the EU. Little by little, its members have come to know intimately this political and institutional system which was as unfamiliar to them as to the lay European citizen. In this respect, one can describe these journalists as the first, and perhaps the only, European public, whose members have acquired a set of perceptions and a political understanding about the workings of the EU system which most European citizens do not possess.

Probably, the most striking example of the nature of the European Union's only public is provided by some opinion polls concerning European Commissioners. When, for example, the French monthly magazine *L'Expansion* decided to try to evaluate the Commissioners' popularity as they would for any other national political figure, there was much debate about the constituency they should survey. Besides the obvious problems of cost and organisation, the main obstacle to such surveys is the fact that, with few exceptions, the political figures in question are for the most part complete strangers to most Europeans. When asked about members of the European Commission, citizens would probably not have been able to pass judgement on individuals whose names they do not even know. EU correspondents were therefore asked to answer the questionnaires in order to establish a 'hit parade' of Commissioners.

It is the means used to collect the results for these opinion polls rather than the results themselves that is most revealing, because it clearly demonstrates the official role of the press as Europe's only real public. This public is in fact made up of people who are bombarded with news and comments about the EU in a way which the average citizen is not. One could even say that the press pool – this microcosm from which individual Commissioners try to obtain assent through regular meetings – is the sole representation of a European public opinion. Indeed, through the questions the journalists are asked, the Commissioners are able to understand how different nations react to individual issues. What can be taken for granted in France may be slightly more difficult to introduce in Germany or in another country. Thus, the press corp's reaction gives a hypothetical idea of how an actual European public opinion, with its various national tendencies and problems, might function.

Having learnt how the EU works, these journalists can develop analytic skills which enable them to write political stories about current affairs. However, most written articles on the subject fail to depict a decision's political implications in spite of the specificity which the EU institutional system represents. In fact, the only conflicts that are given time and space are those involving member states, as is the case for any form of inter-governmental bargaining. While EU correspondents are very well aware of the intense political life in Brussels, this particular European dimension is hardly ever explored, which results in a reinforcement of the public belief – one shared by national editors-in-chief – that Europe is excessively technocratic. There is a distinct difference between what these journalists know about any decision or fact and what they actually write about it.

Three approaches to the politicisation of EU news

Although the Brussels press corps can be largely depicted as a microcosm, this does not mean that a kind of 'Eurojournalism' with its own homogeneous practices and production has emerged. In fact, national boundaries have not disappeared – as one British journalist puts it, 'there are fifteen microcosms' in the press room.[3] There are principles of organisation which are specific to any group of national journalists. One cannot, therefore, understand the EU news produced in any member country without bearing in mind the kind of relationships that exist among the different national groups of journalists. Indeed, apart from the language barrier, national professional and political cultures still determine EU coverage, while each national press continues to organise itself according to its own principles, which in turn produces a particular method of reporting 'Europe'.

On their arrival in Brussels journalists must learn to deal not only with existing patterns of coverage and the development of the institutions' communication strategies, but also with their editorial offices' expectations and their own conception of their work as journalists. It is possible to distinguish between at least three forms of journalism in Brussels which represent the different attitudes to the politicisation of EU news: institutional, investigative/political and domestic/political journalism. This section examines these three approaches, using French and British practices as exemplars.

Different organisational patterns

As far as the French and British press are concerned, two main organisational differences need to be emphasised from the beginning: turnover policy and the influence of the nationally based editorial offices. Both of these have consequences for the coverage produced and especially for the correspondents' room for manoeuvre when deciding what events are relevant for their media.

Let us first look at turnover policy. The primary factor that one must take into account when analysing the way the British journalist group organises itself and the place it occupies in the press corps is the time these journalists spend in Brussels. While French newsmen and women have generally been EU correspondents for quite a long time – even the youngest – British journalists spend barely more than four or five years posted in Belgium. Indeed, their newspapers consider that too long a stay could undermine their readiness to be critical and that they might, as Mrs Thatcher used to say about British officials in Brussels, 'go native'.[4]

This turnover policy has two major consequences: it prevents British journalists from gaining prominent positions among the microcosm's members and stops them from making the most of their socialisation period since they are likely to leave Brussels just as they have learnt the technicalities of the EU system. The British press is quite prestigious and well known in Brussels, particularly the *Financial Times*.[5] Individual British journalists, however, remain quite anonymous. As a result, the British press corps has long had a weak influence on the organisation of the EU institutions' communication policy. For example, up until 1995, even though there were about three times as many British journalists as French, the official languages of the Commission's press briefing was French. Given that they are required to give up the EU job after such a short period, British journalists are unable to become experts on EU matters to the same degree as some French journalists are. This pheno- menon makes it more difficult for them to apply political journalism to the EU, since, as we have seen, the socialisation period is essential to journalists who plan to write news stories explaining what is really at stake, the balance of power that exists and the actors involved in the policy- making process.

A second difference between French and British journalism in Brussels concerns the kind of relationship that exists between the correspondents and their editorial offices. While French journalists are quite free to evaluate the 'newsworthiness' of information and to define their own position, their British counterparts seem to have a much stronger link with their London offices. EU correspondents become experts who are in a strong position to determine what is at stake. Since editors have very little interest in (and knowledge about) EU news, they can hardly contest the choices made by the journalists. Yet British newspapers paint a very different picture since EU news is not only considered relevant solely for those who already have the detailed knowledge of an expert, but is also deeply embedded in national politics. As one journalist put it 'I am an extension of Westminster or rather Westminster is an extension of me' (interview with a British press agency journalist). This concept of a post which is geographically located abroad but which is not a traditional foreign correspondent's job is widely shared among the French as well as the British. However, in the latter case, it has a different signification: while EU news almost exclusively goes to the 'Foreign news' pages in France, British correspondents very often have their articles published in the 'Home news' section. Fundamentally, and above and beyond this revealing insight into the organisation of British newspapers, EU news in the UK is most of the time framed through the prism of domestic politics. Two factors have to be taken into account here. The first concerns the kind of domestic issue that the EU represents. Second, one has to consider the degree of politicisation of newspapers and especially whether European issues occupy a dominant place or not in their news coverage.

Box 5.1 **Differences between British and French members of the Brussels press corps**

France	Great Britain
Long stay	Turnover policy
A group divided between 'institutional' and 'investigative' journalists	Prominent position of Geoffrey Meade
Weak influence of the editorial offices	Strong link with London (especially political editors)
Europhiles	Eurosceptic bias

Institutional journalism

Historically speaking, EU coverage has been dominated by this traditional institutional journalism and it is only in the last few years that new insiders have begun to contest it. Institutional journalism refers to a journalist's professional habits where the main role is that of a 'clerk' documenting EU activities and giving a daily account of current events and issues. This type of coverage is more concerned with 'policies' than 'politics' and is best represented by newspapers such as *Le Monde*. This approach has long been found among French journalists – the turnover policy of British newspapers prevents such a phenomenon occurring – and indeed has long been the dominant definition of the EU correspondent's job. Representatives of this approach have become prominent personalities in both the press corps and the wider EU microcosm. In short, they have become 'institutions' in their own right, as well as part of the institutions they cover.

> I realised in fact that these people who were here for thirty to forty years, who have been here since the beginning, were European campaigners. That is, they believed in the European idea. They have made Europe as much as the Eurocrats themselves. They have popularised the European idea, they have covered it from the beginning. It's their baby. These people aren't journalists in the original sense of the word. That is, they don't see things in a competitive way . . . They are used to seeing things as a family where everybody takes part in the construction of an ideal.
>
> (Interview with a French broadsheet journalist)

Their technocratic coverage of EU news excises the very political nature of events, the power struggles and the clash of interests. Conflicts between the various actors (top civil servants, politicians and lobbyists) never feature, even though, as Hooghe's study of the Commission's top officials clearly shows, political and ideological differences exist inside this institution (Hooghe 1999). Indeed, the only struggles represented are those which oppose member states as in any traditional form of intergovernmental bargaining. This form of European coverage dates back to the period when these journalists first arrived in Brussels (the late 1960s), when Europe's main concern was the Common Agricultural Policy which was of interest to only very few social groups – notably farmers who had gained expertise through their professional involvement. The journalists' self-identification with the European political project provides a further explanation of their reluctance to highlight the EU's controversial aspects.

As far as their sociological profile is concerned, these journalists are also often the veterans of the press corps and are seen as leading experts on European matters: the many years spent covering these institutions and the priceless contacts they obtained while they were junior journalists rubbing shoulders with future top officials have transformed them into the 'best address books in Brussels'. From the group's internal viewpoint, these veterans command respect because of their in-depth knowledge of European affairs and their analytic skills. However, they have also gained influence by helping young, newly arrived journalists, providing them with contacts and introducing them to 'the right people'. While none of them is a 'media star', they have benefited from symbolic rewards in the small world of Brussels: they are influential and looked upon as experts among journalists; they are prominent personalities in the microcosm and talk to officials and Commissioners on equal terms. Present in Brussels since the 1960s or 1970s, they started out as 'believers' who identified themselves with the European institutions and their political project. Thus, one of them can say that he 'considers himself as a fake Eurocrat without the salary' because the discourse and the aims of the Commission have become his own. This assimilation with the aims of the European institutions has been criticised by a new generation of journalists.

> The problem is that, very often these people, the journalists, 'think the right way' because their desire is to be integrated into the machine instead of scrutinising it, criticising it, analysing it, dissecting it. Their dream is to be accepted by those people.
>
> (Interview with a French broadsheet journalist)

This accusation of collusion is fairly routine in the journalistic milieu and, as far as Brussels is concerned, is used by other journalists to describe the kind of ties that exist between the institutional journalists, on the one hand, and politicians and Commission officials, on the other. Given that they arrived very young (it was often their first assignment as a journalist), they met people of the same age who were at that time Commission trainees and who later moved up the hierarchy to become members of *cabinets* or even Commissioners. Yet these kinds of acquaintances imply comradeship and friendship with people whom they are supposed to be able to criticise. Undoubtedly, this relational capital that they have cultivated makes their work easier and is reinforced and legitimised by their 'faith' in the European political ideal. In the past, as long as the press corps was small enough for everybody to know each other, the daily exchanges/communication between journalists and civil servants (especially spokespersons) was very friendly. As one journalist puts it, the daily briefing used to look more like a 'pleasant discussion' than a professional press conference. Nowadays, as the institutional journalists bitterly point out, the will of the spokespersons 'to get a message across' is obvious and they seem to regret the 'good old days' when information was given confidentially between friends who shared the same convictions about Europe.

Rather than insisting on what is in fact a relatively 'natural' collaboration between journalists and their sources, more benefit can be derived from an analysis of this phenomenon in terms of the shared assumptions and beliefs which exist between these two sets of actors (on the phenomenon of shared assumptions, see Padioleau 1976). Since these journalists have both a social and intellectual identification with their sources' world, they develop a 'reaction of protection of the institution', a kind of self-censorship which they justify by their belief that the Commission is acting for the public good, even if there are occasional lapses of behaviour.

Yet, as one German journalist explained, things have changed in Brussels and the Breydel's cosy press centre now welcomes journalists who tend to practise a new kind of journalism:

> Until the early nineties investigative journalism was an unknown species in Brussels. Most of the press corps, myself included, saw ourselves as fighting on the same side as the Commission to build up our common Europe. . . . Only a couple of years ago some journalists, given time and money by their editors, started to dig deeper and to look behind the daily press conferences, declarations and so-called 'background' briefings. Far away from mainstream reporting another truth saw the daylight.
>
> (Nathie 1998)

Investigative reporting and the politicisation of the EU

A second approach to EU coverage recognises that Europe is not just limited to the Common Agricultural Policy, but that it has became a political and institutional system in its own right.

> My contribution to the French press (I think) is to have shown that Europe, the coverage of Europe, isn't 'techno', isn't obviously techno-

cratic. And that you can make investigations, you can make revelations, you can make scoops . . . you can make the news and that's something that wasn't true five years ago. . . . One used to have the impression that only the Common Agricultural Policy existed (which is definitely boring and the less I write about it the better). . . . Now everybody knows things are not boring.

(Interview with a French broadsheet journalist)

This 'new species' of journalist is made up of those who define themselves as 'investigative reporters', since they were able to uncover scandals concerning Edith Cresson and other Commissioners as well as expose the BSE crisis. Unlike most of their peers they do not consider that EU coverage is limited to experts and they refuse to hide behind a specialisation which they see as synonymous with a technical, expert-like and biased coverage. As one academic commentator notes, 'the position of critic of specialisation is a way for those who adopt it . . . to disqualify their colleagues since the worst reproach that can be directed at a journalist is to consider him as a "militant" or a spokesperson, that is someone who goes against journalistic "objectivity" and "honesty"' (Marchetti 2000). As they strike a new journalistic pose in Brussels, investigative reporters accuse their predecessors of being actively involved in the issues that they cover. In contrast, their new approach highlights their self-definition of a journalist's status: their 'objectivity' is demonstrated by their will to reveal scandals and dig out scoops. They have also decided to treat the EU as they would any other political system by giving an account of the internal conflicts and struggles that exist.

These journalists differ from the institutional journalists in respect of their 'late' arrival in Brussels – usually in the period following the signing of the Maastricht Treaty in 1992. Compared with their British colleagues they seem quite established in the job, yet at the same time they represent a new generation. They did not come to Brussels on the strength of their own conviction or faith in the EU's political project but they saw fit to make the most of their socialisation processes within the EU microcosm. Once their training period was over, their intimate knowledge of the functioning of Europe's political system enabled them to go beyond the traditional account of decisions taken in Brussels. Indeed, after a few years in Brussels, they have developed their own informers' network, with whom they enjoy a trustworthy relationship, and are likely to understand what is at stake in every conflict that fuels their investigative and political news stories.

I would say that after four years, I began to be efficient. That is, I began to understand all the internal mechanisms and power struggles. I began to know enough civil servants and then you can dig out scandals . . . [You need] to be completely integrated into the mechanics, to know people who trust in you, who know you'll never break an 'off', that the documents they give you are in a safe and that nobody will lay their hands on them. I mean you need networks to understand what is going on.

>   (Interview with a French broadsheet journalist)

The professional methods of the 'investigative reporters' also differ from those of the institutional journalists. While the latter have developed useful contacts inside the institutions and have reliable sources which they protect, the former do not have the kind of 'reaction of protection towards the institution' that is characteristic of the institutional journalists and they do not hesitate to reveal even their most compromising information. Moreover, in a journalistic circle which has long been characterised by friendly and intimate contacts, they have professionalised their relationships with sources by refusing to dine with officials and develop friendships.

> We aren't friends with these people. We are from different social backgrounds. We'll never belong to their social world: we'll never earn as much money as they do, we'll never be civil servants. So, we should never forget what we are: small.
>
>   (Interview with a French broadsheet journalist)

After arriving in Brussels, which is not in itself a very symbolically rewarding posting, these journalists wanted to redefine the traditional EU correspondent's job in a way that conformed more to their professional expectations. They wanted to show that Brussels was capable of allowing the most legitimate and prestigious form of journalism to prosper, rather than just supporting an institutional approach that essentially offered local symbolic rewards to journalists. As Marchetti emphasises, by refusing to class their older colleagues as 'journalists' the new generation are defending 'a more professional and more autonomous conception of the job, that is, most of the time, a more subversive and moral one' (Marchetti 2000).

> You give the posting the complexion you want. In the past nobody would have imagined that it was possible to undertake investigative reporting.
>
>   (Interview with a French broadsheet journalist)

In order to do so, these journalists have developed routines which are closer to a professional definition of good practice: investigative reporting and political journalism. Although they remain 'Europhiles', they are not seeking prominent local positions in the microcosm, nor do they share the same set of beliefs and assumptions as the institutional sources. Hence, they tend to be more critical towards the functioning of the EU. This intermediary position ('Europhile' yet critical) makes them a privileged beneficiary of any eventual leaks. Since they have gained the reputation of being 'investigative journalists', those who want certain documents and facts to become public go directly to them.

They also tend to analyse EU events in a political way, explaining and describing the internal struggles and conflicts that take place inside the institution. They consider the EU as neither a technical nor an apolitical issue, nor do they regard it as an inclusive fraternity. To them it is a 'continual struggle' which involves member states, officials, Commissioners and institutions, and they want to give an account of this political reality. They therefore develop a style of political journalism in which they portray Euro-politicians and write accounts of daily political life so as to explain what goes on behind the official discourse. One of the best examples of this approach was a regular column called 'Coulisses' [Backstage] published in the French national daily *Libération*.

The introduction of these professional methods into the daily coverage of the EU enables them to turn the Brussels post into a more prestigious and potentially interesting job for other journalists. Even if this new form of coverage is still not widely spread in the French press – it is mainly to be found in *Libération* and the weekly news magazine *Le Nouvel Observateur* – competition between national broadsheets and the retirement of most of the institutional journalists may lead to an increase in the value of EU news.

What is actually taking place here is a symbolic struggle, particularly fierce in the French case, concerning the most legitimate journalistic approach to take in Brussels. The scandals involving nepotism and the resignation of the Santer Commission brought this opposition fully out into the open and helped to harden each group's position. Members of each group traded accusations: institutional journalists were alleged to have connived with EU officials, while investigative reporters were accused of being superficial and of having been manipulated. In fact, this symbolic struggle in Brussels between two conceptions of the journalist's function is a reproduction of what is taking place within the profession in France: the institutional journalists now represent an anomaly in a field dominated since the 1980s by a definition of journalism that tends to privilege exclusives and spectacular news (Champagne 2000).

Finally, one should note that some British newspapers have also developed a form of investigative journalism in Brussels. The case of the *Daily Telegraph* is rather revealing in this respect. Since the start of 2000, Ambrose Evans-Pritchard has been the newspaper's EU correspondent, having previously served as a correspondent in Washington where he became famous as an investigative journalist by uncovering scandals about the Clinton presidency. Before he arrived in Brussels his future colleagues had already nicknamed him 'the Prodi killer'. In fact, a few months before his arrival, he was in Italy to investigate Prodi's political career and the potential scandals he had been involved in. It is clear that the Eurosceptic position of the *Daily Telegraph* played a big part in the decision to send a journalist with such a profile to Brussels.

The 'nationalisation' of EU news

The 'nationalisation' of EU news is one of the main differences between the British and French press.[6] First, political journalists based at Westminster may find themselves regularly involved in coverage of EU news, something which hardly ever occurs in the French press. Second, the coverage produced by these journalists, either on their own or with the regular EU correspondent, is intimately linked to the national political debate. In this respect it differs from a journalistic definition of the post where EU politics are covered on their own terms, with specific actors, conflicts and power struggles. In contrast, such a 'nationalisation' of EU news occurs in the French press only on very specific occasions.[7]

This cross-national difference in approach is connected to the kind of political issue that 'Europe' represents in the two member states. Since the Maastricht referendum in 1992, the EU is no longer a watershed issue in French politics. In fact, among mainstream parties there exists a widely shared consensus on Europe and arguments about fundamentals between leading politicians hardly ever occur. In Britain, however, EU issues are deeply embedded in national political debate and some of the fiercest struggles between (and within) mainstream political parties concern European issues (Wilkes and Wring 1998; Anderson and Weymouth 1999). The only British journalist to have retained a post in Brussels for fifteen years explains how his relationship with his editorial offices has evolved over time:

> It was quite an easy job because as an EU correspondent I was quite important. But there wasn't much to do because the news desk did not want much. When Mrs Thatcher arrived asking 'what is going on in Brussels? We are losing sovereignty' etc.' then it began . . . then it became domestic politics . . . Little by little I've been in continuous contact with my political editor in Westminster. At the beginning there was nothing, it was pointless: nothing to discuss. But since Thatcher, there is always something happening at Westminster which is linked to what is going on in Brussels and the other way round . . . .
>
> (Interview with a British press agency journalist)

After Mrs Thatcher's premiership turned the EU into a domestic political issue, it became not only part of political debate but also of the political positioning of the national press. One of the main differences between the British and French press is the partisan politicisation of newspapers. While British newspapers adopt a clear political line, their French counterparts, using a 'rhetoric of objectivity', refuse to act in a partisan fashion (Marchetti 1997). While French newspapers may have political leanings, no editorial stance is adopted which favours one political party or another. Thus, in the French case the elite political consensus among mainstream parties on

Europe continues to be reinforced by newspapers which, broadly speaking, are all Europhile.

In stark contrast, the British press is not just divided over Europe, but the majority of national newspapers have adopted a Eurosceptic approach (Tunstall 1996: 240–55). The politicisation of EU news is therefore carried out through the prism of domestic politics. As newspapers reflect and reproduce the clear division that exists among political elites, EU news is introduced into debate within a particular national framework. While French coverage is characterised by two rival conceptions of the EU correspondent's job (broadly speaking, institutional versus critical journalist), British coverage of the EU can be depicted as being dominated by a particular newspaper's editorial policy, with the correspondents supposed to cover Europe according to the newspaper's position on the issue of 'Britain and Europe'. For example, in the British case, the role of the sub-editors is to rewrite the pieces produced by correspondents, taking into account the newspaper's stance on the EU. This role is much less important in the French case.

This 'nationalisation' of EU news has affected the way in which the group of British journalists organises itself in Brussels. While the French press corps has two poles of attraction based on the two forms of journalism we have outlined, British correspondents have only one – Geoffrey Meade, the Press Association's correspondent in Brussels. When asked to name the most influential person or newspaper in the British camp, journalists spontaneously and unanimously cited this representative of the national news agency. He is the journalist who determines the 'newsworthiness' of any event. As one of his colleagues remarked, 'when he decides it's a story, it's a story', and Meade himself ironically explained that British journalists consider him as an 'oracle' and that his views and advice are listened to with great respect. His influence is related to three factors. First, it is linked to his seniority: he is the person who has the greatest in-depth knowledge of the European institutional system. Second, each journalist has to bear in mind that Meade's press releases 'are on [their] chief editor's desk'. The final component of his influence – and the most revealing one – is the fact that the media he deals with cover only British current affairs. Given that his entire coverage of EU news is UK-centred, it corresponds perfectly to what the London editorial offices expect.

The 'national filter' which this particular journalist represents is symbolic of the way in which British newspapers deal with EU news. The form this politicisation of news takes is a result of interpretations made on the basis of domestic political frameworks: is a decision of the Commission likely to embarrass the British government or not? Paradoxically, however, though it has the strongest 'Eurosceptic' press, British journalists did not anticipate the political crisis that led to the resignation of the Santer Commission. Since Euroscepticism fuels most of the articles that are written on the EU, corruption and wastage are taken for granted and 'Euro-scandals' are commonplace in British newspaper coverage of Europe. In addition, since British newspapers and journalists have always considered EU news from a domestic perspective, they were unable to detect the existence of a real and specific political crisis. As a result, they did not pay much attention to the changing balance of power between the European Parliament and the politically weak Commission. Moreover, as no British Commissioner was involved and the main informer was 'an unknown Dutchman' (Paul Van Buytenen), the national editorial offices were not interested in articles which might have given an account of events. The belatedness of British journalists to react in this instance is evidence of the kind of politicisation that takes place in their newspapers: a politicisation that fails to take into account the specific political dimension of an institutional system which cannot be compared or reduced to that which exists in individual member states.

***Box 5.2* Three attitudes towards the politicisation of EU coverage**

Institutional journalism

- Older, in Brussels for more than fifteen years
- Self-assimilation to the institution
- Intellectual and political project
- Protection of the institution

Investigative journalism

- Younger
- Distance and reliable sources
- Professional project
- Scandalisation

Politicisation through national politics

- Four or five years in Brussels
- Professionalisation of the source–journalist relationship
- Editorial project (for example, 'Prodi killers')
- Scandalisation through national politics

Conclusion

This chapter has given an overview of the way the EU press corps organises itself, the role it plays in the socialisation of journalists and of the kinds of journalism that can be found in Brussels. Since we have focused on the politicisation of news, many other aspects have not been taken into account. However, by concentrating on the internal organisation of the selected national groups it has been possible to describe the processes of inter-definition and of self-legitimisation that presently take place in the press corps. The comparison we have made also enables us to counterbalance what might be mere national particularities and so to enrich the analysis of each group with factors that relate back to political, professional and cultural differences.

Notes

1 For a critical approach to theories of the democratic deficit, see Smith 1999.
2 This situation is probably changing as investigative reporting develops. However, for most journalists who do not practise this kind of journalism, competition still does not exist.
3 The most striking example of this organisation of the Brussels press corps along national lines is provided by the seats the journalists occupy in the press room. For instance, French and British journalists always sit in the same part of the room alongside their national colleagues. There are very few exceptions to this unwritten rule.
4 One purely economic explanation for the turnover policy among British correspondents is that after five years their companies are obliged to make national insurance and social security payments at the Belgian rather than UK rates.
5 One could ask to what extent the *Financial Times*, especially in its European edition, qualifies as a *British* newspaper.
6 Interview material.
7 This is not to argue that French media coverage never adopts a 'national' approach to EU news. In the French case such 'nationalisation' of coverage may take place under two sets of circumstances. The first concerns a crisis issue which has direct consequences for domestic politics. A good example of this was the BSE crisis in which the French government opposed the Commission and other member states regarding health and safety issues in general and the continuation of the ban on British beef in particular. The second – and more common occasion – concerns coverage of EU summit meetings when the President and Prime Minister of France are presented as defending national interests. At these events, journalists from the national desks and from media that do not have any permanent EU correspondents (which is true of most broadcasting companies) arrive to cover the event and, according to their colleagues based in Brussels, do so from a national perspective, for example only attending press conferences involving French representatives and being much more concerned with power struggles among French officials (especially within the context of executive 'cohabitation') than with the European bargaining taking place.

References

Anderson, P. J. and Weymouth, A. (1999) *Insulting the Public? The British Press and the European Union*, London: Longman.
Champagne, P. (2000) 'Le médiateur entre deux *Monde*', *Actes de la recherche en sciences sociales* 131/132: 8–29.
Guérivière, J. de la (1992) *Voyage à l'intérieur de l'eurocratie*, Paris: Le Monde Editions.
Hooghe, L. (1999) 'Images of Europe: orientations to European integration among senior officials of the Commission', *British Journal of Political Science* 29/2: 345–68.
Marchetti, D. (1997) 'Contribution à une sociologie des transformations du champ journalistique dans les années 80 et 90', unpublished PhD thesis, École des Hautes Études en Sciences Sociales, Paris.

Marchetti, D. (2000) 'Les révélations du "journalisme d'investigation"', *Actes de la Recherche en Sciences Sociales* 131/132: 30–40.

Meyer, C. (1999) 'Political legitimacy and the invisibility of politics: exploring the European Union's communication deficit', *Journal of Common Market Studies* 37/4: 617–39.

Morgan, D. (1995) 'British media and European Union news. The Brussels news beat and its problems, *European Journal of Communication*, 10/3: 321–43.

Nathie, H. (1998) 'Brussels needs its muck-rakers', *La lettre de l'API*, no. 2.

Padioleau, J. (1976) 'Systèmes d'interaction et rhétoriques journalistiques', *Sociologie du travail* 3: 256–82.

Schickel, C. (1995) 'Les journalistes accrédités auprès de l'Union européenne', unpublished thesis, Institut d'Études Politiques, Strasbourg.

Shore, C. (2000) *Building Europe. The Cultural Politics of European Integration*, London: Routledge.

Smith, A. (1999) 'L' "espace public européen": une vue trop aérienne', *Critique internationale* 2/(hiver): 169–80.

Tunstall, J. (1970) *The Westminster Lobby Correspondents: A Sociological Study of National Political Journalism*, London: Routledge and Kegan Paul.

Tunstall, J. (1996) *Newspaper Power*, Oxford: Clarendon Press.

Wilkes, G. and Wring, D. (1998) 'The British press and European integration 1948–1996', in D. Baker and D. Seawright (eds), *Britain For and Against Europe: British Politics and the Question of European Integration*, Oxford: Clarendon Press.

Part II

Towards a cynical coverage of politics?

7 Media escalation and political anti-climax in Australia's 'Cash for Comment' scandal

Rodney Tiffen

Occasionally scandals transfix public attention. They generate saturation news coverage, with every day seeming to bring dramatic new accusations and surprising revelations. Sometimes they achieve such intensity that the sense of crisis dominates the political agenda and the pressures for a resolution are enormous. Some scandals have a devastating impact on the individuals involved, and lead to electoral defeat or far-reaching policy changes. On other occasions, however, dramatic allegations seem to pass without substantial follow-up. Or after a brief controversy, where partisan opponents exchange accusations and denials, seemingly serious transgressions disappear, without authoritative resolution.

This chapter seeks to specify the factors which make some scandals escalate dramatically, and to examine the characteristics which enhance the likelihood that a scandal will achieve this intensity. It does so by exploring a recent scandal in Australia, which generated saturation media coverage, led to an effective and penetrating official inquiry and achieved a clear resolution of the salient transgressions, but which then left the offenders largely unscathed.

The most common focus in the study of scandals is on what we might call the initial stage, how the scandal becomes public. This is a natural and interesting focus. Corruption and other scandalous behaviour by their nature typically involve concealment. As Walter Lippmann wrote sixty years ago, 'it would be impossible for an historian to write a history of political corruption in America. What he could write is the history of the exposure of corruption' (Sturgess 1990: 3).

Whether the secrecy surrounding corruption can be penetrated is logically the first question in the study of the public life-cycle of scandals, especially so if the first public disclosure has been achieved through investigative reporting or the actions of whistleblowers inside government or major corporations. Sometimes this is taken as the most important test of the media's ability to act as an independent force for disclosure, and indeed in some major scandals determined investigative reporting has been pivotal in achieving such exposure. In fact, this is a less common way for scandals to begin than other avenues of disclosure. Often some public event, perhaps a disaster – financial or physical – dramatises previously hidden wrong-doing. Sometimes through the actions of regulatory agencies or political opposition the alleged transgression surfaces first in a public forum.

However, to allow the analysis to stop at this point leaves many of the most important aspects of the development of scandals unexplored. Scandals are not simply a matter of a single moment of exposé, of heroic investigations single-handedly puncturing the shield of secrecy and achieving an instantaneous and inevitably cleansing impact. Sometimes this is so. However, frequently allegations pass, their claims unresolved, their political consequences negligible. As Harold Evans said, 'There are occasions when it is no use publishing the truth once' (Evans 1983: 62).

Initial disclosure leads to further news attention in a variety of outlets only if other organisations can easily follow up, if there is a ready supply of newsworthy developments. No matter how heroic it may be, investigative reporting, even in those cases where it was pivotal, forms only a small part of any prolonged or intense reporting of a scandal.

The early stages of scandals are often marked by enormous uncertainty. If the initial reporting of corruption does not stem from a privileged forum, such as courts or parliament, it is a fraught and problematic process. Even scandals which later developed into major episodes sometimes threatened to peter out, when it seemed, for example, that other media were going to ignore the initial revelations.

In what we might call the second stage in their public development, scandals become subjects of routine news coverage. There are two major avenues by which this occurs. The first and most prolific is if the alleged transgression becomes an issue of political controversy, where a major party seeks to score points against another by prosecuting aspects of the scandal. In this case, the reporting of the issue is determined to a considerable degree by the publicity interests and strategies of the key players. The other major route is the launching of judicial proceedings. This provides a steady, although circumscribed, stream of news stories through covering the daily proceedings, although because of contempt of court provisions, it also reduces the media to a passive role until the verdict is given. In both these ways, stories about a scandal can become staples of the news agenda.

However, the most momentous scandals escalate beyond predictable lines of reporting. Fully blown scandals inspire saturation coverage. This dominance of the news agenda in turn generates enormous political momentum. Developing scandals set in train an open-ended, unpredictable process that envelops issues and provokes responses which could not be foreseen at the outset, a political roller-coaster whose direction and speed are beyond the control of any individual.

The development of scandals is an unruly process. While it remains all but impossible to predict how scandals will develop, in retrospect the combination of three broad factors has often characterised those which came to dominate the media agenda (Tiffen 1999).

The first is a central forum facilitating disclosure. An indispensable source for intense coverage by a range of competing media is a public forum, normally either parliament or a judicial or quasi-judicial setting, such as a Royal Commission, which provides prolific revelations which all media can cover easily. In the absence of such a forum, which can compel information, or where new questions and accusations can be raised, it is much easier for the accused to resort to stonewalling and hope that with their silence news interest will dissipate and the public spotlight move elsewhere.

The second is a constellation of conflicts escalating the scandal. The single most important factor is an opponent determined to pursue and exploit the scandal. This comes most commonly from a political opposition seeking partisan gain, a central reason why, for example, the tone of political scandals is distinct from those in the business world. However, the factor which often elevates a scandal from normal partisan controversy into an acute and unmanageable crisis is when the defending side is split amongst itself. Three-sided and many-sided conflicts are much more difficult to manage politically.

The third involves scandals which resonate with diverse elements of newsworthiness, where issues of high principle are fortuitously spiced with personal drama and human interest. Often this involves revelations of backstage behaviour, normally shielded from public view, which puncture the persona of those under scrutiny. In addition, the news media are particularly receptive to scandals which appear to be 'moving forward', which promise some impending resolution, and the anticipation of this climax induces a media 'feeding frenzy'.

It is not necessarily the most serious transgressions which produce the most intense attention or provoke the most severe consequences. The study of scandals is the study of social reactions, and the forces of reaction have their own logic only loosely related to the gravity of the alleged offences, as Pujas demonstrates in her study of the response to contaminated blood supplies in France and Spain, where the reaction was stronger in the former country, although the extent of the contamination was greater in the latter (see Chapter 8 by Pujas).

The response to the proliferation of scandals in Western democracies in recent decades has taken two main forms in media scholarship. The first is to concentrate on the necessity for investigative reporting, and the ability of the media to uncover serious wrong-doing as the most important test of its performance (for example, Protess *et al.* 1991; Schultz 1998). A very different tradition has emphasised the media's appetite for scandal. Especially in post-Watergate America, this has led to several works emphasising the deleterious role that scandals play in public life, laying the central blame for this at the door of the media (for instance, Sabato 1991; Garment 1993; Sabato *et al.* 2000).

While there have been excellent individual works in both these genres, both are partial in their perspective. The latter in particular tends to explain media coverage merely in terms of editorial or journalistic wilfulness and to see the media acting in a vacuum. Instead the processes outlined above seek to trace the interactions between the media and the political environment to which they are reacting.

The processes fanning the escalation in media coverage were well encapsulated by a scandal which erupted in Australia in 1999. There was much for connoisseurs to savour in the 'Cash for Comment' scandal, especially because it raised large issues of principle and gross hypocrisy, but without anyone suffering too much. The subject matter is doubly interesting because it concerned a scandal within the media themselves. Apart from its intrinsic fascinations, the case invites analysis because it is an unusual mixture – the scandal escalated enormously and there was an authoritative resolution of the major issues, yet the perpetrators escaped with minimal sanctions following.

'Cash for Comment': the ingredients

The 'Cash for Comment' scandal focused upon two very prominent presenters on commercial radio – John Laws and Alan Jones – and the secret payments by various sponsors to them. These payments aligned with seemingly spontaneous and sincere comments in praise of viewpoints favoured by their secret patrons, not only about their products but in public controversies involving them. It was essentially an exercise in black propaganda. The statements were not signalled in any way to the audience as being paid advertisements.

As we shall explore below, the scandal was fuelled by several sources of supply – a lively public controversy, several revealing searches by journalists pursuing the new agenda, and finally and most importantly, a penetrating official inquiry. However, to understand the scandal's impact, it is necessary to begin with the demand side, with why the scandal was so newsworthy and had such public resonance.

When a scandal involves already well-known figures, and perhaps especially if they have a quasi-celebrity status, like movie stars, sporting heroes or media figures, this can greatly enhance its newsworthiness. If the scandal runs against their established persona, and this persona is itself contentious, it makes it juicier still. The misdeeds of the firebrand American tele-evangelist Jim Bakker and his wife Tammy in the 'Pearly-Gate' scandal gained so much greater currency because of the well-known public pretensions and images already established. A generation earlier, the quiz show scandals – in recent years the topic of a feature film – had similarly attracted wide attention because the public was already familiar with the programmes and personalities. The scandals led to the demise of quiz shows and the elevation of other programming especially Westerns (Barnouw 1975).

Laws and Jones were famous figures in Sydney, and to an extent in Australia nationally (see Box 6.1). Laws was the highest paid person in Australian radio, with an annual income estimated at Aus$11.6 million a

***Box 6.1* The players**

The radio station and its employees

- 2UE, a high-rating, successful commercial radio station in Sydney, specialising in 'talk radio'
- Alan Jones, 2UE breakfast announcer
- John Laws, 2UE and nationally syndicated morning announcer
- John Conde, 2UE chairman and chief executive
- Mike Carlton, 2UE afternoon announcer

The regulators

- The Australian Broadcasting Authority (ABA), the official regulator of Australia's commercial media. Following the passing of the Broadcasting Services Act (BSA), it replaced the previous regulator, the Australian Broadcasting Tribunal. The BSA marked an important change in Australian broadcasting policy, with much more emphasis on co-regulation and industry codes.
- David Flint, Liberal Government appointed chair of the ABA. A staunch monarchist, Flint was replaced as chair of the inquiry by Michael Gordon-Smith
- Julian Burnside, leading barrister and counsel assisting the inquiry

The sponsors

- Qantas, Australia's national airline
- Optus, Australia's second telephone carrier, operating since partial deregulation in the early 1990s.
- Australian Bankers' Association, the industry association representing Australia's major banks
- NRMA, the New South Wales Motoring Association and a major insurance company

The news media

- ABC, the Australian Broadcasting Corporation. Its programme *Media Watch* disclosed the scandal, and its presenter Richard Ackland won Australia's top journalism award for doing so
- *Sydney Morning Herald*, a quality newspaper based in Sydney. Its major journalists covering the inquiry were Anne Davies, Bernard Lagan, David Marr and David Leser. Its editor in chief was Greg Hywood
- *The Australian*, Australia's national quality daily, owned by Rupert Murdoch. Its major journalists covering the inquiry were Amanda Meade, Mark Day and Errol Simper
- *Australian Financial Review*, Australia's major business daily
- *Daily Telegraph*, Sydney's tabloid morning newspaper, also owned by Murdoch

year. His morning programme was syndicated to seventy-seven radio stations across the country, with a total audience estimated to be as high as two million (*Sydney Morning Herald*, 16 October 1999). Not only had he been a prominent and high rating personality for some decades – forty-four years as a broadcaster, the inquiry was told – he was also paid handsomely for his advertising prowess, starring in both radio and television ads. In his radio programme, advertisements and personal endorsements often merged into each other.

Jones was equally famous. The Sydney radio market contains thirteen stations, with the highest audience listening at breakfast time. Jones for several years has won this most important time slot. On average he commands around 17 per cent of the audience, running just ahead of two FM stations which combine rock music and comedy. The Jones slot, however, is an all-talk format, with news, interviews and the presenter's commentaries. Far more than most other radio programmes in Australia, and certainly far more than any with a comparable audience, Jones's programme is one of unashamed advocacy. A staunch monarchist, Jones did not have a single republican viewpoint expressed on his programme in the six weeks leading up to the referendum on the issue in November 1999.

Like the shock jocks of American radio, Jones combines very one-sided presentations and a right-wing populism. But unlike them, his audience and his own personal networks are well within the mainstream of Australian conservative politics. Jones is extremely well connected in the Liberal Party, a personal friend and former adviser of Prime Minister John Howard. Liberal Party strategists believe that the Jones factor was worth 2 per cent of the vote to them in New South Wales during the 1998 Federal election. When the Liberals were in government in that state, ministers would talk openly around the Cabinet table of the 'Jones test'. What would Alan think? What had he been saying about a particular issue? One former minister said Jones and John Laws were the twenty-first and twenty-second members of the Cabinet during that time. 'A lot of time was spent considering their views and trying to predict what their reaction to decisions would be' (*Sydney Morning Herald*, 20 November 1999).

Although viewed by the Liberals as a great political asset, Jones's views have sometimes veered much further towards right-wing populism. He supported the corrupt Queensland Premier, Joh Bjelke-Petersen, in his ludicrous and soon aborted 'Joh for PM' campaign. Similarly he was a strong advocate for the controversial populist-cum-racist One Nation Party of Pauline Hanson, which flourished in the years after the 1996 election. During the 1980s he had been an advocate for the South African apartheid regime. This probably derived at least partly from the personal contacts built up from his role as coach of the Australian Rugby Union team. Later he also became a coach in the National Rugby League competition.

Jones has survived controversies that might have sunk someone with a thinner skin. In the mid-1990s, it was revealed that a newspaper column he wrote about oil politics was a passage of fiction taken from a Frederick Forsyth novel. Jones's excuse was that he had been set up – a reader had sent him a letter which he had reproduced. Earlier he had been arrested in a public toilet in London, but all charges were dropped before any court proceedings. He had also been a leading advocate for an investment company, Estate Mortgage Corporation, which went bankrupt in the late 1980s, obliterating the savings of many small investors (*The Australian*, 20 November 1999).

There is a personal feud between the two super-stars, which one suspects 2UE, the top rating commercial 'talk' radio station in Sydney, used to play up to increase interest in their programmes. Although there are some contrasts between them, the similarities are also strong. Laws's pedigree is not as overtly political as Jones's, and has a much more directly commercial profile. He cultivated an image of toughness – for example often speaking admiringly of truckies and the trucking industry. However, in reality he is a very soft interviewer, preferring to save his harshest comments for occasions when he is unchallenged.

Like Jones's, Laws's views are right-wing populist. He is vociferously anti-trade union, unfriendly to aboriginal causes and suspicious of big government and bureaucracy. While for most of his career he has been much closer to the Liberal Party than to Labor, the right-wing of the New South Wales Labor Party put great effort into wooing him during the 1980s. Since then – and perhaps partly as product differentiation from Jones – he has not been as clearly aligned in party terms.

Political strategists fear both Jones and Laws because of the size of their audiences, and because both express their antagonisms in unrestrained blanket condemnations, allowing those they disagree with little chance to express their views. The venomous nature of Jones's style is well captured in his attacks on the then Primary Industry Minister, John Anderson, in late 1997. The local fruit juice industry was lobbying hard against the importation of cheap orange juice concentrate from Brazil. At various times, as the controversy raged, Jones charged that Anderson was lying, mad, not serious, 'a complete fool', 'absolutely off the wavelength', 'an absolute and arrant dope', 'a joke, an absolute joke'. Jones said he must be 'suffering from a serious kick in the head. Some cows must have got on to him'. He lumped Anderson in with 'bureaucratic buffoons' and the victims of 'some sort of stupidity infecting people in Canberra'. He urged Anderson to hand in his 'guernsey'. Jones told his 2UE listeners: 'Our citrus industry couldn't be more efficient. It is only the politicians who are inefficient.'

Even by Jones's unique standards, the personal vitriol was extravagant. Some thought it derived from a personal animus dating from the time when early in his career Jones had been an English teacher at one of Sydney's leading private schools and Anderson one of his students. However, during the ABA inquiry two years later, it also emerged that Jones, unknown to his listeners, was during this dispute over trade protection on a retainer from the Sunraysia Citrus Growers (*Sydney Morning Herald*, 19 November 1999).

It is obvious that the first ingredient in making the scandal so newsworthy was that the principals were such famous personalities, well known for pontificating on a wide range of issues. There was a wide constituency who disliked the influence and the anti-intellectualism and political prejudices of these two 'tall poppies'. But it was not just the personalities involved. It was the nature of the charges, and the forceful way in which they became public, that made the scandal so newsworthy. The revelations came as a huge shock. No one had any sense of just how large or prevalent was the scale of payments in talk radio, and the way in which its influence extended well beyond personal commercial endorsements and into matters of public policy was a stark revelation.

The first phase: public controversy and media inquiries

The scandal began on Monday 12 July on the Australian Broadcasting Corporation TV programme, *Media Watch*, a weekly quarter-hour look at media misdeeds. Presenter Richard Ackland, who later won Australia's top journalism award, a Gold Walkley, for his story, began a very biting and precise presentation by counterposing sound clips of Laws during his earlier bank bashing phase with some much friendlier references afterwards. Then he played the rather clumsy on-air phone call from the head of the Australian Bankers' Association ('Hello Tony, this is a surprise') in which Tony Aveling of the Australian Bankers' Association asked Laws to tell 'the whole story' – the name for what became a regular segment promoting the banks' virtues. Months earlier, Ackland had visited this about-face on banking by Laws. In response, Laws had attributed criticisms to envy by others less successful. He also said that the banks were paying for the series on the whole story ('I'm a saleable commodity'), and claimed the banks had approached him to do the series. The story soon died.

Now, however, Ackland produced a confidential internal document from the Australian Bankers' Association. It began by contradicting Laws's claims about who approached whom. The banks had been approached by an associate, on Laws's behalf, offering them the deal. The document also contradicted Laws's claims that his opinions could not be bought, because as part of the agreement, 'there can be no criticism of banks'. Indeed, a key aim of the banks, according to the document, was to reduce the negative comments from the previous level of four a week to zero and to receive positive comments instead.

As Ackland concluded, 'in the middle of a concerted campaign against the banks by the most widely listened to broadcaster in the country, his agents approach the banks and say he'll drop the criticism, for money'. Then came the *coup de grâce*, the banks had paid 1.2 million dollars for this change of direction (*Media Watch*, 12 July 1999). (It was later asserted that Aus$500,000 would go directly to Laws.)

It was too late for the next morning's newspapers to follow up. Laws initially seemed relaxed about the revelations. He denied approaching the banks, but reiterated that there had been a commercial deal for the segments. The following day, a listener told Laws: 'I'm just dismayed. . . . I don't know where the ad starts and where the ad finishes with your programme.' Laws confidently replied: 'No, well, nobody does. That's why they're so good' (Johnson 2000: 20). A series of celebrities and associates rang Laws's programme in an orchestrated show of support (*Sydney Morning Herald*, 16 July 1999).

Journalists from other news organisations began to pursue the story. In the following days, both the *Sydney Morning Herald* and *The Australian* had page one reports. As with many scandals, the central accusation led to an intense search into the whole area, and there followed a rash of other revelations (including some about leading announcers in other states). Saturday's *Herald* (*Sydney Morning Herald*, 20 July 1999) revealed that Laws had an agreement with Qantas, and also had the first story involving Alan Jones. The country's second telephone carrier, Optus, confirmed that it had a deal, currently worth half a million dollars a year, and dating back to 1994, for Jones to read advertisements on air and to provide editorial comment from notes provided by Optus. The continuing explorations of the deals prompted Laws to say he was going to call in the police to investigate stolen documents (*Sydney Morning Herald*, 20 July 1999), although sadly no arrests followed.

The story was now a self-sustaining controversy. Not only was it a period of active, diligent exploration by several journalists, but the accelerating public developments generated considerable news coverage. Moreover, the story soon acquired a damaging, catchy epithet – cash for comment – which accompanied most future coverage. News also fed on the proposals by various official bodies to investigate further. Up to six possible inquiries by different bodies were canvassed. Eventually only one proceeded – that by the Australian Broadcasting Authority (ABA).

An inchoate but lively public controversy broke out, as commentators, editorialists, interest groups and politicians all joined the fray. Prime Minister John Howard was travelling in America. His staff asked the accompanying journalists to put a question to the Prime Minister, who duly proclaimed that he was 'surprised' and 'disappointed' (*Sydney Morning Herald*, 16 July 1999). Labor politicians also sounded critical themes (*Sydney Morning Herald*, 20 July 1999), although not generally vilifying Laws directly.

The head of 2UE, John Conde, proclaimed the station would investigate, and if 'facts are established which entitle 2UE to terminate contracts and which make it appropriate to do so, then 2UE will act so to make clear its determination to uphold 2UE's policy' (*Australian Financial Review*, 20 July

1999). He did not mention Laws by name, but it was hardly a ringing defence of his star performer (*The Australian*, 24 July 1999).

Once the deal became public, the Bankers and Laws began a race to drop each other (*Sydney Morning Herald*, 17 July 1999). While there were tensions between the leading banks over how to respond (*The Australian*, 20 July 1999), Laws said he would stop the arrangement because of the campaign of smear and innuendo (*Australian Financial Review*, 20 July 1999). That night the Bankers' Association also terminated the deal (*Sydney Morning Herald*, 20 July 1999). Its chairman, Frank Cicutto, seemed to regret mainly that they had been caught – 'I am apologetic for the concern and embarrassment the affair has caused for our employees, industry and customers', he said (*The Australian*, 25 July 1999).

As is common in scandals, the flurry of revelations, accusations and confused defences resulted in a splintering of accusations, and soon included broader reflections on the role of junkets and advertorials in journalism. Fellow 2UE broadcaster Mike Carlton intervened, apparently both trying to deflate the seriousness of the offences ('John Laws advertises things on the wireless and makes a lot of money doing so. Who would have thought it?') and to spread the blame. In particular, he charged that some prominent ABC personalities had a conflict of interest because they had interviewed on air people they had given media training to. (An ABC investigation subsequently reprimanded one presenter, who then chose to resign.) Meanwhile the ABC reported a 2UE memo from station manager John Brennan saying that all announcers were not to make derogatory comments about McDonalds on air because the fast food chain had committed Aus$170,000 of advertising money to the station (Johnson 2000: 59).

Laws was soon on the counter-attack against this 'unbelievable feeding frenzy', against 'the sharks in the water mad for blood' (*Sydney Morning Herald*, 20 July 1999). He charged that the journalists pursuing him were opening a Pandora's box. For example, he alleged that the *Herald's* travel writers wrote favourably about places that looked after them well and that magazines were full of advertorials (*Sydney Morning Herald*, 21 July 1999). In a brave move by editor-in-chief Greg Hywood, the following Saturday's *Herald* (24 July 1999) included a feature which examined all the free gifts, offers of travel, lunches and other special favours that had flowed into the *Herald's* offices and to its journalists in recent weeks. Later he brought down a draft code of ethics (*The Australian*, 4 November 1999).

After some weeks, the news focus moved elsewhere, dominated by the momentous events in East Timor (Tiffen 2001). Occasional revelations still occurred, for example, that Laws had been paid by Rupert Murdoch's Super League, the latter's attempt to start a breakaway rugby league competition to thwart the existing TV deals surrounding the official competition (*Sydney Morning Herald*, 2 October 1999). But the immediate threat to the announcers had abated. Despite the widespread chorus disapproving of their hypocrisy, they remained on air and unrepentant. The initial burst of intense public attention had been exhausted and there was a hiatus until the inquiry's public hearings began in October.

The second phase: the ABA inquiry

On 20 October, the inquiry began in dramatic fashion. The opening statement of counsel assisting the inquiry, Julian Burnside, outlined a series of six-figure deals between the two broadcasters and several of Australia's leading companies, with Laws's personal deals amounting to over Aus$3 million and those of Jones to over Aus$1 million. It revealed many memos and correspondence between the various players, leaving no one in any doubt about the extent and gravity of the deals. In news terms, it was the perfect start for an inquiry. The journalists in the audience were all in a state of shock at the revelations. On television that night one referred to 'these vast, obscene amounts of money'. None of the journalists had had any inkling of the stupendous scale of the pay-offs (Johnson 2000: 88–93). The next morning, the tabloid *Daily Telegraph* devoted its whole front page to the deals under the headline 'Struggle Street' (21 October 1999). Jones had always referred to ordinary Australians as those on 'Struggle Street', whom the big players forgot, while Laws always urged his listeners to 'keep the dream alive'. Commentators during the scandal made great play of such invocations.

In the following weeks, the ABA inquiry was an ideal forum for generating media coverage. Neither the procedural nor reporting constraints that accompany a criminal trial were present. Moreover, there was an array of lawyers representing diverse interests – each of the individual parties at 2UE individually represented, but also several public interest groups and corporations – and often these barristers wanted to move in different directions that undercut each other.

The hearings provided a rich spectacle. The interrogations of the radio stars, the station managers and the sponsors often had huge entertainment value. Although, by the end, the parade of venality and secret deals had become familiar and predictable, many of the revelations en route were surprising and shocking, even for close observers of Australian politics.

Moreover, there was ample evidence that not only did their on-air comments constitute personal endorsements for products, but time and again were in fact paid political advertisements masquerading as commentary on current affairs. One of the most vexed issues in Sydney for the last quarter century has been the need for a second airport. In the early 1990s, the Hawke Federal Government after much internal division decided instead, or at least as an interim measure, to build a third runway. This meant greatly increased noise for residents of many of Sydney's suburbs, resulting in great discontent, drops in real estate values in the most affected areas and a huge political furore. Both major parties promised moves to minimise noise and to proceed with increased urgency to build a second airport. The most likely site was outside Sydney at a place called Badgery's Creek. Jones was a constant and vociferous critic of the proposal: 'It's laughable, absolutely laughable'. 'His abuse rolls on month after month. It's Jones at his most declamatory, most repetitive' (*Sydney Morning Herald*, 8 January 2000). The two major airlines have poured millions into re-developing their facilities at Sydney Airport and are publicly circumspect, but privately determined, opponents of proposals for a second major airport. Jones's comments helped fuel the politics of veto, which made it impossible for any definite other proposal to be implemented. This was not a simple advocacy for the virtues of Qantas as an airline, but an intervention into an extremely difficult policy area, where the airline's corporate interests did not necessarily coincide with other public interests.

Like Jones, Laws often strayed into matters of public policy and debate, including examples of him betraying his listeners in the interests of his sponsors. In late 1998, for example, callers to his programme were complaining about the insurance companies. Following floods in Wollongong, it transpired that most of the victims were going to receive much less compensation from the companies than they had expected. Laws replied by praising NRMA insurance, saying how they had set a 'fine example' to other insurers and had behaved 'very, very well'. Laws was secretly receiving Aus$300,000 a year from the NRMA (*The Australian*, 2 December 1999).

Similarly, the social harm caused by gambling has been an acute public issue in recent years, as governments have expanded various avenues for people to engage in it. Star City Casino, the only licensed casino in Sydney, which opened about two years ago, sponsors Laws for Aus$200,000 a year, plus various perks. During a dispute he wrote to placate them, by telling them how he censored his listeners: 'I believe that I have displayed my loyalty to Star City constantly and perhaps in a way of which you are unaware. We get reasonably frequent calls wanting to be critical of Star City, as we do with faxes and e-mails. I either dismiss them totally or defend Star City.' He also avoided any on-air discussion of the death of a patron in the car park following a scuffle with security guards. The agreement was also said to contain a clause preventing Laws from denigrating gambling (*Sydney Morning Herald*, 20 and 23 October 1999).

The most newsworthy scandals not only involve a serious moral issue at their centre, but are accompanied by fascinating side-shows and by-play which enhance media attention to the issue. Apart from the disclosure of matters of clear public importance, this one generated much voyeuristic fascination with revelations of backstage behaviour. As the scandal developed, established public boundaries around the two broadcasters were penetrated. Tales of greed and quirkiness emerged both in the inquiry's documents and by other (usually anonymous) sources. For example, the inquiry revealed a note from Alan Jones to his manager, Harry M. Miller, following the Walker Corporation's announcement of a greatly increased profit: 'Are we being paid enough!! Let's face it, they wouldn't be in the public place without moi!' (*Sydney Morning Herald*, 18 November 1999).

As in all scandals, the nature of the defences had an important influence on the tone and development of the coverage, and as in many scandals, the alliance among the defenders was soon subjected to severe stresses. As the *Media Watch* journalist Richard Ackland commented, although the actions of the two had been very similar,

> their lines of defence to the ABA have been quite different. Laws adopted the position that he is an old commercial rake, that everyone knows what he's all about and that his listeners can tell in a matter of moments whether he's selling something or giving them the benefit of his views for free. Jones, on the other hand, asked the ABA to accept the proposition that he doesn't editorialise as a consequence of these commercial agreements, that if there is a favourable mention of a client then that is just a coincidence. His 'mindset' is different from his contractual obligations. . . . Jones says that he's never, ever changed his opinion for money.
>
> (*Sydney Morning Herald*, 19 November 1999)

This difference led to contrasting issues in the interrogations of each. Laws took the line essentially that there was no ethical issue, no matter of public interest, beyond normal commercial dealing and salesmanship. He said 'I'm not a journalist and I don't pretend to be a journalist. I'm an entertainer. . . . There isn't a hook for ethics' (*Sydney Morning Herald*, 8 February 2000).

On the other hand, Jones maintained that the payments had not influenced his behaviour at all. He claimed that he was unaware of contractual arrangements which obliged him to make on-air comments. He claimed that it was pure coincidence that he started making comments in favour of the Walsh Bay development the day after he signed a lucrative contract to do so (*Sydney Morning Herald*, 18 November 1999). His self-righteousness was immune to all contrary evidence.

> He might be brutally contradicted by learned counsel and even attract guffaws of incredulity from the public gallery. But Jones has hung his credibility around this persona of reasonable charm . . . The apparent contradictions are numerous. Yet Jones' high moral ground is elevated to the point of dizzying vertigo.
>
> (*The Australian*, 18 November 1999)

Not only did the main defendants take contrasting routes of self-justification, but they had both shared and conflicting interests with their employer, the owners of 2UE. John Conde, the executive chairman of the station, was a well-known business figure, who, for example, had been a principal figure in the St James Centre for business ethics. As the broadcaster licensed under the Act, the company was responsible for their announcers' actions. It was the party which (eventually) might be sanctioned under the Act. On the other hand, it was Jones and Laws who had built 2UE's commercial success. If they were fired and went to another station, 2UE could find its income severely reduced.

On the issue of how much he knew of his star announcers' actions, Conde was in a no-win situation. If he knew, he was implicated. If he didn't know, he was ineffectual, perhaps even stupid. Evidence presented to the inquiry demonstrated that Conde had intervened after a March 1998 *Media Watch* programme had exposed the Laws–NRMA agreement and had made some small moves to ensure the station's propriety on that issue. But largely his attitude was that he did not want to know. There was no attempt to investigate other agreements, or to enforce the policies he had promulgated. He 'chose not to confront the obvious' (*The Australian*, 2 December 1999).

For a time in November, there was a direct conflict between Conde and Laws. The situation was ripe for each to be taking umbrage at the self-justifications of the other. Laws was offended by Conde's comments professing his ignorance and implying his disapproval of some of the star's behaviour. He then leaked to a national weekly news magazine, *The Bulletin* (9 November 1999), that he would extend his testimony, saying how, when Conde had issued a policy statement about endorsement agreements on 28 July 1998 in response to the *Media Watch* accusations, he had come to Laws's office. According to Laws, Conde told him: 'This memo is not necessarily for you. It's for you-know-who' and pointed down the hall to Jones's office. Conde denied this conversation ever took place.

The breaking of their solid front further heightened news interest. At the end of November, after weeks of enormously damaging publicity, 2UE was desperate to repair its image and show its willingness to initiate corrective action. They broadcast a station announcement on Laws's programme, telling listeners that the station would identify Laws's sponsors and the annual fees paid by them. This apparently caught Laws by surprise. As the announcement was broadcast, he immediately attacked it, saying 'Is that right? Really? I see. Well that's really very interesting. You mean you're going to put on the website how much money I'm paid? Are we going to have all the executive salaries on the website too? Are we going to ask barristers? . . . To hell with that.' Later in the day, the station retracted the commitment to disclose fees (*Australian Financial Review*, 4 December 1999).

Following the public schisms, there was much public speculation that 2UE would stand by Jones, but cut Laws adrift (*Sydney Morning Herald*, 13 November 1999). It would have been all but impossible to find any rationale on which to justify differential treatment. In any event, it seems that tempers cooled over the summer break between the end of the hearings and the handing down of the decision. At least at a public level, the relationship seemed to be repaired.

A common occurrence in scandals is the development of secondary themes. Scandals provoke events which otherwise would not have occurred. It is a commonplace in public commentary to say that the damage from scandals was caused more by the cover-up than by the original offence – although this leaves open why a cover-up might have been necessary in the first place. Sometimes the *coup de grâce* for offenders comes not from the original offence, but when they are caught out having engaged in duplicity. A scandal gains new momentum if secondary themes – concerning the appropriateness of the responses – develop. Beyond the common issue of cover-ups and duplicity, one of the most challenging aspects of scandals is that the response to them so often enters relatively uncharted territory, where there are few guidelines or precedents about procedures and penalties. Secondary themes also develop because once the fate of the accused is decided, the focus often changes to an exploration of how the offence could have occurred and the adequacy of policing provisions and penalties.

The 'Cash for Comment' inquiry was by far the biggest public event the Australian Broadcasting Authority had ever staged. The chairman, David Flint, was unfortunate that it coincided with the republican referendum. Flint was prominent in the monarchist case. During the inquiry he appeared on the Laws programme to answer a charge that former Prime Minister Bob Hawke had made about his claims on the republic. Laws treated him to a very soft, very respectful interview. There was an immediate outcry, heightened further by Flint giving an interview to a Perth radio announcer Howard Sattler, who was to be the subject of a future inquiry. After some initial resistance, on 8 November Flint disqualified himself from presiding over the inquiry.

Aside from this brief circus, the much more serious concern was the inadequacy of the Broadcasting Services Act (BSA) and the ABA. From the time the inquiry was called, the ABA had announced that they had no power to punish the individual announcers. The inquiry brought into sharp public focus the changes that were introduced with the BSA in 1992 in the name of greater self-regulation. Earlier what the radio station had allowed to occur could have resulted in the loss of their licence, and there had also been provisions for the punishment of individual broadcasters for breaches of the Act. After 1992 these sanctions disappeared. Rather, the framers of the Act seemed to view it as incredible that any broadcaster would commit an offence of sufficient seriousness that it should deserve immediate punishment. If after specific warnings and conditions were laid down they broke the code again, then they could be punished.

The inadequacy of this 'first offence is free' doctrine could not have been more sharply highlighted than by the parade of misdeeds and hypocrisy that had now been revealed. Similarly, the new agency had a mandate to engage in co-regulation, but in practice this meant that in seven years of existence its record was one of almost complete passivity. Indeed, at one stage, Laws's barrister argued that his client should not be punished because of the Authority's long 'silence and inaction' on the offences (*The Australian*, 27 October 1999).

As a result of this disjunction between the seriousness and size of the offences and the lack of powers residing with the ABA, the closing addresses had a somewhat schizophrenic character. Julian Burnside's closing submission was a scathing indictment of the stars and the station. Alan Jones's evidence strained credibility; Conde's position was one of either guilty knowledge or wilful blindness (*Sydney Morning Herald*, 25 November 1999). Burnside charged that Laws had committed 183 breaches of the radio code and Jones around half that number (*The Australian*, 24 November 1999). But the common theme among his and the other closing submissions was the impotence of the ABA to administer any substantial sanctions. Several public interest groups instead focused on possible amendments to the Act.

Resolution

The inquiry's findings were announced on 7 February. In a 522-page report it found that the two broadcasters had breached the code ninety-five times. It maintained the principle that 'the ordinary reasonable listener should be able to assume in the absence of appropriate disclosure, that the presenter of a current affairs program is disinterested' (*Sydney Morning Herald*, 8 February 2000). It introduced a new disclosure regime, which from the beginning of its new licence period, dating from 1 April, became part of 2UE's licence conditions. Later, this became part of all other radio stations' licence conditions, and in fact the industry body called for this (*Australian Financial Review*, 8 February 2000). 2UE was also ordered to clearly distinguish between advertisements and other programme matter (*The Australian*, 8 February 2000).

After the scandal, although their wider public reputations were severely tarnished, and one suspects that their extra-curricular income was severely reduced, the two broadcasters carried on as before. Alan Jones commented after the inquiry: 'There's not one word in this report which in any way could establish the notion of cash for comment' (*The Australian*, 9 February 2000). Laws, at least for the initial weeks of the new disclosure provisions, tried to turn the sponsorship announcements into on-air entertainment, accompanying his statements with cow bells and raspberries, and saying how proud he was to be associated with the great companies involved.

Their ratings were not substantially reduced. It is possible, for example, that ABC listeners would have taken such offences far more seriously and deserted the announcers *en masse*, but that the habitual audiences of these two either believed in their announcers or did not take the moral issue so seriously. Throughout, despite the abundant evidence that Laws and Jones had treated their listeners with contempt, their on-air protestations mawkishly proclaimed that whatever the ill-intentioned critics said, all that mattered was the loyalty of their listeners.

In late March 2000, pay-TV station Foxtel staged a lavish party in honour of John Laws to celebrate three years of his chat show on their network. Many politicians attended, including former Labor Prime Minister Gough Whitlam and New South Wales Premier Bob Carr. It was hosted by Rugby Union player turned journalist Peter FitzSimons, and speakers included Germaine Greer and John Newcombe. The scandal had become simply an occasion for making jokes about Laws's money-making appetites and abilities. Newcombe paid tribute to the guest of honour: 'They can knock you down on the ground, but every time you stand up, you stand taller' (Johnson 2000: 238–41) – a hero, a victim, certainly not a villain. In late 2000, the issue of banks came up again on Laws's programme. He concluded his observations with the tart 'banks are bastards' (*Media Watch* 30 October 2000).

Conclusion

The 'Cash for Comment' affair prompts several reflections upon the public development of scandals. First, it was breathtaking that such wrong-doing could have been occurring on such a scale without earlier exposure. It showed again that, given the inadequacies of many of Australia's regulatory watchdogs, both in their institutional vigilance and in the strength of the laws they enforce, the media, despite their foibles and erratic nature, still often play an indispensable role in bringing important abuses to public attention.

Media coverage of the scandal developed enormous momentum. On two of our three criteria – a public forum facilitating disclosure and resonating with diverse elements of newsworthiness – it scored very highly. In particular it was one of the juiciest scandals for several years with the hypocrisy of its high profile offenders and the developing drama around them. The third factor – a constellation of conflicts escalating the scandal – was present to some degree with feuds and stress between the defendants, but the scandal lacked the peculiar intensity of persecution which comes with the zero-sum, winner-take-all conflicts of party politics.

In the weakness of its resolution, it showed how different such private sector scandals are from political ones. In the zero-sum, winner-take-all two-sided contest to form government in Australian politics, the game is played with great toughness and cynicism. Anyone who had committed the offences which Jones and Laws had would have been subjected to constant sniping, extravagant rhetorical condemnation and the frequent posing of parliamentary questions as every aspect of every deal was pursued. No political party would have long supported them.

Instead, there was no convention that forced them to resign, no forum like parliament where they could continue to be cross-examined. Moreover, although no politicians publicly approved their behaviour, neither did they vigorously pursue them as they would have done a member of an opposing political party. This was largely because of fear of the damage the broadcasters could still do to them.

The larger implicit stake in the development of scandals is whether or not their resolution confirms the public sense of justice. Instead, this scandal showed how, because of changes made in the early 1990s, the existing regulatory codes did not match the community's sense of morality. Although the scandal had dominated the news agenda, in the end it dissipated because of the weakness of the Act. Despite its high drama for so long, and the abundant and incontrovertible evidence of serious breaches of the public trust, in the absence of a regulatory mechanism to punish the offenders, they were able to continue on air without tangible consequences. The larger issue of secret payments in the persuasion industry disappeared again from the public agenda.

References

Barnouw, E. (1975) *Tube of Plenty*, New York: Oxford University Press.

Evans, H. (1983) *Good Times, Bad Times*, London: Weidenfeld and Nicholson.

Garment, S. (1993) *Scandal. The Culture of Mistrust in American Politics*, New York: Anchor Books.

Johnson, R. (2000) *Cash for Comment. The Seduction of Journo Culture*, Sydney: Pluto Press.

Protess, D., Lomax Cook, F., Doppelt, J.C., Ettema, J.S., Gordon, M.T., Leff, D.R. and Miller, P. (1991) *The Journalism of Outrage: Investigative Reporting and Agenda Building in America*, New York: The Guilford Press.

Sabato, L.J. (1991) *Feeding Frenzy: How Attack Journalism has Transformed American Politics*, New York: Free Press.

Sabato, L.J., Stencel, M. and Lichter, S.R. (2000) *Peep Show: Media and Politics in an Age of Scandal*, Oxford: Rowman and Littlefield.

Schultz, J. (1998) *Reviving the Fourth Estate: Democracy, Accountability and the Media*, Cambridge: Cambridge University Press.

Sturgess, G. (1990) 'Corruption: the evolution of an idea 1788–1988', in S. Prasser *et al.* (eds) *Corruption and Reform: The Fitzgerald Vision*, Brisbane: University of Queensland Press.

Tiffen, R. (1999) *Scandals. Media, Politics and Corruption in Contemporary Australia*, Sydney: University of New South Wales Press.

Tiffen, R. (2001) *Diplomatic Deceits. Government, Media and East Timor*, Sydney: University of New South Wales Press.

8 Explaining the wave of scandal

The exposure of corruption in Italy, France and Spain

Véronique Pujas

Although much has been written about the scale of corruption and the proliferation of scandal in Italy, France and Spain, no work to date has investigated conceptually the reasons for the explosion of public indignation at the time it occurred: why the late 1980s and early 1990s and not before? The aim of this chapter is not to chronicle these scandals or describe the institutional contexts from which they originated, but rather to provide a conceptual analysis of the nature of scandal and the conditions under which it emerges. Scandals are the result of conflicts of legitimacy involving three major elements of the democratic polity: the representation of the electorate, the legality of political behaviour and the mobilisation of public opinion. Understanding the emergence of these conflicts requires an investigation of the tensions or 'strains' occurring within and between the three arenas of democratic polities that embody these key elements: politics, the judiciary and the media.[1] Only by analysing this complex process of interaction can we understand why scandal has emerged on such a wide scale in these countries since the late 1980s and why its implications for the future of these democracies are so important.

This chapter is organised as follows. Section one shows how scandal results from the mobilisation and manipulation of core social values by strategic social actors in a particular context. This section focuses on a case-study of a failed scandal in Spain to demonstrate the central role of the media in determining the success or failure of this mobilisation. Section two considers why and to what extent the media, judiciary and politics are at the cross-roads of contested politics in the public sphere and demonstrates how strong tensions within and between these arenas helps explain the recent wave of scandals in these polities. The chapter concludes with some reflections on the implications of widespread scandal for these democracies.

Understanding the emergence of scandal

It is well known that the same event or development may provoke a scandal in one country but not in another. We also know that in the same country the same set of political practices may provoke a scandal at some point in time but not at another. This strongly suggests that scandal is a socially constructed phenomenon.[2] It emerges against the background of a specific set of norms and values and its public/collective impact involves the mobilisation of particular resources by social entrepreneurs or 'skilled social actors'.

As this section demonstrates, scandal emerges on to the public agenda only when certain preconditions are satisfied. Scandal occurs only if the denunciation of corruption takes place in a sensitive context and is able to mobilise public opinion. Thus, scandal is also the product of a social enterprise, which defines and persuades public opinion that public order is being threatened. This is especially true of situations in which scandal is no longer an isolated event but a widespread phenomenon, undermining – as in southern Europe in recent years – the legitimacy of the existing social and political order. The violation involved in this case is the betrayal of political confidence – confidence, that is, in the political institutions that link electoral mechanisms with the representation of the public interest. The perception that the trust underpinning this relationship has been violated threatens a central pillar of democracy and throws into question the entire system of democratic governance.

This section does not develop the different stages of the 'public careers' of scandals (see Chapter 7 by Tiffen). Briefly, it would appear that four broad, interrelated conditions are required if scandals on the scale of those which have emerged in southern Europe and France in recent years are to occur. These are:

1   a general atmosphere of distrust with regard to politics;
2   tensions between social and political values and eventually the breakdown of some social norms in a new social context;
3   a recognition that a violation of standards has occurred, implying the active definition of events/facts as scandalous (or not) in the public sphere; and
4   a breakdown in the basic bargains which regulate political relationships.

While the first two conditions may be characteristic of many societies, they do not necessarily produce scandal. The third and fourth conditions are the critical ones, since they require the active mobilisation of public opinion by skilled social actors. In effect, a scandal will not emerge until the feeling of betrayal and threat to social order is widespread among the public. Journalist and media coverage are the key factors in this process. This is why the rest of this section focuses on the media's failure to provoke an outcry on the issue of contaminated blood in Spain in comparison to the highly public scandal that erupted in France.

Contrasts between France and Spain over the contaminated blood affair: the central role of the media

One of the best ways to understand scandals, as a denunciation of facts judged unacceptable by public opinion, is to study the role of the media in public mobilisation.[3] Comparing the scandal surrounding contaminated blood in France, where 38 per cent of haemophiliacs transfused with blood were contaminated by AIDS and 1,300 died in 1993, with the failure of the scandal in Spain, where the number of contaminations was higher (47 per cent and 1,563 deaths respectively), is very useful in understanding the conditions essential to the creation of a scandal.[4] Why was the Spanish case different from the French? Why did the denouncers not succeed in creating a popular mobilisation on an issue that was both a national tragedy as well as a personal tragedy for the transfused group? This section does not develop all the features which explain the mobilisation failure in the Spanish case (Pujas 1999). Instead, it focuses on those factors that lead to the creation of a 'virtuous spiral of noise' around a contested issue.[5]

A scandal becomes concrete when it enters the media arena and goes beyond the polemical subjectivity of the actors directly involved in the conflict, thereby becoming visible for everyone. The mobilisation of the media is an essential condition in the creation of a scandal because this gives the actors an opportunity to diversify their resources through access to other arenas. For example, if the media talk about the problem of contamination, political actors are obliged to react and anonymous informants in possession of secret information may communicate this to the media to defend their position. Above all, the simplification of information relative to the issue allows its dissemination to the general public, while at the same time it deprives technocrats of their expert discourse. Finally, the development of the argument by the media leads to a loss of control by those who first leaked the information. The argument here is that success in mobilising public opinion depends on at least some minimum coverage by the most important newspaper. On the contaminated blood issue, the failure of the Spanish newspaper *El País* to act as a mobilising force with regard to public opinion, in contrast to the active voice of *Le Monde* in France, explains to a significant extent the overall lack of mobilisation in Spain and the failure of the issue to become a scandal.[6]

Analysts of the French case have identified the starting date of the scandal as April 1991, simultaneous with the publication of a report in the monthly magazine *L'Evénement du Jeudi*. The value of this report was that it showed that in May 1985 the National Centre of Blood Transfusion (CNTS) knew that its blood stocks were contaminated by AIDS, but nevertheless continued to distribute them. It was only at this time that French haemophiliacs, convinced that their trust had been violated, began to mobilise, and the issue became public due to extensive nationwide media coverage. In the Spanish case, in February and March 1983 two doctors representing a medical trade union sent out two press releases in which they denounced the administrative delays in the enforcement of a legal obligation of the minimum recommended time for heating blood as a means of decontamination. They soon realised that the national media of press and broadcasting were not giving coverage to this information. They decided therefore to adopt an alternative strategy: to mobilise the international press. A second press release was sent to a German newspaper, the *New York Times* and other media. In this way, they tried to force the Spanish media to speak about the tragedy of the massive contamination of Spanish haemophiliacs and more widely of transfused people. However, this tactic was not sufficient to create a scandal.

It seems that the construction of scandals depends on two factors working together: media coverage, crucial in the mobilisation of public opinion, has to be accompanied by a judicial prosecution. In the Spanish case, however, there were no collective legal complaints by haemophiliacs. The issue of AIDS contamination was the object of media coverage only in the case of specific judicial prosecutions by contaminated individuals. The psychological burden (public revelation of AIDS often creates cases of rejection and socio-economic isolation for the individuals concerned) and the financial costs of a prosecution very often discouraged individuals from starting a lawsuit. In addition, people infected with AIDS frequently died before the end of the court proceedings. Two main factors, therefore, explain the failure of public mobilisation in the Spanish case: the concentration of press coverage on the representatives of a medical trade union rather than on the haemophiliacs directly concerned combined with the absence of a collective judicial complaint to legitimise their grievances.

To understand more precisely the reluctance of the Spanish media to cover this issue, it is useful to examine the role of Spain's main official newspaper *El País*. For a variety of reasons, *El País* is regarded by Spaniards as the main legitimate source of information. First, the newspaper takes a serious view of its news function, showing a preference for information which comes from official sources, to the extent that some critics call it the 'BOE' (Boletin Official del Estado – Official State Bulletin). Second, its journalists do not engage in sensationalist coverage or focus on tragic events; rather they are very controlled and reserved in their writing. Third, as in the case of *Le Monde* in France, *El País* is considered to be the dominant media reference nationally. This explains why the newspaper largely ignored and denied the contaminated blood story: the preference for official information tends to exclude non-official sources. For example, the representatives of the medical trade unions were accused of pursuing political goals with their denunciation. Finally, the strong desire to stay out of 'gutter press' and sensationalistic ways of covering the news meant that the editorial line of the newspaper tended to play down the human importance of the tragedy. In the case of the coverage of the first death by AIDS contamination, journalists even denied that AIDS was the reason for the death. In addition, it should be noted that *El País* is well known for its anti-corporatist stance. The 1980s were characterised by strikes in the medical sector. Llovet (1992) has shown that *El País* never supported the demands from medical staff for more funds, status and recognition.

In the West European media landscape the nature and dissemination of information are largely determined by a 'dominant referent', an actor who acts as the reference point for other media, such as *Le Monde* in France and *El País* in Spain. In these circumstances, it is understandable that the low profile coverage of the contaminated blood affair by one of these crucial media sources meant that the issue was ignored. While this was the case in Spain, in contrast *Le Monde* had an active, albeit in some ways contested, position regarding the AIDS contamination issue in France (Champagne and Marchetti 1994; Marchetti 1996). However, in the French case there was an important difference: a prosecution was launched in 1992, legitimising the denunciation.

At this stage, it is important to emphasise two consequences of the coverage's intensity (number of articles and rhythm of diffusion) by a 'dominant referent' in the media: the leakage of secret information which feeds the scandal and the multiplication of witnesses which increases the importance of the scandal. With regard to the first consequence, it is contended here that the repetition of information in all national media (newspapers, radio and television) creates a 'virtuous circle' of noise around the issue. In the Spanish case, however, since the dominant actors did not know of the relevant information, this prevented the legitimisation of the issue and created a 'silent circle' which resulted in its being kept out of the public domain.

To allow us to draw conclusions about the lack of a scandal in Spain in contrast to France, we need to focus on the nature and mechanisms of the 'virtuous circle of noise'. During the initial stages of the issue's coverage in France, the leakage of secret information to the media was important. Obviously, if the media talked about the issue, a lot of people were automatically involved: the staff of the National Centre for Blood Transfusion, the Ministry of Health, all those individuals who had received a blood transfusion and were then affected by AIDS, their relatives and friends, doctors and medical experts, and representatives of the political opposition among others. Very quickly, therefore, many actors were directly concerned and had to take a position. They had to formulate an opinion and acquire expertise on every dimension (technical, political, economic and financial) of the issue. Those who refused to talk were suspected of hiding the truth. In a very short space of time, therefore, a lot of actors became directly involved in a public debate in which the aim was to reconstruct the facts and to find those accountable for the tragedy.

At this stage of social awareness and divergent opinions on the scandalous character of the issue, some people were accused of mistakes and of being responsible for the infection and death of hundreds of people. Secret information arrived on the desks of newsroom staff working for newspapers and magazines. Reports, internal bureaucratic directives, expert opinion on the techniques of blood treatment, all this material evidence provided anonymously aimed to impose a rational interpretation of the facts. These actors also pursued other objectives. They did not want to be seen as responsible or they may even have wished to impute responsibility to opponents or competitors. Hence, individual interest was at the basis of the decision to speak or remain silent. Media outlets solicited anonymously can be regarded as indirect mediators of personal objectives. Journalists and newsroom staff would decide on the basis of their professional and personal interest and with reference to the competition with other media. Finally, the flow and diffusion of a greater quantity of information and witness accounts in the public sphere amplified the debate and led to the recognition of the issue as a scandal as a result of its wide communication within public opinion and the involvement of three main sectors of society: media, judiciary and politics (see next section).

This first section has emphasised the role of the media in the formation of public opinion, in the creation of an orientation as to what people think and how they think about an issue. There can be no scandal without a massive diffusion of denunciation in the public sphere. This is why the media occupy a strategic position of gate-keeper on what becomes a public issue. Moreover, the media increasingly adopt a critical position toward state power, even if the 'dominant media agencies' often neglect non-official sources. Success in the mobilisation of public opinion in the creation of a scandal (or in other areas of public life) is mostly dependent on the attitude of the media. In the case of scandals generally, this success is located at the crossroads of two other fields directly involved: the judiciary and politics. Thus, we need to treat scandals as the product of competition among actors both within and across these fields.

The competitive mobilisation of scandal

This section focuses on the erosion, or in the Italian case collapse, of traditional bargains between politics, the judiciary and the media as an explanation of the wave of scandals which occurred simultaneously in Italy, Spain and France during the 1990s.

The breakdown of key political bargains

Rather than emerging from any one of the above arenas, scandal is always the result of relations of conflict and co-operation between them. In many ways interdependent, these arenas are also engaged in a struggle over relative power, influence and legitimacy in the public sphere. In the three countries studied, the mobilisation of scandal stems from the complex interaction between these arenas, which were simultaneously also going through a phase of internal instability. In complex societies where the contemporary public sphere is undergoing a transformation, such conflicts of power and legitimacy are inevitable. How then have traditional bargains between politics (parties and the state), the judiciary and the media in these countries broken down?

First, with regard to the interaction between politics and the media, this longstanding relationship has been going through a period of change in these countries, but with ambiguous results, given that the tradition of a free and independent press is still far from strong. Politicians and journalists find themselves structurally interdependent. In societies where the media take a central communicative role in structuring the public sphere (Gitlin 1980; Turow 1992), the two arenas are intrinsically linked because they have a common focus: the production of information and interpretation of words/events (Bourdieu 1994). Politicians have always tried to control information given to journalists. This control can take the form of direct censure or an indirect, more insidious, form of disclosing certain information to hide other facts. Political ownership of the press has also brought journalists within the sphere of political consensus, making them bulwarks rather than subverters of the status quo.

This old 'bargain' has broken down in a number of ways. Greater competition in the political sphere has led politicians to exploit the media as a means of denouncing the corrupt behaviour of their political opponents. At the same time, new methods of 'political marketing', which forces politicians to communicate through fixed codes, consequently changes the nature of the message and political competition. Specialists in communication deliver 'sound bites' aimed at all media outlets and also create 'media events' which represent a new way of conducting politics (Sorrentino 1995). These developments have also made transactions between politicians and the media much easier, especially as the liberalisation and privatisation of television have multiplied the opportunities for voicing denunciation and using scandal to delegitimise opponents (Diaz Nosty 1994). Thus, more than ever before, scandal is produced at the crossroads between the two arenas of politics and the media.

Second, in the relationship between the judiciary and the media, the judicial sphere has traditionally been governed by strict rules of secrecy and discretion and, unlike relations between politicians and the media, there has been little interaction, let alone interdependence. Consequently, this is less a case of a deal being broken than of a new interpenetration between these two spheres, which has had the effect of precipitating the decline of the traditional politics/media and politics/judiciary bargains. Since the

1980s, more investigative and competitive media have forced greater transparency on a previously closed profession. They have also given crusading magistrates a new power resource.

The strain between the discretion necessary for the effective application of judicial procedures and the use of the media for publicising judicial actions raises a number of problems (Leclerc 1997). First, in some instances the treatment of judicial information by the media can be strongly criticised: the media have used judicial data to inform the public, though often reporting trials in a dubious and partial fashion (Commaille 1994). The media also use investigative techniques to report scandalous events by copying judicial procedures, often reaching the stage where it becomes difficult to distinguish between judicial/official and journalist investigations. The widening role of the media, from strictly reporting events to actually conducting private investigations, at a time when investigating magistrates are also exploiting the press as a resource, creates ambiguities as to the status of information.

One effect has been a 'personalisation' of such information, presenting judges as 'media heroes' and leading to a closer proximity between the judiciary and ordinary citizens. This can detract from the supposedly impartial status of such figures and make them vulnerable to attack. The media have also tended to assume a new quasi-judicial function in claiming the legitimacy to judge what is and what is not fair in a given dispute. Intense media involvement in this respect has contributed to a growing incompatibility between the demands for justice presented and demanded in the media and the speed of due legal process. Judicial rhythms are not adapted to fast-flowing demands, especially when faced with the needs of the media (Bessin 1998). This gap between the objectives of the media and the judicial pursuit of corruption can also lead to unjust treatment in systems where scandal has become widespread. Usually, the media report at the beginning of the case, focusing on the personalities under investigation, who are not necessarily guilty, but are regarded with acute suspicion by public opinion. At the end of the trial, the media rarely emphasise the vindication of those found to be innocent. This can have a damaging effect on personal reputations and also damage the integrity of the judiciary.

Finally, the strains between the judicial and political spheres relate to both their theoretical independence and their 'sociological' proximity. In other words, the traditional collusion between both sets of elites has recently become conflictual. In terms of the principle of the separation of powers, the magistracy is an independent part of the constitution and considered politically impartial. In practice, however, in most democracies politicians have tried to produce mechanisms which allow political interference in the activities of the judiciary, while politicisation of the judiciary in the three countries covered in this chapter means that the application of the law may be politically motivated.

As far as political crimes are concerned, the magistracy's efficacy is, to a large extent, determined by its degree of independence from political authority. Political power has always tried to influence the judiciary and magistrates have always attempted to deal with these political pressures, whether under direct political constraint or because of class collusion. Since the early 1990s, movement towards liberalisation seems to have changed the nature of judicial guardianship. In Italy, for example, the conflict between members of the political class and the magistracy has become ferocious: witness that between the media tycoon and leader of Forza Italia, Silvio Berlusconi, and Antonio Di Pietro, a judge and later a minister, dismissed from his post partly as a result of a successful campaign of personal de-legitimisation. To speak of 'strain' in relation to this kind of open conflict is almost euphemistic.

Understanding the breakdown of these bargains requires further investigation of changes occurring *within* each of the respective arenas. The 'strains' within these arenas – greater competition among and within political organisations, new competition in the media following liberalisation, conservative versus radical approaches to judicial prosecution – have fuelled a growing interaction and co-operation/friction between them. It is from this nexus of relations of interdependence and conflict that the social dynamic of scandal has emerged in France, Italy and Spain in recent years.

The political arena: intensified competition

The political arena is the prime locus of scandal since it combines both the reproduction of democratic norms via the electoral process and the exercise and maintenance of power. Problems of bribery, bureaucratic malfunctioning and the misuse of public power emerge within the state machine. These are frequently linked with both the struggle to gain power (for instance, illegal party finance), since that power is constantly at stake due to frequent elections, and the desire to conserve and extend it (for example, building support networks via the corrupt allocation of public contracts). What is interesting about the late 1980s and 1990s is that the exposure of such practices, combined with the increasing personalisation of politics and the marketing tools used to create media events, became a resource for parties seeking to overcome or eliminate a political opponent in the competition for power.

There has been much general speculation about the role played by the changing ideological climate in the explosion of corruption scandals in recent years. The fall of the Berlin Wall is frequently alluded to in the Italian case as a fundamental external cause of the crisis that afflicted the country's political class after the wave of scandals in the early 1990s (Ginsborg 1996). The mechanism is assumed to be the 'loosening up' of the domestic political system due to the consequent return to respectability of the Italian Communist Party which was then able to make a full transition to social democracy. From a comparative perspective, however, it becomes clear that it is the changing nature of political competition in all three countries studied here that contributes – in combination with other developments – to the eruption of scandal.

As already discussed, a scandal is created through a dispute over the definition of facts denounced as scandalous. Political actors are particularly active in this definitional debate: some are directly concerned with the accusations, because the issue which caused scandal underlines a problem of public/political management which falls within their competence; others have to take a stand in the public dispute according to both their ideological beliefs and their position in the political arena. The capacity for scandal to disturb the status quo and radically de-legitimise political actors in the eyes of the public makes it a powerful weapon in the hands of politicians, to be combined with other instruments of political competition. In all three countries, it is possible to demonstrate the contribution of intensified political competition to the emergence of scandals.

In the political arena, the intensification of tensions and competition can derive from shifts in the political spectrum, the restructuring of political organisations or changes in the balance of power. At the electoral stage, there are often multiple denunciations involving politicians. Triggering a scandal when the electoral stakes are high can distance a candidate from the competition. More often than not, scandal has been used toward this end. An election or a political changeover may instigate denunciation and the search for political mobilisation around a scandalous issue. This was the case, for example, in the 1995 presidential elections in France when more than fifteen corruption cases were exposed in the media in the run-up to the elections. These related to members of the right-wing government, a number of whom had to resign. Eventually the spiral of scandals led to Prime Minister Edouard Balladur himself, who was competing directly with Jacques Chirac for the presidency. His chances of winning the election were finally put paid to when he was forced to explain his own sources of income from acting as a consultant for an informatics company (Pujas 2001).

A change in the configuration of political forces can instigate competitive behaviour amongst new players, as was the case in Italy. Since the early 1990s, the nature of political competition has been totally transformed in Italy. Not only did the Communist Party change into the social democratic PDS, while losing its hard-line rump which became the far-left *Rifondazione comunista*, but a new party formation, standing on a regionalist, populist, anti-Southern, anti-corruption platform, seriously threatened the already crumbling Christian Democrat vote in the North. The main reason for voting Christian Democrat (to keep the Communists out of power) had already lost much of its potency. The Lombard (later Northern) League's meteoric rise tore through the fabric of the old party system. In the general elections of April 1992, before the full extent of scandals was known, the voters punished the old parties but did not destroy them. The emergence of new 'protest' parties like the Northern League (perceived to be outside the established 'partyocracy' system of power sharing) and Forza Italia (the new party created by businessman Silvio Berlusconi in early 1994) exploited the disclosure of corruption involving the Christian Democrats, who were still in power, thereby intensifying political competition. These new forces instigated the use of 'hidden means', such as scandal, to better de-legitimise their opponents.

Finally, as is shown in the Spanish case, changes in the internal structure of political organisations can also facilitate scandal. When a long-standing strong leadership is denounced and contested by newcomers, or when an ideological break takes place within the party structure, an array of methods will be employed to discredit rivals. The 1993 explosion of the Filesa affair in Spain (which revealed that two elected Socialist Party [PSOE] representatives ran a 'front' company which paid party bills by charging businesses and banks for fictitious consultancy work) has to be explained not just with reference to the party's prominence in the public arena and media attention (see below), but by internal strains in the party itself. The years 1990–1 were marked by a struggle between two wings of the party, the *Guerristas* and the *renovadores*. The scandal of the PSOE's illegal financing emerged in this context of internal and external party weakness. In this period, the PSOE's dominance in parliament also came under a great deal of pressure from opposition forces.

The media arena: competing conceptions of journalism

None of the tensions in the political arena discussed above would be scandalous without the transmission of information to the public via the media. This is an obvious but important point given that, traditionally in southern Europe and France, the press has been anything but an active and independent critic of political behaviour.

The media are necessary to trigger scandal. For instance, the first big French scandals, the Dreyfus Affair and the Panama Scandal at the beginning of the twentieth century, were contemporaneous with the growth of the press. If information is concealed from the public, the denounced infringement of standards does not amount to scandal. Not only do the media reveal such information, but they fuel scandal by sensationalising it. Scandal, as a socially constructed phenomenon, is propitious to the needs of the mass media. The sensationalist nature of scandal, its surprising character and the ease with which an event can be personified (with a scandal it is easy to identify the guilty party and the denouncer) are features particularly adapted to mass media production. The definitional dispute and labelling of infringement involved in scandal makes good copy. To a large extent, the public sphere is now coterminous with the media sphere (Habermas 1976), given the media's strong agenda-setting impact on both the political and judicial arenas. Actors will, of course, provide their own independent interpretations of the core issue at stake, but the perception of the facts themselves will be mostly influenced by media representation.

The likelihood that the media will fuel scandal depends on their organisation and the journalistic tradition in a particular country. These have both been undergoing important changes in the three countries considered here. Competition within this arena, the media's economic and financial needs, ownership structures and the ideological preferences of the press are all relevant to an understanding of the role of the media as both democratic check and balance, and exploiter of scandal for their own purposes. Media competition has proven to be particularly important in recent years, following liberalisation and privatisation in the sector. Intense competition has resulted in the predominance of audio-visual media in the production and dissemination of information. A new commercial logic has imposed its own criteria on cultural production and the result is the search for 'scoops' and ever more sensationalist ways of presenting events. In Spain and France, the entry of new competitors and the increasing liberalisation of the media throughout the 1980s created a cleavage in journalism: between journalists as mediators of institutional news supplied by official agencies, on the one hand, and investigative journalism seeking hidden information and aiming to bolster its audience or readership levels, on the other.

The strain between these two different conceptions of journalism can itself create propitious grounds for scandal. In France, for example, a businessman, Pierre Botton, infiltrated the political environment and the media through donations of gifts, and later used his media relationships to promote the rise of a political personality, Michel Noir, a leading member of the Gaullist *Rassemblement pour la République*. The subsequent scandal was named 'l'Affaire Botton-Noir', after the leading figures involved. The relationship that the businessman had with Patrick Poivre d'Arvor, the well-known television news presenter on the privatised channel TF1, and the way in which the case was presented on that channel revealed the potential incompatibility between market logic and professional ethics.

The media's relationship with political parties and government varies from country to country and this determines the role they play in the struggle against corruption. For example, Italian newspapers have traditionally provided ideological support for particular political forces and were not prepared to play a key role in the denunciation of systemic corruption. By the early 1990s, however, they had become an outlet for information provided by anti-corruption judges about trials in progress, and papers and magazines of the Espresso-Repubblica group were used almost as means of prosecution, provoking accusations that this was corrupting the legality and legitimacy of the legal process (Burnett and Mantovani 1998). In Spain, the emergence of *El Mundo* in 1989 provided a vehicle for the denunciation of the PSOE through the systematic exposure of information regarding the corruption of the Socialist elites and their abuse of power during their fourteen years in government. For the first time in Spain this newspaper introduced a form of investigative journalism which was interested in hidden information and the disclosure of scandals. However, this was not exactly an impartial and independent role. Behind *El Mundo*, political and financial lobbies and the friendship between its director and the opposition leader of the *Partido Popular* influenced the editorial line of the newspaper and focused its attention overwhelmingly on affairs which weakened the legitimacy of the PSOE. Finally, in France, while the management of television channels is regularly subject to political intervention in the state sector and commercial pressures in the private sector, the press, and especially the newspaper *Le Monde*, occupies a special place.[7] The latter's prominent investigative journalist and now chief editor, Edwy Plenel, has played an important role as an opinion leader in defining 'affairs', such as Botton/Noir (Pujas 1994) or the more recent Dumas Affair, as scandals.

Two major trends in the 1990s explain the changing nature of competition within the media arena and as a result their more auspicious attitude in welcoming political denunciation in our three selected countries. First, the growing commercialisation of the media and the resultant competition for audiences has helped underpin spectacular and clamorous allegations against politicians in a climate of political dissatisfaction. Second, in covering the prosecutions led by emancipated and fearless judges, some newspapers have taken on the function of watchdog for the first time in decades.

The judicial arena: new notions of independence and investigation

The judiciary is a key actor in the production of scandal for three main reasons. First, the judicial arena has two general functions: the normative producer of rules and the guardian of social order through the implementation of sanctions. The law determines standards as to what is legal and illegal. Infringement of the law, therefore, will determine whether denunciation leads to scandal. As discussed above, the production of scandal is determined in part by the definition of legality and the sanction of law. Given that illegal acts committed by public agents are usually breaches of criminal law, the eventual punishment of corrupt politicians is closely bound to the existence and visibility of criminal prosecution. The exposure and prosecution – and eventually incrimination – of individuals engaging in particular forms of political behaviour as corrupt depend on how these functions are managed and deployed in any particular country.

Second, the denouncer of a violation expects both formal and symbolic sanctions to be applied. The formal sanction operates by recognition in law that a crime has occurred; the symbolic sanction operates through trial and punishment and is experienced by the community at large as a form of catharsis. This latter aspect is related to the visibility of scandal. Although the investigative capacity of the media has been previously referred to, in our three countries most of the information they deal with comes from official sources. Therefore, when scandal enters the higher judicial institutional arena, it is often the product of intense media scrutiny. By dealing with scandal in formal and 'rationalised' terms, above the fray of partisan argument and debate, the legal process gives greater visibility to the potential scandal, because the media feel legitimised by the judicial 'framing' of the violation to deal with other aspects of the scandal outside of the court setting.

Third, the judiciary's institutional competence and practice affect the probability of scandal. Judicial investigations have increased the rewards of corruption for other actors (politicians and journalists using it for their own ends) and magnified its potential social consequence as a political scandal. Magistrates perform a crucial function in corruption control and the penal accountability of politicians. They are the 'natural' adversaries of the corrupted and their corrupters. The effectiveness of judicial intervention, however, depends on the quality of the legislation produced. In Italy about 150,000 laws are currently in force compared to little more than 7,000 in France (Cazzola and Morisi 1995). As a result, the extent, range, and relevance of laws and regulations increase the efficacy and the speed of judicial response to litigation. As far as political crimes are concerned, the efficacy of investigating magistrates is also to a large extent determined by their degree of independence from political authority. Recruitment based on competitive examinations and open to those who have a university degree in law increases judges' autonomy. In southern European democracies, the development of the 'Mani Pulite' [Clean hands] investigations led to greater intervention by magistrates in the political sphere through the development of an autonomous strategy of communication with the citizenry. In Italy in particular, in the fight against terrorism and the Mafia, magistrates exercised proactive power bolstered by new legislation. The probity of judges has been in stark contrast with the involvement in criminal activity of numerous members of the political class and, as a result, the magistrates have won direct legitimacy for their activities in the eyes of public opinion (Giglioli *et al.* 1997; Pizzorno 1998; della Porta 2001).

The likelihood that the denunciation and legal investigation will result in prosecution depends on the organisation and use of the legal system. If one considers prosecution in two different legal systems, France and Italy for example, one can see not only that the procedural aspects are different, but also that they affect the probability of the case reaching trial. In France, the prosecution is managed through the 'principle of discretion': the public prosecutor [*chef du parquet*] is free to exercise his discretion to prosecute, depending on the nature of the offence. In Italy, the Ministry of Justice does not have the institutional means to influence the public prosecutor. Judges govern themselves through the *Consiglio Superiore della Magistratura*.

The 'principle of legality' of the prosecution gives them some guarantees of independence because they can prosecute every type of denunciation that comes before them. In France, many magistrates [*gardes des sceaux*] have acted in a political way themselves, from the left to the right of the political spectrum, provoking conflict with the judiciary by trying to hush up 'affairs' linked to the political parties they are connected with. In contrast, politicians (and some independent commentators) in Italy have accused the most zealous anti-corruption magistrates of waging a political war against the right-wing establishment.

While this view may be exaggerated, it is true that a different type of judge has entered the Italian magistrate profession since the 1970s and this changing sociology of the profession has been crucial in the spread of the prosecution of corrupt politicians and the proliferation of scandals. Mass education opened the universities to the lower classes and the protest cycle of the late 1960s influenced the political attitudes of a whole generation (Folena 1996). In the legal profession, a new generation of so-called *giudici ragazzini* [young kid judges], lacking any sense of deference towards political power, began a series of investigations into administrative misconduct. In 1992 the disclosure of the Mario Chiesa case (the first in the long series of *Tangentopoli* revelations) had an explosive effect because of the accumulation of corruption facts linked to this affair and their revelation in the press. Neither newspaper editors nor the political class could control the subsequent flood of allegations and indictments from this new form of strategic judicial investigation. Politicians at a higher level of society who were previously considered 'untouchable' were now prosecuted almost in the same way as other people for the crimes they had committed. This is a new development in the history of justice in the countries under study.

This clearly evident change in the role of the judiciary in our three countries allowed some observers to present these new judges as defenders of political legitimacy (Guarnieri and Pederzoli 1997). Moreover, the new independent attitude of the judges vis-à-vis politicians, the innovative investigations carried out by some of them and a greater coverage of politically sensitive prosecutions have all brought the judiciary to the fore as a new independent power – indeed the only one in such a climate of denunciation capable of providing the means to make politicians publicly accountable.

Comparative considerations

Corruption scandals have witnessed and reflected the emergence of the media and the judiciary as much more powerful actors in all three countries covered in this chapter. The judiciary in particular has enjoyed a transfer of legitimacy from traditional political representatives, although this may be short lived if the judiciary itself comes to be seen as partisan and politically motivated. While journalists use increasing media coverage of the judicial process to expose corrupt political behaviour, judges have exploited the media as a means of asserting their presence in the public sphere. In turn, public opinion, once alerted to the sometimes venal nature of politicians, has become increasingly dissatisfied with political conduct. This creates a transformation in political ethics because the media and judiciary propose a certain type of legitimacy (legal rules and transparency) to ensure social order and democracy, while the representative and contested nature of parliamentary politics has been degraded. The consequences of this re-configured relationship between judiciary, politics and the media are important for the future of democracy.

That said, the impact of the various factors analysed in this chapter has differed in each case. Hence, the implications of the recent wave of scandal for these democracies also differ. The judicialisation of politics has been the major factor in revealing corruption in the Italian case. The Italian judiciary and in particular the 'Clean hands' pool of magistrates revolutionised the role of the judges vis-à-vis politicians, provoking successive calls and campaigns to reduce their powers. Taking advantage of the political crisis and new political context created by the disappearance of the Communist Party as the major pole of attraction on the left, the judges began to bring politicians to account in a particularly virulent fashion after years in which they had been virtually immune from prosecution. This new phenomenon began to impact heavily on public opinion when journalists, and at the beginning especially Canale 5 (a new private channel), began making broadcasts to publicise the first major affair, the Mario Chiesa Trial. In fact the media tycoon, Silvio Berlusconi, initially wanted to exploit the failure of the old political elite of the First Republic and to replace it. Unfortunately for him, he was soon also to become a victim of the burgeoning revelations of corruption at all levels of the political system, though this did not prevent his re-election to the premiership in the 2001 elections.

In Spain, the media have played the major role in the disclosure of corruption. During twelve years of Socialist Party government there was an absence of a particularly active political opposition. Only the media, particularly after the entry into the market in 1989 of a new actor, *El Mundo*, fulfilled this function by exposing the corruption of Socialist elites. The problem is that behind *El Mundo*, some political and financial lobbies (for instance, the role of Mario Conde in the Banesto Affair) influenced the editorial line of the newspaper and its focus on affairs and scandal.

In France, it is more probably a combination of the judiciary and the publicity given to corruption trials by the media which explains why corruption has become a public issue. For its part, the judiciary has tried to emancipate itself from political pressure at different levels – for example, on the openness of investigations – and to move away from a general passivity in the face of political power. These changes stem from a new form of socialisation of magistrates (such as those from the École Nationale de la Magistrature de Bordeaux), a more heterogeneous social background than before (Garapon and Salas 1996), and new modes of interaction between magistrates and other social actors, including journalists. As for the media, newspapers have increasingly focused on the judicial process when public representatives are involved. The chief editor of *Le Monde* has invigorated investigative journalism in the major French media, while the entire political class remains remarkably silent (and collusive?) on these exposés, making the press in France a new and critical check on the abuse of power (Pujas 2001).

In short, behind the proliferation of scandals and the prosecution of politicians in the three countries studied here lies an increase in the importance of (new) checks and balances combined with invigorated political competition. The consequent competitive mobilisation of scandalised public opinion is the major driving force in the wave of scandal that has swept across these countries. Public interest in the disclosure of the politics of corruption appeared strongly in the 1990s, although these illicit practices emerged much earlier, principally in the 1970s. Public interest appears in the context of broader political change in which parties and other traditional political institutions lose legitimacy, and confidence in political elites declines. This chapter has argued that the major factor behind disclosure is the appearance of new and/or more confident political actors (the judiciary and the press), which have in turn helped generate wider public demands for greater transparency in party funding and in the public sphere (Pujas and Rhodes 1999). Political power in southern Europe is more contested in the late 1990s than at any time in the postwar period. In principle, one result should be a reduction in levels of corruption and greater faith in the political class. But given that the main protagonists of a democratic polity – the political parties – still suffer from a serious legitimacy deficit, there is some way to go before that confidence is fully restored.

Notes

1 The concept of 'arenas' refers to the competition within and between sectors where problems evolve. Here we examine the effect of these arenas on both the evolution of problems and the actors who influence their definition and perception. See S. Hillgartner and C.L. Bosk (1988) 'The rise and fall of social problems: a public arenas model', *American Journal of Sociology* 94: 53–78.

2 On the notion of scandals and 'affairs' as socially constructed phenomena see N. Yanai (1990) 'The political affair: a framework for comparative discussion', *Comparative Politics* 22/2: 185–97; C. Charles (1997) 'Naissance d'une cause. La mobilisation de l'opinion publique pendant l'affaire dreyfus', *Politix* 16: 11–18; A. Garrigou, 'Le scandale politique comme mobilisation', in F. Chazel (ed.) (1993) *Action collective et mouvements sociaux*, Paris: Presses Universitaires de France; J.B. Thompson (2000), *Political Scandal. Power and Visibility in the Media Age*, Cambridge: Polity Press; L.J. Sabato, M. Stencel and S.R. Lichter (2000) *Peepshow. Media and Politics in an Age of Scandal*, Oxford: Rowman & Littlefield Publishers.

3 We focus on the role of the press for one main reason. It appears from research on scandals that the role of the press is much more relevant than that of the broadcasting media in initiating a successful mobilisation of actors around a

controversial issue. Denunciation in the newspapers has a significant social impact above all when the broadcasting media relay the information. We can talk of scandal only when all media actors cover the controversial issue. For a deeper analysis of the press' role in being at the origin of scandal see D. Marchetti (1996) 'La genèse du "scandale du sang contaminé"', *Ethique, Sida et société*, Rapport de l'activité du Conseil National du Sida 1989–1994, Paris: La documentation française.

4 The case of Italy is not covered in this part of the analysis for lack of evidence of the existence of any AIDS-related contaminated blood scandal.

5 This contrasts with the spiral of silence conceptualised by Elisabeth Noelle-Neumann (1993) *The Spiral of Silence: Public Opinion, Our Social Skin*, Chicago: University of Chicago Press.

6 Of course, other factors also contribute to an explanation of the lower likelihood of a successful mobilisation of haemophiliacs around a common denunciation of their contamination in the Spanish case. These include the fragmentation of haemophiliacs as a social group and the lack of a centralised blood transfusion authority in Spain. Notwithstanding these factors, the central argument of this section focuses on the important role of the media in the failure to mobilise opinion in Spain as compared to France.

7 This is probably because it is the newspaper's journalists who are the main shareholders in *Le Monde*.

References

Bessin, M. (1998) 'La temporalité de la pratique judiciaire: un point de vue socio-logique', *Droit et Société* 39: 331–43.

Bourdieu, P. (1994) 'L'emprise du journalisme', *Actes de la recherche en sciences sociales* 101/102: 3–9.

Burnett, S.H. and Mantovani, L. (1998) *The Italian Guillotine: Operation Clean Hands and the Overthrow of Italy's First Republic*, Lanham, Maryland: Rowman & Littlefield.

Cazzola, F. and Morisi, M. (1995) ' Magistrature et politique', *Politix* 30: 76–90.

Champagne, P. and Marchetti, D., (1994) 'L'information médicale sous contrainte', *Actes de la recherche en sciences sociales* 101/102: 40–62.

Commaille, J. (1994) 'L'exercice de la fonction de justice comme enjeu de pouvoir entre justice et médias', *Droit et Société* 26: 11–18.

Diaz Nosty, B. (1994) 'Mario Conde et l'oligopole mouvant', *Médiaspouvoirs* 36: 113–18.

Folena, P. (1996) *Il tempo della giustizia*, Rome: Editori Riuniti.

Garapon, A. and Salas, D. (1996) *La République pénalisée*, Paris: Hachette.

Giglioli, P.P., Cavicchiolo, S. and Fele, G. (1997) *Rituali di degradazione: Anatomia del processo Cusani*, Bologna: Il Mulino.

Ginsborg, P. (1996) 'Explaining Italy's crisis', in S. Gundle and S. Parker (eds), *The New Italian Republic: From the Fall of the Berlin Wall to Berlusconi*, London: Routledge.

Gitlin, T. (1980) *The Whole Word is Watching*, Berkeley: University of California Press.

Guarnieri, C. and Pederzoli, P. (1997) *La democrazia giudiziaria*, Bologna: Il Mulino.

Habermas, J. (1976) *L'espace public*, Paris: Payot.

Leclerc, H. (1997) 'Justice et médias, un affrontement nécessaire', *Médiaspouvoirs* 1 (new series): 74–9.

Llovet, J.J. (1992) 'El Control del prensa sobre la profesion médica: el caso de *El País*', *REIS* 59: 261–85.

Marchetti, D. (1996) 'La genèse médiatique du "scandale du sang contaminé"', *Ethique, Sida et Société*, Rapport de l'activité du Conseil National du Sida 1989–1994, Paris: La documentation française.

Pizzorno, A. (1998) *Il poetere dei giudici. Stato democratico e controllo della virtu*, Rome: Laterza.

Porta, D. della (2001) 'A judges' revolution? Political corruption and the Judiciary in Italy', *European Journal of Political Research* 39: 1–21.

Pujas, V. (1994) 'Le scandale comme mobilisation: L'Affaire Botton-Noir', unpublished PhD thesis, Institut d'Études Politiques, Grenoble.

Pujas, V. (1999) 'Les scandales politiques en France, en Italie et en Espagne. Constructions, usages et conflits de légitimité', unpublished PhD thesis, European University Institute, Florence.

Pujas, V. (2001) 'Corruption in French politics', in A. Guyomarch, P.A. Hall, J. Hayward and H. Machin (eds), *Developments in French Politics 2*, Basingstoke: Palgrave.

Pujas, V. and Rhodes, M. (1999) 'Party finance and political scandal in Italy, Spain and France', *West European Politics* 22/3: 41–63.

Sorrentino, C. (1995) *I percorsi della notizia. La stampa quotidianna italiana tra politica e mercato*, Bologna: Baskerville.

Turow, J. (1992) *Media Systems in Society*, New York: Longman.

9 The ambivalent watchdog

The changing culture of political journalism and its effects

Kees Brants and Hetty van Kempen

When French President Jacques Chirac came to visit the Queen and Prime Minister of the Netherlands in early 2000, he turned down all requests for advance interviews. Dutch television news got 'no' for an answer, current affairs programmes begged in vain and the political editors of all national newspapers received only a short reply from the President's information office: terribly sorry, but no interviews. There was one exception, however: the *TV Show* of the public broadcasting station TROS, hosted by Ivo Niehe, the Dutch equivalent of David Letterman. His shows are usually filled with entertainment stars or (non-political) people in the news. The format is that of a friendly chat, with exchanges which shed light on the human side of the interviewee and eschew any confrontational approach. Although hardly a political programme, it was an ideal platform for the French President to say what he wanted to say and to keep silent about any hot potato that he apparently feared all the other interview applicants were dying to chew on – and to say it with a smile, unchallenged by the Jeremy Paxmans of the Lowlands.

Talk shows like these, or their somewhat more political but no less human interest focused counterparts which Chirac would be familiar with – like Michel Drucker's *Vivement Dimanche* on France 2 – are often considered to be the nail in the coffin of serious political communication or, even worse, of democracy itself. They are supposed to give us more of the images and personalities of politics than of the issues and opinions that (should) concern us. It is, as Swanson has put it so vividly for the United States, 'a style of coverage driven by entertainment values and a desire not to be left behind by the tabloids in attracting the mass audience' (Swanson 1997: 1269).

Though the evidence for such an infotaining of political communication in Europe is rather ambiguous (Brants 1998), Chirac's smiling his way out of potential trouble points to two other things, or rather to two sides of the same coin. One is the so-called bypass strategy of politicians, a trend apparently set by Bill Clinton in the 1992 US presidential election campaign.

This is aimed at avoiding television programmes involving serious political discussion and critical interrogation by political journalists who hold decision-makers and power holders accountable for their promises, policies and deeds. The other is the apparent assumption that, as a politician, you cannot expect to receive fair treatment from political journalists. They are more interested in scandal and negativism, in 'exposing' the 'ugly' than the 'true face' of politics and politicians, and they do not give politicians a chance to inform, to explain or to react.

This 'blaming the messenger' has for some time now been part of a heated debate in the US and it finds a growing resonance in Europe, where it is claimed that the cynical approach of journalists creates a more general political cynicism among the public. This contributes to a picture of a tuned-in but turned-off voter, with growing civic disengagement and mistrust of governments. Soundbite journalism and scandal orientation of the news media are blamed for this state of affairs. This view is so widespread that Norris even claims that it has developed into something of an unquestioned orthodoxy in the popular literature, particularly in the United States (Norris 2000). The successive political marketing and spin-doctoring of parties and politicians has in turn angered political journalists, thus leading to a 'spiral of cynicism' evolving into a 'crisis of democracy' or in 'civic communication' (for the US, for example, see Cappella and Jamieson 1997; Kerbel 1999; and for the UK, see Franklin 1994, 1997; Blumler and Gurevitch 1995).

What evidence is there in Europe for such a spiral of growing cynical journalism and public opinion, both caught in an almost unstoppable amplification process? In responding to this question, this chapter examines the case of the Netherlands.

The spiral of cynicism thesis

The anti-political attitude of American journalism, though present since the founding of the new republic, can be traced back particularly to the arrival of immigrants to the cities. This fostered the rise of machine politics and displaced middle Americans from power at the local level (Protess *et al.* 1991: 35). As an instrumental part of the Progressive movement at the end of the nineteenth and beginning of the twentieth century, muckraking journalism was a reaction to the exhortation of the citizenry. It aimed at reform as well as civic awareness and, in the end, at mobilising an outraged public against the political bosses. Journalists and writers like Ida Tarbell, Upton Sinclair and Lincoln Steffens reported on the corruption of senators and city authorities and exposed the criminal practices of large corporations. They waged a moral crusade against the concentration of power in a political or economic form, which, they claimed, had pervaded American society as a whole. At the onset of the First World War, the excesses of some of its practitioners, diminishing media rivalry and the growing importance of objective journalism for newspapers aiming to attract and satisfy a mass audience resulted in the demise of this radical form of investigative journalism.

It took more than half a century to reappear, albeit in a slightly different form, triggered by Vietnam and Watergate. As it turned out at the time, Presidents Johnson and Nixon had not only lied about America's role in Southeast Asia and the break-in and consequent cover-up of the head-quarters of the Democratic Party, respectively, but the objective style of reporting had lulled the majority of journalists almost into passivity. Apparently they could be easily fooled with appetising chunks of news fed to them by the well-staffed information offices of the President and political parties. Fortunately, investigative journalism had not died out completely; the romantic hero of the young and daring reporter emerged in the double bill of Woodward and Bernstein at the *Washington Post*. In showing that the press could still perform its watchdog role, sceptical of major institutions and politicians, they inspired a whole generation of journalism students. Dubious political practices, professional news management and their own revelations increasingly convinced political journalists that most, if not all, politicians were suspect. What the latter claimed as the factual truth should never be taken for granted. The post-muckraking professional rules of separating facts and opinions prevented, however, a new wave of the old moral crusaders: incriminating revelations had to be checked and double-checked, and press attacks to be substantiated with facts.

According to Patterson (1993), the US media were unable to sustain this exacting type of scrutiny, as it requires time and knowledge and sometimes results in the well-paid reporter not having a story at all. Patterson claims that, in the wake of Vietnam and Watergate, the media have moved from a descriptive to an interpretative style of reporting. This is a substitute, however, for true investigative journalism, in that it uses opponents as a means to undermine a politician's claim. 'When a politician made a statement, they turned to his adversaries to attack it. Conflict, always an element of political coverage, became the predominant theme'. Moreover, 'attack journalism had come to include reporters as direct participants; they regularly worked their own criticism into their interpretative reports' (Patterson 1996: 103):

> The interpretative style elevates the journalist's voice above that of the news maker. As the narrator, the journalist is always at the centre of the story. . . . Interpretation provides the theme, and the facts illuminate it. The theme is primary; the facts are illustrative. . . . Reporters question politicians' actions and commonly attribute strategic intentions to them, giving politicians less of a chance to speak for themselves.
>
> (Patterson 1996: 101–2)

According to US research, interpretative journalism shows itself in several forms, particularly in election campaign reporting. First, it expresses itself in a move away from issue-based reports to poll-driven *horse-race* stories that emphasise which candidates are ahead and behind, and to *strategic game frames*, which remind the audience of the self-interest of actors and highlight the strategies and tactics of the candidate's campaign. Patterson (1993) found a sharp increase in strategy coverage in the front-page headlines of the *New York Times* between 1960 and 1992. He also showed that between 1988 and 1992, horse-race coverage of election events on the nightly television news rose from 27 to 35 per cent.

Second, political news provides excessive focus on the conflictual and the negative. Looking, for instance, at the weeklies *Time* and *Newsweek* over a period of more than thirty years (1960–92), Patterson (1993) found an increase in negative references to the major party nominees, up from 25 per cent of the campaign coverage in 1960 (the Kennedy–Nixon campaign) to about 50 to 60 per cent in elections from 1980 to 1992. According to Sabato, political reporting has turned into blood-thirsty attack journalism, whereby 'the news media, print and broadcast, go after a wounded politician like sharks in a feeding frenzy' (Sabato 1991: 1). The practice of 'pack journalism' – journalists running after each other to cover the same story in the same manner – thereby strengthens the image of politics being about conflict and scandal.

Finally, the journalist becomes more important in the interpretative style than his political news source. So much so, that during the network coverage of the 1992 US election campaign, journalists spoke six times as long as the candidates who were shown speaking. A viewer who watched the television news every night during the election campaign would have heard less from the mouths of Clinton, Bush and Perot than from viewing one single presidential debate (quoted in Patterson 1996: 102). Moreover, tabloid television has, according to Hallin (1998: 46), further eroded the ethic of objectivity in favour of one of emotional involvement 'The journalist must show that he or she shares the emotions of the viewer'.

The assumption with the quoted authors is that this type of news coverage has a decisive impact on voters' perceptions of candidates and politics; in fact it activates, if not breeds, political cynicism. This assumption is not new. Back in the 1960s, Lang and Lang (1968) were already claiming that television's style of chronicling political events could stir up in individuals defensive reactions by its emphasis on crisis and conflict instead of clarifying normal decision-making processes. Robinson (1976) was the first to refer to it as 'videomalaise', to describe the link between the dominant style of television journalism and feelings of political cynicism, mistrust and lack of efficacy. He claimed that the greater exposure to the negative and conflictual television news reporting, the more cynicism, frustration and malaise among the viewing public.

In several researches since 1992, Cappella and Jamieson (1997) found that strategic frames for election coverage activate audience cynicism in both print and broadcast media; issue-based frames do not consistently depress cynicism, though neither do they elevate it. In an experimental research project, Ansolabehere and Iyengar (1995: 112) showed that the use of negative or attack television campaign ads 'drives people away from the polls . . . breeds distrust of the electoral process and pessimism about the value of an individual's own voice'. There are some dissenting voices outside the dominant orthodoxy. Political scientists like Bennett (1998) disagree with the supposed 'death of civic culture' and take issue with the view that 'television and related media of political communication are implicated in various political crimes and misdemeanors'. However, the likes of him are few and far between in the United States.

The situation in Europe is somewhat different. While in many countries the same criticism exists about the content (or lack of it) of political reporting, systematic and longitudinal research is scarce. Moreover, substantive empirical proof of a growing videomalaise or of political cynicism has been virtually absent or at best inconclusive. At the beginning of the 1990s, for instance, Holtz-Bacha (1990) found no evidence for Germany; in fact she reported positive effects of news media on political knowledge, interest and understanding. In contrast, in a later study on the same country, Schulz (1997) did find a relation between 'tabloidisation tendencies' in public and private channels and growing political cynicism among the public. The direction of the causality, however, remains uncertain; people who are less interested in or negative towards politics to begin with may well prefer the more tabloidised television genres.

For Great Britain, Norris (1999) demonstrated from large-scale experiments during the 1997 election campaign that exposure to negative television news about the major parties had no influence on party images or propensity to vote; positive news, however, did have a significant impact. In addition, in a longitudinal research on participation in the European elections and media use between 1989 and 1999, she found no evidence for the claim that those most exposed to negative news coverage during the campaign were demobilised by the experience. There was a substantial, and in some countries even dramatic, decrease of voter participation, but Norris argues that the most plausible interpretation of this evidence is that there is a 'virtuous circle', whereby watching the news activates existing predispositions and prior tendencies lead people to turn on the news (Norris 1999, 2000).

What is the relevance of this debate for the situation in the Netherlands?

Three phases of political communication in the Netherlands

The coming of age of political journalism in the Netherlands can best be described in terms of three periods in which changes in (party) political culture, the relationship between the mass media and politics, and journalists' attitudes towards audiences have resulted in varying changes in media content and journalistic style and behaviour. The phases bear resemblance to the three 'ages' that Blumler and Kavanagh (1999) have distinguished in (Anglo-American) political communication. In their first age, political communication was mainly subordinate to relatively strong and stable political institutions and beliefs. In the second age, the electorate was cut adrift while parties professionalised and adapted their communications to the news values of television. In the (still emerging) third age distinguished by Blumler and Kavanagh – that of media abundance – political communication is shaped by intensified professionalisation of political advocacy, increased competitive pressures, anti-elitist popularisation and populism, centrifugal diversification and 'tailored' communication and, finally, changes in how people receive politics. The 'ages' of Dutch political journalism, though often likened to the Anglo-American example, have different elements and characteristics.

The first phase: pillarisation

For a long time the Netherlands has been renowned, at least among political scientists, for its 'pillarised' structure: political parties, labour unions, associations of employers and other voluntary associations, sports clubs, schools and mass media were all organised on the basis of religious and ideological cleavages. Since before the Second World War, but more especially after it, four large social blocs – Roman Catholic, Protestant, Social Democratic and Liberal – dominated and segregated Dutch society; people of one bloc hardly mixed with those of another. Communication and consultation took place only via the respective elites, who told their followers what, and particularly what not, to think and believe.

With diversity at mass level, accommodation and conflict resolution in the political system were possible only because the leaders of the different pillars agreed to certain rules of the game. Business-like politics, tolerance (more or less as a gentlemen's agreement to respect each other's 'territories') and secrecy were the main components. In order to create and maintain this culture of quiescence among the citizenry, the diversity at mass level necessitated an almost consciously created 'information gap' about what was going on. Until the mid-1960s, the postwar period was characterised by a high degree of harmony in both the political and economic spheres.

The media were part and parcel of this cleavaged structure, showing an extreme form of partisanship or pillar advocacy, comparable to the situation of a fragmented consociational party system and the 'arrangement' of *lottizzazione* in political communication found in Italy prior to 1989 (see Chapter 4 by Roncarolo). The press included a fair number of neutral papers, but the majority (by circulation certainly) were clearly connected to the major pillars, with the Catholic and Social Democratic pillar most strongly represented. In broadcasting the different pillars had their own organisations, each with its own structure and with specific broadcasting time to 'spread the message'. Both pillarised newspapers and broadcasting organisations had interlocking directorships with the other organisations within the pillar. It was not unusual, for instance, for the editor-in-chief of the Catholic newspaper or the chairman of the Socialist broadcasting organisation also to be a Member of Parliament for the respective political party or the leader of the relevant labour union. Moreover, the political journalists of these media would be specially informed by the party leader or attend, and even participate in, the meetings of 'their' Members of Parliament.

Generally speaking, the media formed the mouthpieces of the party elites within the pillars, rather paternalistically telling people what they 'had to know', not caring what the latter might want to see, hear or read. The media oriented themselves towards the elite, communicating the 'right message' from leaders to rank and file. The electorate formed a stable group on which the political parties could count at election time, while the media had a strongly integrating function which both showed and confirmed the correctness and cohesiveness of the pillar's ideology. Political communication formed an almost closed system. If, in describing political journalists, one were to use a metaphor from the animal world, *lapdogs* would probably be the most appropriate species: journalists followed obediently and communicated more or less what they were told to. Political conflicts might exist, but these would be mostly kept in-house. With a stable electorate, horse races did not exist and there was no necessity for hoopla and photo opportunities in election campaigns.

The second phase: depillarisation

The description of this neat arrangement has to be somewhat ideal – because otherwise one cannot explain why around the mid-1960s it came to an end. A decline of religious feeling and depillarisation, fed by socio-cultural developments around most of the democratic world, shook the stable foundations of both political and media systems. The organisations, associations and political parties became less segmented and more pluralistic, while interactions between the members of the pillars increased rapidly. Television opened up the world for them and triggered many developments. The rank and file, locked up for so long in the internal closeness of the pillar, caught a glimpse of how the 'other half' lived. The political parties lost their relatively fixed electorate, the floating voter appeared and the parties were now forced to go in search of them. Newspapers with pillarised origins lost readers and several had to close. The broadcasting system was opened up to newcomers, most of whom had no links with traditional pillars; they appealed to the new and young generation of the 1960s that cared little about traditional belief systems.

The closely knit co-operation between party and medium eroded and the 'natural' platform for politicians to spread the word was suddenly inhabited by young and critical journalists, boldly asking questions that had been anathema under the closed culture of pillarisation. The uncertainty of the party elites regarding this changed political culture was shown by the medium, to which the old party politicians were not yet accustomed. Until then there had been no need, as the medium had been their platform. Now the nature of political communication changed from a top-down one-way street to one of critical interaction: journalists tried to hold politicians accountable for their deeds and the latter had to answer questions never previously asked, about political differences, issue stances and policy records. In the past, the questions had been predictable; now politicians had to be on their guard.

Depillarisation, one might say, emancipated political journalism. No longer the lapdog of politicians, sharing in the politics of secrecy towards the citizenry, journalists became the *watchdog* of politics. They informed, gave space to the expression and exchange of ideas and opinions, and critically followed and analysed the claims and policies of power holders. They scrutinised the responsibility of those running the country and, though respectful of the position of political parties and politicians as the initiators of political news, in the end regarded themselves as responsible only to the public. Journalism was an independent performance carried out in the public interest.

The third phase: competition

Although no systematic, longitudinal research has been done, there are several reasons to believe that at the end of the 1980s/start of the 1990s a new phase in Dutch political communication began. This could be regarded as a mix of Blumler and Kavanagh's third age and of Roncarolo's transition from a supposed videocracy to increasing politico-journalistic tension (see Chapter 4 by Roncarolo).

Looking at the political system we see that ideology is less the cement that holds society together and hardly a basis for electoral choice. If they vote, the politically uninterested do so more on the basis of a rather vague image of party and party leader. Political style – shown in the unity, push and openness of the party and in the credibility, expertise, sympathy and humaneness of the party leader – has become an element of political performance aimed at, but also largely defined by, the media. With growing numbers of floating voters and declining numbers of party members, loyalty has also become a problem. Strengthened by the consensual nature of coalition governments under a so-called 'poulder model', differences in party stance become less clear, making it difficult for the public to decide their vote on this basis. 'Party-voter distances have become more stretched, while party-party differences have become more attenuated, with both processes combining to reinforce a growing popular indifference to parties and, potentially, to the world of politics in general' (Mair 1998: 164). This lack of decisive difference forces parties to emphasise the quality of their parliamentarians and their party leader in particular, increasing the importance of media–political interactions.

In the media a process of commercialisation has set in since the appearance of the first commercial television station RTL in 1989. With a cable density of 95 per cent, there are seven Dutch-language commercial stations alongside the three public channels. The former have a market share of around 42 per cent, while the public broadcasters have seen their near monopoly from the pre-1989 period dwindle to a mere 40 per cent. The rest of the audience share goes to around fifteen foreign, special interest and local channels. The prime-time public news programme, *NOS-journaal*, reaches some 1.2 million viewers, one third more than its competitor *RTL-nieuws*, which in content and style is not much different from the NOS. *RTL-nieuws* attracts an over-representation of the less well educated and the politically less interested. The composition of *NOS-journaal* viewers is more or less the mirror image of *RTL-nieuws* (van Praag and Brants 2000: 60).

In the past ten years we have seen an increase in entertainment programming. However, in the context of more hours being broadcast by public channels and commercial stations, both of which have chosen not to neglect news, in absolute terms political information has grown as well. At the same time there has been an increase in programmes of the infotainment genre, such as talk shows and breakfast programmes, where personalisation is often more important than policies and structural developments. With audiences fragmented over all these channels, genres and programmes, it becomes more and more difficult for political parties and politicians to reach audiences. They have to knock on the doors of more than one channel to be able to address the same number of people they reached ten years ago via one. Politicians also have to think more about the package in which to wrap their message.

Television competition has led to a remarkable journalistic paradox: political journalists display both imitative behaviour and a desire for uniqueness. With more channels and more programmes, including the infotainment genre, there are now more journalists covering politics. They do not want to miss what their competitors have and the result is a form of pack journalism – all waiting in line to interview the same politician, asking the same questions. At the same time, the bread and butter of journalistic culture is the scoop, which tickles the ego and pleases both editors and bosses. Journalists, from the traditional lobby correspondent to the new infotainment star and commercial *paparazzo*, thus go in search of what is different, often to be found in conflicts and scandal.

The assumption is that political communication in this period is driven by a media logic in which the content and style of reporting are decided by a frame of reference in which the media make sense of facts and people (Altheide and Snow 1979). By this logic, mass media identify with the public, that is to say with what they think people deem important and entertaining; at the same time, politics becomes highly dependent on the functioning, production routines and news values of the media (Mazzoleni 1987). Where journalists under pillarisation could be labelled lapdogs and between the mid-1960s and the end of the 1980s performed more like watchdogs, we now see the confusing and uncertain elements of a post-modern, eclectic species. There is no single dominant journalistic style, but there seem to be different and often competing types, less driven by notions of the public interest but more by what they believe the public is interested in. If one were to use a metaphor for this modern species, Cerberus, the multifaceted dog of Greek mythology, comes to mind. In the many 'faces' we can distinguish the informer, the interpreter, the investigator as well as the entertainer, sometimes happily but often competitively living together (see Table 8.1). Under such circumstances one might expect the spiral of cynicism to get a foothold in the Netherlands.

Table 8.1 Political journalism in the Netherlands

	pre-1965	*1965–90*	*post-1990*
Characteristic	pillarisation	depillarisation	competition
Role of journalist	docile	critical	multiple
Logic	partisan	party	media
Identication with	party elite	public interest	public
Agenda set by	politics	politics	media
Metaphor	lapdog	watchdog	Cerberus

Political journalism in recent Dutch elections

On the basis of data from the Dutch parliamentary election campaigns of 1994 and 1998 we now look at possible changes in the content and style of political communication and judge whether we can see in the Netherlands a move from a descriptive to a more interpretative form of journalism. Content analyses of the 1994 and 1998 campaign coverage of both RTL and NOS prime-time news programmes were carried out, based on the the final three weeks before the election (van Praag and Brants 2000). Among other things, the percentage of substantive (party stances and disagreements on issues, policies, etc.), hoopla (ritual and pictures of canvassing, etc.) and horse-race news (opinion polls, winners and losers, party strategies, etc.) were investigated, as well as the framing of news items.

Election campaigns have always been treated in political reporting as a news item worth lowering the news threshold for. The coming of commercial television has not changed this. Both *NOS-journaal* and *RTL-nieuws* increased their coverage of the campaign between 1994 and 1998: 37 per cent of the main NOS news in the three weeks prior to the 1998 elections was devoted to the campaign, while for RTL the comparable figure was 30 per cent.

In spite of this increased media attention, television coverage of elections in the Netherlands over the past ten years has seen a steady decline in issue-orientation, particularly on the part of the public broadcaster NOS following the introduction of commercial televison in 1989. While the percentage of substantive news declined, horse-race news climbed and hoopla news remained at around 30 per cent until 1994 (see Table 8.2). In the light of both political and academic critiques of their lack of substantive reporting during the 1994 election campaign, however, the editors of NOS TV news decided to change their approach during the 1998 campaign. The result was remarkable: substantive news, with more than half of political news items, rose to the 1986 level, horse-race items remained at around a third and hoopla news fell from a third to 15 per cent.

Table 8.2 Campaign news on public television (NOS) (in %)

	1986	*1989*	*1994*	*1998*
Substantive news	51	41	36	52
Horse race news	18	31	35	33
Hoopla news	32	27	30	15

In the case of RTL also, the effect of public criticism on their first campaign coverage in 1994 was remarkable. Whereas in 1994 RTL had broadcast less substantive news than NOS – which was to be expected from a commercial channel – they beat NOS in 1998 in content-orientation, albeit by a mere 1 per cent (see Table 8.3). Hoopla items fell substantially, as did horse-race news. Opinion polls, which had been more or less absent in 1994 (the emphasis was on speculation as to who would win and lose and who would form a government with whom), rose to 18 per cent, because in the last two weeks RTL gave the results of its own daily poll every night.

In the opening statements of the news anchor or the political editor of the two news programmes, however, we did find an emphasis on strategic game frames: with NOS 54 per cent of the 'inswingers' referred to the parties' strategies ('The floating voter and the risk of a gaffe are the two elements that campaign teams fear the most' – *NOS-journaal*, 29 April 1998), while with RTL 42 per cent was on winning or losing (question by the anchorman: 'You assume there will be a new Lab–Lib government?' Answer by the political editor: 'For the time being yes, since most opinion polls give that impression'). The fact that RTL tried to set the agenda of the campaign by having an opinion poll every day strengthened their emphasis on horse-race openings.

A second element of cynical news reporting is the framing of the news in terms of conflicts. In the Netherlands, too, conflict frames form a part of electoral reporting. According to Kleinnijenhuis *et al.* (1998: 94ff.), this trend has increased over the past ten years, more so in the case of

Table 8.3 Campaign news in NOS and RTL news programmes (in %)

| | 1994 | | 1998 | |
	NOS	*RTL*	*NOS*	*RTL*
Substantive news	36	28	52	53
Horse race news	35	31	33	24
Hoopla news	30	42	15	23

newspapers than television. They claim (but give little hard evidence) that having to perform as a watchdog is more and more interpreted by journalists as a passport for negativism.

In our research on the 1994 elections we found that the campaign was dominated by the internal strife of the Christian Democrats (CDA), whose party leader was pursuing a more American-style campaign of which MPs and the rank and file disapproved. When it turned out he was (only distantly) connected to a company fraud, it marked not only the end of his political career, but also a dramatic defeat for the CDA party. The 1998 election campaign had much less scandal to report. With regard to conflict, there was regular reference to a (mostly media-constructed) confrontation between the party leaders of coalition partners PvdA (Labour) and VVD (Liberal). We found that 30 per cent of the substantive items of NOS TV news contained such a conflict frame; with RTL news this was 10 per cent less. The tone of this conflict reporting, however, was more ironic than cynical, while the conflict orientation seemed to have been inspired more by an absence of differences between the political parties than a cynical view of the political process.

In line with US research, there was a noticeable change in another style element of television news reporting, which moved towards a more interpretative form. The talk ratio between politicians and journalists was strongly in favour of the latter. In NOS news, Labour leader and Prime Minister Wim Kok was the central actor for only 35 per cent of the total time in items where he was being interviewed. With RTL this was not much different. Liberal leader Frits Bolkestein spoke for only 26 per cent of the time in items in which he was the central actor. Finally, we found remarkably short soundbites from politicians who are usually known for their lengthy statements: Koks quotes on *NOS-journaal* lasted ten seconds on average and on RTL seventeen seconds. For Bolkestein these figures were thirteen and twelve seconds respectively. In comparison, Hallin (1992) found that the length of soundbites in US campaign reporting dropped from forty-three seconds in 1968 to nine seconds in 1988.

With such an ambiguous picture on the possible existence of a journalistic spiral of cynicism in the Netherlands, how is this reflected in the public's attitude towards politics?

Mediamalaise in the Netherlands?

In looking at political cynicism in the Netherlands, we are again left with a feeling of ambiguity. As in other liberal democracies where Pharr and Putnam (2000) found a general pattern of disillusionment with politicians, over the years there has been a slow but steady increase in political cynicism in the Netherlands. With one difference: the trend reversed between 1994 and 1998 (Dutch National Election Studies [DNES] 1977–98).[1] Contrary to other liberal democracies, the Dutch have become less cynical in the last few years. We have also witnessed a related trend and reversal in election news reporting, with the relative amount of substantive news declining until 1994 and sharply increasing in 1998. This raises the question of a causal relationship between media use and political cynicism. Does exposure to non-substantive television news lead to an increase in political cynicism? In other words: is there evidence for 'mediamalaise' in the Netherlands? Using DNES data, we will test this by investigating the connection between political cynicism and exposure to *NOS-journaal* and *RTL-nieuws* for 1994 and 1998.

The results are presented in Table 8.4, in which political cynicism is regressed on media use. The effects show relationships between variables in terms of direction and size; a negative sign means that this variable lowers cynicism and vice-versa.[2] The significance of the effect shows how probable it is that the effect holds true for the complete population. As it turns out, in both years the frequency of watching the newscasts of the commercial station RTL4 had a positive effect on political cynicism, i.e. people regularly watching *RTL-nieuws* were, on average, more politically cynical than those who did not. At the same time, the better educated preferred the public *NOS-journaal* and were less likely to watch commercial newscasts. However, controlling for this and other possible explanatory variables (like political interest and party adherence), the finding still holds. The table also shows that another important predictor of cynicism is adherence to a government party: those feeling strongly attached to a government party are less politically cynical than those who do not feel very close. In addition, educational attainment had an impact on cynicism (although solely in 1994): the higher educated the viewer, the less cynical they were about politics and politicians. At the same time, regular viewing of NOS news did not affect political cynicism.

Though the analysis seems to indicate that exposure to specific (commercial) television news has in itself an effect on political cynicism, the assumed causality is very doubtful. Looking at the content of the two news programmes (Tables 8.2 and 8.3), one would expect to see a similar effect on cynicism of watching the *NOS-journaal*, as in both years there was not that much difference in the amount of substantive, horse-race and hoopla news between the two channels. Yet cynicism among the two groups of viewers was quite different; being better educated, the NOS viewers were

Table 8.4 Political cynicism regressed on media use

	Political cynicism 1994 (0 = 'low', 3 = 'high')	Political cynicism 1998 (0 = 'low', 3 = 'high')
Frequency watching RTL newscast (1 = 'less than once a week', 4 = 'daily')	0.084**	0.055*
Frequency watching NOS newscast (1 = 'less than once a week', 4 = 'daily')	−0.015	−0.032
Political interest (0 = 'low', 4 = 'high')	0.002	−0.018
Adherence to government party (0 = 'no', 1 = 'yes')	−0.133**	−0.101**
Education (1 = 'low', 5 (1994) / 10 (1998) = 'high')	−0.094**	−0.030
Age (scale variable)	0.208**	0.203**
Constant	1.644**	1.478**
R-square	0.087	0.097
n	1812	2101

Notes
The table represents OLS standardised regression coefficients (betas) of television news exposure variables and a selection of control variables.
* Significant at 0.05 level; two-tailed test.
** Significant at 0.01 level; two-tailed test.

less cynical. Moreover, with the increase in substantive news between 1994 and 1998 in both news programmes, a smaller effect on cynicism should have been expected. The effect, however, was exactly the same for both channels in both years in terms of direction and significance. Therefore, it does not seem to matter what the news is about, but rather who watches what: RTL viewers were more cynical to begin with. This is probably a process of self-selection: RTL viewers have different characteristics than NOS viewers, one of which is cynicism towards politics and politicians. Political cynicism decreased slightly between 1994 and 1998, but it seems not to have been caused by watching television news or by the content (or lack of it) of either of the two news programmes.

According to these results, there is no reason to assume that the theories of either Patterson or Cappella and Jamieson apply to the Netherlands. In fact, there is some evidence that trust in politicians has even been strengthened, in spite of indications of somewhat more interpretative, conflict-oriented and strategic reporting. Van der Brug and van der Eijk (2000) found that support for all parties and politicians in the last months before the elections of both 1994 and 1998 increased. Although support is not exactly the opposite of political cynicism, they found that sympathy scores for the five largest parties and the three party leaders of the coalition parties correlated negatively with the political cynicism score.

Conclusion

With growing popular indifference to parties and politics in general in the Netherlands and an increasing commercialisation of and competition in the Dutch media, one would expect a certain 'Americanisation' of political communication. On a limited scale, we have tried to test for the Netherlands US findings that journalism is developing a negative and cynical approach towards politics and politicians and that this has resulted in a more general political cynicism among citizens.

Political journalism in the Netherlands is clearly changing, though it is not always moving in a clear direction. In campaign reporting we did find some signs of a more interpretative style of reporting, with journalists dominating politicians in their newscasts and reliance on relatively short soundbites. Inter- and intra-party conflicts are popular with Dutch journalists and there are examples of scandals being dug up in investigative reporting. On the other hand, election communication gained in length and, comparing the 1994 and 1998 campaigns, the level of substantiveness in both the public and commercial television newscasts increased substantially in 1998. The impression of Dutch political journalism at the start of the century is, therefore, one of ambiguity. There are signs of more market-driven journalism as well as a re-orientation of the traditional professional logic: on the one hand, more strategic game frames, soundbites and dominating journalists, on the other, more substantive and not so cynical news. A critical watchdog role is combined with interpretative elements.

At the same time and in contrast to most Western liberal democracies, we found a general decrease in political cynicism among the Dutch electorate after 1994, indicating a possible effect of the changes in the substantiveness of television news. A clear causal link with watching news programmes, however, could not be found. Watching commercial RTL news seemed to increase cynicism, but as it turns out, RTL viewers were more cynical to begin with. The ambiguity in political journalism is repeated, if not reflected, in the attitude of the Dutch to politics. So, is the Netherlands the odd one out in a general climate of malaise in political communication? Let us look at a few possible explanations.

First, contrary to developments in Italy (see Chapter 4 by Roncarolo), the Netherlands is still very much characterised by consensual politics. There is hardly any negative campaigning or, in general, an adversarial political culture such as exists in the USA and UK. The country combines a multi-party, first-past-the-post, coalition government political system with, ultimately, a popular belief in the benevolent state, entrusted with guaranteeing the public interest. With a changing media system and non-adversarial politics giving little food for scandal, this may explain why journalists adopt more the interpretative mode than a scoop-and-entertainment form of market-driven political journalism.

Second, Dutch television journalism is still very much embedded in the strong tradition of public broadcasting. The cultural–pedagogic logic of reporting on what people are supposed to 'need' to participate as informed citizens in a democratic society, rather than what they may want to see, is still a socialising factor, even for journalists working for commercial television. That may well change, as new generations of journalists not 'tainted' by that tradition enter the profession. The news output of the second commercial channel, SBS6, in the 1998 elections did point to much stronger entertaining elements in news reporting: their news values were based on what people wanted, or at least what they assumed their viewers liked or would enjoy. With declining political interest, especially among the young, and competition for viewers, this change in political reporting styles may well be followed by the other news programmes.

Third, we may be looking at the wrong programmes and the wrong journalists. Is the future of political communication, and the cynical approach for that matter, not to be found in and influenced by the info-tainment genre? As it turns out, in both 1994 and 1998 Dutch politicians made only limited appearances on talk and entertainment shows which contained elements of political information. More than two-thirds of their television exposure was on traditional news and current affairs programmes. Moreover, when they did appear on the breakfast, coffee and evening talk shows, they got a better chance to say what they wanted to say: they had more time and were seldom critically interrupted. They often used these opportunities to substantiate their views on issues and their empathy with problems phoned in by viewers (Brants, Cabri and Nijens 2000).

Finally, does this mean that we are looking at the wrong elements? Cynicism and conflicts are concepts which are highly culturally determined. The journalistic approach to politics in the Netherlands seemed to us, if anything, to be more ironical than cynical. The style could be confrontational – interviewing politicians with questions that in other cultures might look cynical. However, often these seemed more driven by a desire to get a clear picture of party political differences than an expression of distrust or, even worse, disgust. That may well be the background of the conflict-orientation we have seen in much campaign reporting as well. Are differences fought out in the public sphere not the bread and butter of politics, certainly at election time? And is bringing this out in a culture of consensus which tends to cover up disagreements not the obligation of every political journalist? If that is so, the picture of political journalism in the Netherlands may not be so bad after all.

Notes

1 Dutch National Election Studies 1977, 1982, 1986, 1989, 1994, 1998. These can be obtained from Niwi (www.niwi.knaw.nl). The measure of political cynicism is based on a 4-point scale (zero is 'low', three is 'high political cynicism'), developed from three questions: 'politicians promise more than they can deliver',

'ministers are primarily self-interested', and 'to become an MP, friends are more important than abilities'. Media use is based on a 4-point scale (one indicating 'watches programme less than once a week' and four indicating 'watches programme almost daily').

2 There are other variables controlled for, but these are not included in the table because of lack of space. These are adherence to an opposition party, gender, religion, income, occupation and social class.

References

Altheide, D. and Snow, R. (1979) *Media Logic*, Beverly Hills, Calif.: Sage.

Ansolabehere, S. and Iyengar, S. (1995) *Going Negative: How Political Advertisements Shrink and Polarise the Electorate*, New York: Free Press.

Bennett, L.W. (1998) 'The UnCivic Culture: communication, identity, and the rise of life style politics', *PS: Political Science and Politics* 31: 741–62.

Blumler, J.G. and Gurevitch, M. (1995) *The Crisis of Public Communication*, London: Routledge.

Blumler, J.G. and Kavanagh, D. (1999) 'The third age of political communication: influences and features', *Political Communication* 16: 209–30.

Brants, K. (1998) 'Who's afraid of infotainment?', *European Journal of Communication* 13/3: 315–35.

Brants, K., Cabri, E. and Nijens, P. (2000) 'Hoe informatief en hoe leuk? Infotainment in de campagne' ['How informative and how entertaining? Infotainment in the campaign'], in P. van Praag and K. Brants (eds), *Tussen Beeld en Inhoud: Politiek en Media in de Verkiezingen van 1998* [Between Image and Content: Politics and Media in the Elections of 1998], Amsterdam: Het Spinhuis.

Brug, W. van der and Eijk, C. van der (2000) 'De campagne had effect, het mediagebruik niet' ['The campaign had effect, media use not'] in P. van Praag and K. Brants (eds), *Tussen Beeld en Inhoud: Politiek en Media in de Verkiezingen van 1998* [Between Image and Content: Politics and Media in the Elections of 1998], Amsterdam: Het Spinhuis.

Cappella, J.N. and Jamieson, K.H. (1997) *Spiral of Cynicism: The Press and the Public Good*, New York: Oxford University Press.

Franklin, B. (1994) *Packaging Politics*, London: Edward Arnold.

Franklin, B. (1997) *Newzak and News Media*, London: Routledge.

Hallin, D. (1992) 'Sound bite news: television coverage of the elections 1968–1988', *Journal of Communication* 42/2: 5–24.

Hallin, D. (1998) 'A fall from grace', *Media Studies Journal* 12/2: 42–7.

Holtz-Bacha, H. (1990) 'Videomalaise revisisted: media exposure and political alienation in West Germany', *European Journal of Communication* 5/5: 73–85.

Kerbel, M.R. (1999, 2nd edition) *Remote & Controlled. Media Politics in a Cynical Age*, Boulder, Colo.: Westview Press.

Kleinnijenhuis, J., Oegema, D., De Ridder, J.A. and Ruigrok, P.C. (1998) *Paarse Polarisatie. De slag om de kiezer in de media* [Pink Polarisation: The Battle for the Vote in the Media], Alphen aan den Rijn: Samson.

Lang, G.E. and Lang, K. (1968) *Television and Politics*, New York: Thomas Y. Crowell.

Mair, P. (1998) 'Representation and participation in the changing world of party politics', *European Review* 6/2: 161–74.

Mazzoleni, G. (1987) 'Media logic and party logic in campaign coverage: the Italian general election of 1983', *European Journal of Communication* 2/1: 81–103.

Norris, P. (1999) 'Blaming the messenger?' *Demokratiutredningens Skrift* 32: 99–117.

Norris, P. (2000) *A Virtuous Circle: Political Communications in Post-Industrial Democracies*, New York: Cambridge University Press.

Patterson, T.E. (1993) *Out of Order*, New York: Vintage.

Patterson, T.E. (1996) 'Bad news, bad governance', *The Annals of the American Academy of Political and Socials Science* 546: 97–109.

Pharr, S.J. and Putnam, R.D. (eds) (2000) *Disaffected Democracies: what's troubling the trilateral countries?*, Princeton: Princeton University Press.

Praag, P. van and Brants, K. (2000) 'Het televisienieuws: inhoud en strijd' [TV-news: content and struggle'], in P. van Praag and K. Brants (eds), *Tussen Beeld en Inhoud: Politiek en Media in de Verkiezingen van 1998* [Between Image and Content: Politics and Media in the Elections of 1998], Amsterdam: Het Spinhuis.

Protess, D.L., Lomax Cook, F., Doppelt, J.C., Ettema, J.S., Gordon, M.T., Leff, D.R. and Miller, P. (1991) *The Journalism of Outrage. Investigative Reporting and Agenda Building in America*, New York: The Guilford Press.

Robinson, M. (1976) 'Public Affairs Television and the Growth of Political Malaise', *American Political Science Review* 70/3: 409–32.

Sabato, L.J. (1991) *Feeding Frenzy: How Attack Journalism Has Transformed American Politics*, New York: Free Press.

Schulz, W. (1997) 'Changes of mass media and the public sphere', *Javnost/The Public* 4/2: 57–69.

Swanson, D. (1997) 'The political-media complex at 50: putting the 1996 presidential campaign in context', *American Behavioral Scientist* 40/8: 1264–82.

Part III

Changes in political journalism

An opportunity or
threat for democracy?

10 Journalism and democracy in contemporary Britain

Brian McNair

The general election of 2001 came at the end of four years of Labour government, concluding a political cycle in which several issues regarding the condition of the political public sphere in Britain remained prominent on the scholarly and journalistic agenda.[1] In relation to press bias, for example, there was once again a huge newspaper 'deficit' in the coverage of the campaign. By this I mean that only one daily newspaper (the *Daily Telegraph*), representing a mere 7.6 per cent of national daily circulation, supported a party (the Conservatives) which for all that its defeat was historic in scale still won 32.7 per cent of the vote. In contrast, Labour's 42 per cent share of the vote was backed up by editorial endorsements from newspapers representing some 56 per cent of national daily circulation. The fact that the press deficit in 2001, as it had in 1997, benefited a party of the left rather than the right (a reversal of the pattern observed during most of the preceding century) does not change the fact that there was a major discrepancy between the newspapers' voting preferences and those of their readers.

For some commentators, like Hugo Young of *The Guardian*, this pattern of editorial bias was a quite fair reflection of the Conservatives' failure to deserve the support of the people and of serious journalists. Young, indeed, found it odd that the Conservatives had been treated with anything like seriousness in newspaper coverage. 'In defiance of all the evidence', he wrote in his column towards the end of the campaign, 'the worst priced outsiders in modern political history have been given equal and massive time with the most emphatic winners since the 1983 election' (Young 2001). On the other hand, as I argued in *Journalism and Democracy* (2000a), even the most ardent opponent of the Conservatives might think it appropriate, and indeed necessary for the health of the democratic process, that a party which even at its electoral nadir still claimed the loyalty of one third of the British people should have its views and policies treated with appropriate care and attention in press coverage. Left-wing critics of pro-Conservative press bias expressed legitimate concern for the health of British democracy when they complained in the 1980s and early 1990s about the treatment dished out to Labour by Rupert Murdoch, Conrad Black and the rest. It would be shortsighted not to acknowledge the potentially damaging effects on British political culture of an overwhelmingly pro-Labour press bias, especially in an era when there is little effective parliamentary opposition to the government.

It seems certain, however, that the press deficit of 2001 will not be repeated at the next general election, whenever it comes and whatever state the Conservative and Liberal Democratic parties happen to be in. The on-going debate on the merits of Britain's entry into the Euro will put strains on the pro-Labour position of many titles, especially those like the Murdoch-owned *Sun*, which in the pre-Blair era were solidly Conservative in their editorial allegiances. The anti-Euro *Sun*, while declaring for New Labour early in the 2001 campaign (on the basis that 'our readers are not ready to give the Tories another chance – yet') was frank about its intention to declare 'all out war' on the party should it seek to bounce Britain into the single currency following its historic second-term victory. 'An early referendum [on entry to the single currency] would', its editorial warned during the election campaign, 'represent an act of political suicide' (*The Sun*, 23 May 2001). 'If Blair called one', it added a few days later, 'our opposition wouldn't just be unprecedentedly ferocious – it would be deeply, even mortally damaging to Tony, Gordon and everybody connected with the project. Don't make us do it, Prime Minister' (*The Sun*, 28 May 2001). As the Euro referendum approaches, *The Sun* and other Eurosceptic newspapers will apply their intimidating political muscle to the utmost, and New Labour will find itself at the receiving end of the same kind of treatment old Labour experienced in the 1980s and early 1990s. How this prospect might impact on Tony Blair's European policy will be one of the most interesting features of British politics in the coming years.

Meanwhile, in the debate about 'spin' – a political communication practice unjustifiably demonised by journalists who, I have suggested,[2] have their own self-interested reasons for resenting the communicative work of the political public relations practitioners – the 1997–2001 Parliament provided much food for thought. On the one hand, the sheer size of the government's political public relations apparatus grew under New Labour as the number of special advisers increased and huge sums (even greater than those allocated by the Conservatives when they were trying to sell their big privatisations in the 1980s) were spent on the marketing of governmental initiatives and schemes. The infrastructure of political information management expanded, and the behind-the-scenes power of Alistair Campbell as the Prime Minister's official spokesman was a frequent theme of critical journalistic commentary (see Chapter 3 by Kuhn).

On the other hand, the 1997–2001 government was marked by many spectacular failures at the level of presentation and the image of the invincible spin-doctor was irreversibly damaged. The latter half of the first Blair administration was marked not just by public relations disasters, such as the Prime Minister's badly received speech to the Women's Institute in 2000 and the on-going catastrophe that was the Millennium Dome, but also by the dismissal from government, for the second time, of arch-spinner Peter Mandelson. Not once, but twice in the course of a single Parliament, the much-mythologised master of the black arts of news management was brought down in a media feeding frenzy of rumours and allegations which seemed to fly in the face of his reputation as a political communicator *par excellence.*[3] Mandelson's ministerial demise was only the most obvious example of how those whom New Labour minister Clare Short once called 'the people who live in the dark' looked rather less threatening to democracy when confronted with the realities of ministerial power and governmental responsibility than they had appeared (to some, at least) in opposition. In the 2001 election, most commentators agreed, the spin-doctors had a bad campaign, and by its end the sinister aura which had long surrounded their activities was replaced with a more pragmatic acceptance that these were fallible human beings, just as capable of screwing up as anybody else.

The 1997–2001 Parliament also generated much new material in the discussion – high on the evaluative agenda of *Journalism and Democracy* – of how and with what effect on the quality of democracy journalists exercise their normative 'watchdog' role of scrutiny, or critical publicity, in coverage of the political process. Do they – did they in 1997–2001 – concentrate on the appropriate themes and issues in their political news? Did they prioritise the 'serious' matters of public life over the trivial concerns of 'infotainment'? Did they prefer to report matters of style over substance, and performance over policy, or were they striving to do their best to exercise their Fourth Estate responsibilities in the face of what some commentators perceived to be an unprecedentedly manipulative governmental information machine? Are the competing emphases mutually exclusive, or can coverage of performance be a valuable resource in the assessment of policy, and reviews of political style help us to assess substance?

In a letter to the *Daily Telegraph* published during the 2001 campaign, the Deputy Director of BBC News noted that 'we expect our political journalists to provide context and interpretation. The audience is properly served by journalists attempting to disentangle the claims and counter-claims that characterise political debate, particularly at election time' (*Daily Telegraph*, 1 June 2001). Were these expectations met in the course of the 1997–2001 Parliament and in the June 2001 election campaign? Before addressing these questions[4] let me briefly recap on the arguments central to *Journalism and Democracy*.

The *Journalism and Democracy* thesis

This work emerged from a growing awareness amongst political communication scholars in Europe that by the late 1990s the still commonplace application of what is sometimes characterised as the 'critical paradigm' to the study of political communication – a paradigm which imposes a framework of cultural pessimism on both scholarly and journalistic thinking about the subject[5] – was overlooking some important and positive changes in the structure and content of the public sphere. The critical discourses encapsulated in terms such as 'dumbing down', 'Americanisation' and 'tabloidisation' and the anxieties expressed by so many about the rise of 'infotainment' and the decline of 'serious' political journalism seemed curiously reminiscent of the elite disdain for popular culture which goes back to the emergence of mass literacy in the nineteenth century, and is so eloquently critiqued in Carey's *The Intellectuals and the Masses* (1992).

Although I took care to distinguish my rejection of this paradigm from the nihilism of Baudrillard's dismissal of all 'bourgeois' concerns for the quality of liberal democracy (and the associated demand for 'rational communication') (Baudrillard 1983), I sympathised with his view that there is something deeply condescending in the presumption that we – the intellectual elite, in the academy, the media and elsewhere – know what is best for the mass of the people in political communication or indeed any other form of culture. I shared his impatience with the frequently expressed view that the public sphere is in some kind of 'crisis', preferring to characterise this as a 'crisis of mass representation'. By this I was referring to on-going elite anxiety, or moral panic, about the cultural consequences of mass democracy.

Journalism and Democracy questioned the normative foundation on which most assertions about the decline of political communication were based (which I argued to be judgements based on taste and aesthetics rather than objective criteria of what kinds of political communication were optimal for the health of the democratic process), and presented an alternative, more positive evaluation of the political public sphere as we approached the end of a century of unprecedented democratic progress. The twentieth century, one should remember, saw the extension of voting rights to women in advanced capitalist societies, to blacks in the USA and South Africa and to the populations of the former USSR and its Warsaw Pact allies in Europe. It witnessed transitions from right-authoritarianism to democratic governments in Central and South America, Taiwan and South Korea. How could the evidence of such progress be reconciled with the pessimism of those, such as Blumler and Franklin in the UK (Blumler and Gurevitch 1995; Franklin 1994), Fallows and Hart in the USA (Fallows 1996; Hart 1987) or Bourdieu in France (Bourdieu 1998), that we were living through a 'crisis' of political communication which was undermining democracy? My argument was that it could not, and that the pessimists were wrong in their assessments of the trends.

That conclusion was based on an extended quantitative and qualitative evaluation of the public sphere. Quantitatively, I pointed out what was beyond dispute even to the most pessimistic of commentators – that the public sphere had expanded exponentially in the final years of the twentieth century, as multi-channel and digital communication technologies were introduced to mass consumer markets comprised (in relative historical terms, at least) of highly-educated, choice-rich citizens with unprecedented access to the new technologies of information and communication. Cable and satellite television and radio, in the first instance, and then the internet had created a public sphere of 'practically infinite size', containing within it more information than any individual could possibly access or absorb. As Pavlik noted, 'news junkies have never had it so good' (1999: 54), and media audiences in general now had 'access to much more news and information than any previous generation'. More recently, Barnett and Gaber's *Westminster Politics*, a book which is generally pessimistic in tone, acknowledges that 'there is more space given to politics over the airwaves or through the computer cable than has ever been the case' (2001: 81).

Some critics argued that this access was and would remain far from universal, since advanced capitalist societies continue to harbour two-tier information spheres in which the relatively less-educated, lower-income groups do not participate fully. But by the late 1990s this traditional objection to the democratising effects of new information and communication technologies was outdated – a pessimistic 'rhetoric of recurrence' which has accompanied every leap in communication technology since the invention of the printing press. When cable and satellite television were introduced in the 1980s similar arguments were voiced. Only the affluent middle classes would be able to afford these services, it was predicted, or be interested in using them. As it turned out, of course, the success of Rupert Murdoch's Sky operation in the UK was founded on blue-collar and working-class demand for the enhanced access to televised football and light entertainment which it provided (and the profits from which, ironically, subsidised Murdoch's 24-hour news channel). Elsewhere, home shopping and lifestyle channels fuelled the development of multi-channel television. The biggest users of cable and satellite in its early years were precisely those who the intellectuals had predicted would be marginalised by the information revolution.

Similar concerns were raised by the emergence of the internet a few years later. The poor and the poorly educated would be excluded from the digital revolution, as they had been excluded from all previous waves of technological development. Optimistic projections of its spread were said to be naive and utopian. By 2001, however, following the pattern of cable and satellite, computers and internet access were commonplace consumer items across income and social class categories throughout the advanced capitalist world, and certainly not the preserve of the well-educated middle classes. In developing countries such as India and China, faced with particular economic and geographical problems, the internet was proving to be a powerful educational tool (although, of course, economic constraints and – in the case of China – anxieties about its destabilising political effects inhibited its spread). If it is still too early to predict quite how the internet will be used in the longer term, and by whom, there can be no doubt of its emerging status as the newest mass medium, and that access to it will shortly be as commonplace as the telephone, the television and the video cassette recorder.

Moreover, none of this has been at the expense of the traditional media of political communication. In Britain, for example, despite the dire warnings of the 'death of print'[6] frequently heard in the late 1990s, there was no evidence of serious decline in the circulations of broadsheet newspapers (McNair 1999), nor of declining journalistic interest in 'serious' matters like politics. Politics, as interviews with political editors and others cited in *Journalism and Democracy* revealed, remained the backbone of 'quality' British print journalism, routinely dominating the news agenda. The editorial resources devoted to politics, in both print and electronic media, had if anything increased since Jeremy Tunstall's *Newspaper Power* (1996) noted a rapid expansion in the number of political journalists supported by the UK press. This increase was a consequence of the simple fact that, in the more intensely competitive media market which the information revolution had generated, credibility in this area of coverage was a key 'brand' factor for media organisations which wished to be perceived as 'quality'. The 1990s had seen an explosion of political commentary and analysis, as well as an increase in the numbers of correspondents and reporters dedicated to coverage of the political process. In this sense, and in opposition to the opponents of journalistic commodification or commercialisation, I argued that the economics of cultural capitalism were working in favour of political journalism, not against it.

Although some traditional forms of political journalism, notably the verbatim coverage of parliamentary debates which once occupied substantial portions of the broadsheet newspapers, had indeed disappeared from the British press in the 1990s, they had turned up on the internet (the on-line version of *Hansard*), and on BBC Parliament (formerly the Parliamentary Channel) – a cable channel devoted exclusively to coverage of legislative debates not just in the British parliament, but in the Scottish, Welsh and European legislatures. The USA has long had C-Span, and similar media outlets for 'gavel-to-gavel' coverage of representative assemblies exist in many countries.

However, to show that the political public sphere is expanding is not the same thing as demonstrating its improvement as a tool in the pursuit of democratic government. To do that required qualitative evaluation of the extent to which this rapidly evolving communicative space could service what Chambers and Costain call 'deliberative democracy', by constituting 'a healthy public sphere where citizens can exchange ideas, acquire knowledge and information, confront public problems, exercise public accountability, discuss policy options, challenge the powerful without fear of reprisals, and defend principles' (2000: xi). *Journalism and Democracy* assessed the quality of political journalism in relation to such indices as the proportion of its subject matter devoted to policy matters as opposed to political process or the 'trivia and fluff' of public life. It assessed the extent to which political media extended what Habermas called critical publicity, or scrutiny (account-ability) to political elites. It considered the degree of access to information, analysis and debate which the contemporary public sphere provided to the citizenry as a whole. And it examined the implications for political journalism of the rise of 'spin', and the changing dynamics of the relation-ship between journalists and the political news managers on which the demonology of spin is founded.

These qualitative dimensions in the performance of political journalism were assessed through analyses of a range of journalistic genres, includ-ing 'straight' news reportage, commentary columns, interview and access formats. At the end of it all, I concluded that, if things were far from perfect (resource constraints and economic pressures were signalled as a serious threat to the capacity of political media to do their job properly), neither were they nearly as bad as the pessimists thought. Indeed, the political public sphere was both bigger (in quantitative terms) and better (qualitatively) than at any previous period in capitalism's cultural history. Whether measured by the decline of journalistic deference towards political elites, the quantity of political information in circulation, or the ease of access to that information which proliferating media channels provided for the population as a whole (regardless of whether or not audiences chose to access it), turn-of-the-millennium capitalism was a very different beast from the disenfranchised mass ignorance of just a hundred years ago.

In the light of this assessment, the start of a new millennium was a good time to break out of the critical paradigm and begin to consider not just what the political media were doing *to* the people that was bad, but what they were doing *for* them that was good (or at least beneficial to the democratic process). And to ask, too, what the people might henceforth do with their political media. 'Now that the people have unprecedented access to information about politics', I asked, 'what do they do with it?' I had no answer to that question, of course (nor, to be fair, has anyone else), though the elections of 2000 and 2001 in the US and the UK respectively provide some new data which might help in providing one. Despite the widespread availability in both Britain and the United States of huge quantities of political information, both contests produced historically low voter turnouts, read by some as clear evidence in support of the pessimistic 'crisis' thesis (I will return to the phenomenon of voter apathy below).

Cultural pessimism or panglossian optimism?

One reviewer described *Journalism and Democracy* as 'tinged with millennial optimism'[7] which I can live with, and 'panglossian', which I will respectfully contest, since the book's argument was not that 'all is for the best in the best of all possible worlds' but simply that a critical re-orientation away from the unrelenting pessimism of most scholarly analysis of the contemporary political media is overdue. And in arguing for that shift of perspective I do not thereby advocate, to quote another reviewer, 'acceptance of a media ordering of the world, disabling of any alternative view',[8] but intellectual engagement with the democratic possibilities offered by the emerging media environment. If the public sphere has been transformed in ways which are significant, the critical project must adapt to that change if it is to retain any political relevance (and it must be relevant, if it is to be deserving of an audience beyond the elite ranks of the scholarly community).

That means, in practice, being much less dismissive of the new forms of mass engagement with politics which the evolving public sphere provides and, instead of always reaching for the lazy rhetoric of 'dumbing down', 'Americanisation' and their related terms, recognising that in contemporary conditions the institutions of the media are increasingly where politics happens, for better or worse, and that political communication in a democracy must be permitted to reflect the languages and registers of the ordinary people who comprise the modern democratic polity.

In the British general election of 2001, for example, journalists were rightly critical of the degree of media control exerted by the parties in their respective campaigns. Political reporters complained that they were shepherded around the country in battle buses and campaign planes, kept at distance from the candidates and prevented from asking the kinds of probing questions which elections are ideally supposed to allow. The journalists were bored with the predictability of the campaign, and so were their audiences – a factor which probably did not cause (but certainly did nothing to counteract) the historically low turnouts recorded on polling day (below 50 per cent in many constituencies).

Thank goodness, then, for the kind of political infotainment thrown up by the aggressive political interview (a feature of broadcast journalism in the UK since Robin Day invented it in the 1960s, but which became much more prominent a feature of the political public sphere in the late 1990s). In *Journalism and Democracy* I had argued that because of their unpredictability and 'liveness' in an era of 'hyperactive news management' such interviews were becoming 'an increasingly important forum, where political actors can be confronted with questions and issues they might rather see left alone' (McNair 2000a: 104). I defended the democratic contribution of the adversarial political interview against those who have dismissed the 'hyperadversarialism' of the form and the increasingly confrontational, gladiatorial style of its best-known practitioners.

This issue arose again in the course of the 2001 British general election, when an apparently invincible Labour government lacked any serious obstacle to its onward march, except for the vigorous probings its representatives received at the hands of broadcast interviewers whenever they entered a television or radio studio. In those conditions, the aggressive political interview came into its own as a source, not just of more than usually entertaining campaign coverage, but of serious democratic scrutiny. Jeremy Paxman's *Newsnight* interviews with William Hague and Tony Blair put both on the defensive. Hague's demeanour of weary resignation in the face of Paxman persuaded many pro-Tory commentators who saw the interview that the game really was up. Blair's defensive, evasive answers to Paxman's questions about inequality and taxation contrasted with his generally polished and typically 'nice' performances at press conferences and other staged media events.

One of the UK's most experienced political interviewers, John Humphrys of the BBC, asked in his *Sunday Times* column a few days after Labour had been granted a record second term majority of 165 by the British voters: 'who will save the nation from elective dictatorship?' To which he replied, with tongue only slightly in cheek, 'We will. We broadcasters, with our fearless interrogation of those in power, will champion the cause of freedom' (Humphrys 2001), though he accepted that adversarial journalists were not a substitute for an effective parliamentary opposition: 'Journalism should be about something quite different. It is about trying to illuminate what politicians might want to keep in the dark. It is about providing an extra means by which to make politicians accountable.'

And if, in the pursuit of that accountability, some interviewers have a tendency to grandstand, and may occasionally overdo their expressions of world-weary cynicism (as Jeremy Paxman once put it, when describing his approach to politicians in interviews, 'why is that lying bastard lying to me?'), better that than the deferential, supine interviewing styles of a few years ago. This democratic function was exemplified by the tenacity of Paxman, Humphrys and others in the course of the 2001 campaign.

Humphrys conceded, in a gesture to the critics of his and others' 'hyperadversarialism', that the broadcast interview had become more 'demotic' in recent years. But, he went on to argue, this was an inevitable and probably necessary by-product of the form's emergence as a key channel of popular political communication in a modern public sphere. If the political interview is increasingly expected to attract and engage the people in scrutiny of their political elites, he argued (and who disputes that this is at least one of its goals in a liberal democracy?), 'it must include the widest audience, and not go over the heads of the majority. It must link to their world, to the world in which tabloid newspapers are read, as well as the *Telegraph* and *Times* and *Guardian*. And the more demotic political interviewing becomes, the more likely it is that that it will adopt some of the values of showbiz' (Humphrys 2001). And if that is the price of attracting an audience, he implies, so be it. 'Interviews should tell us a bit more about policies. They should also tell us a bit more about personalities.'

Politicians know the potential value to their campaigns of spontaneous, 'live' media appearances in which they are visibly facing down no-nonsense journalists like Paxman and Humphrys. But these are only valuable as tools of political communication to the extent that they are 'live' and spontaneous, which means that they always carry the potential for disappointment and even disaster. The off-the-cuff response to a difficult interview question may produce the impression of strength and determination, or it may come across as arrogant and ill-judged. Broadcast as it was just a few days before the election on June 7, and given the relatively small audience of *Newsnight*, Paxman's interrogation of Blair was never likely to have much of an impact on the outcome of the campaign. But for those who watched it, there was insight into an aspect of the Prime Minister's personality and leadership style which this viewer at least considered to be of value in assessing him and, what is more important, his party's election platform.

The contribution of access programmes

Alongside the political interview, and for many of the same reasons, public access to politicians, channeled through the media, has an important and increasing role to play in the democratic process, as the 2001 election illustrated. *Journalism and Democracy* noted a trend in political communication which is by now obvious: in an age when the tradition of public meetings and town hall hustings has largely gone, and when politicians are generally protected from spontaneous encounters with ordinary people, mediated access – mediated chiefly through the electronic channels of television, radio and the internet – is the closest most people come to engaging with those who are competing for their votes. There is in British electoral politics an emerging tradition of political leaders facing media audiences in adversarial, interrogatory contexts where they must answer to the people, or at least to a sampled public. Bourdieu called French access television a 'charade' in his pessimistic book-length essay *On Television and Journalism* (1998). In Britain, however, and especially during elections, access broadcasting has become a key moment in the critical scrutiny of politicians.

Where the American campaign highlights the 'live' presidential debate, British political leaders shy away from head-to-head confrontations outside the highly ritualised chamber of the House of Commons (where, of course, they regularly debate with each other in parliamentary debates). Unlike US presidential candidates, however, they do submit themselves to encounters with small groups of people who have been selected as representative of the population as a whole. They may not want to do so because, as with broadcast interviews, the form removes much of the control over presentation which the modern politician is used to. They must appear on these programmes, nonetheless, because the UK's political culture expects it of them, and because their competitors are doing so.

BBC television has the flagship *Question Time*, presented by David Dimbleby, on which all the main party leaders appeared during the 2001 campaign (special programmes gave the leaders of the nationalist parties in Scotland and Wales the same opportunity). On ITV the other Dimbleby, Jonathan, hosted a series of *Ask the Leader* debates. On BBC network radio there were *Election Call* and the *Nikki Campbell Show*, where listeners phoned in with questions to the various leaders as they took their turn on 'live' unedited air. Scotland and other localities had similar programmes for their local candidates.

These programmes, often backed up with on-line question-and-answer sessions, provided significant moments of public access to the political leaders during the 2001 contest, if only because there were so few such moments elsewhere in the campaign. To an even greater degree than in the carefully choreographed election of 1997, these programmes provided venues in which candidates met 'real people', as unsuccessful Tory leader William Hague took to calling the great British public in his doomed effort to portray himself as the bearer of a 'common sense revolution'. They were the only times, in fact (apart from the aforementioned political interviews), when the spin-doctors and the news managers had to be left at the door and the politicians were obliged to deal with unpredictable situations (with some notable examples, such as the infamous moment in the 2001 campaign when Deputy Prime Minister John Prescott punched a protesting farmworker who had thrown an egg at him; or the occasion when Tony Blair was confronted in the full glare of the cameras by an irate relative of a cancer patient who had, she believed, been let down by the NHS). The following exchange took place during the BBC's *Question Time* interrogation of Tony Blair:

Questioner: Your manifesto promises for the health service are very much echoes of four years ago. Given this is a clear indication of your failure to achieve the results you wanted, why should we trust you again?

Blair: We made, actually, pretty limited promises four years ago, in respect of waiting lists in particular. But I've got absolutely no doubt at all we've still got a massive amount to do in the National Health Service –

Dimbleby: You said 48 hours to save the National Health, didn't you?

Blair: I said 24 hours, in fact.

Dimbleby: Well that's quite a big promise.

Blair: But I didn't say within 24 hours I'd transform the whole of the National Health Service. What I said was . . . [Blair goes on to defend his record in government].

This was polite compared to a later intervention from a woman whose child urgently required specialist health care.

Questioner: Will you make a commitment tonight that you will put some funding into the bone marrow registries? Our child is desperately needing a bone marrow transplant. She's gonna die without that. Will you make that commitment and help us save her life?

Blair: I can't give you a specific commitment on bone marrow. I can give you a commitment on health service spending. I'm sure . . . .

Questioner
(angrily):   No, it's not good enough, Mr Blair, it's not good enough. We've heard this time and time again . . . [goes on to recount negative experience in securing access to bone marrow treatment on the NHS]. It should not be down to individuals like us campaigning to get donors on registers. It is not good enough. Your government needs to do the campaigning.

I am not suggesting that these exchanges, and the performances of the politicians as they seek to deal with them (and performances they were, reviewed as such by media commentators and audiences alike), made any difference to the outcome of the election on June 7. As had been the case in 1997, the pattern of actual voting in 2001 was very similar to that predicted in opinion polls weeks, even months, in advance of polling day. Most people, it seems, had made up their minds about which party they would be voting for, and why, long before they had a chance to rate the performance of Blair, Hague or the Liberal Democrat leader Charles Kennedy in a 'live' media situation. New Labour never looked like losing in 2001, and there seems little that the party leaders could have done in these programmes to change that fact. But the broadcasts provided rare opportunities, for political journalists on the one hand and public audiences on the other, to deviate from pre-rehearsed campaign scripts. They allowed those people who wished to do so to engage, albeit by proxy, in real dialogue with those who would be their Prime Minister and who were otherwise largely protected from the inconveniences of 'reality intrusion'.

The significance of this engagement increases in an era when traditional forms of democratic participation, such as voting and party membership, are in decline. In June 2001, as noted above, only about 60 per cent of those British citizens entitled to vote did so. This has been interpreted by some as evidence of broad public satisfaction with the state of things in Labour's Britain, such that many people simply did not feel the need to vote. Others see it as an index of deep dissatisfaction with politics, which is leading now to conscious withdrawal from the democratic process by unprecedented numbers of people. This trend is often attributed to the negative effects of 'mediated democracy' in all its forms – the relentless spin, soundbites, and 'promotional rhetoric' masquerading as policy debate; the political marketing and focus groups; and the presentation which often obscures political honesty. It may of course be that with European and devolved assemblies now up and running, there are just too many elections for people to follow with enthusiasm. Or it may be that in Britain, as has long been the case in the USA, the policy and ideological differences between the parties have become so minor that people genuinely feel it does not matter who they vote for.

It is too soon to assert with any confidence which, if any, of these explanations for the low turnout of 2001 is correct, and we must await the next electoral cycle to see if the trend will be confirmed. But the critical re-orientation to which I have referred means recognising that people cannot be force-fed democracy, and that even in an age of enhanced media coverage of and access to politics, people may have good reasons for choosing not to vote. Access to information about politics may turn people off voting as much as it turns them on. If it does so, it is probably not the fault of the journalists, though the media clearly have a role in engaging and mobilising citizens to the greatest degree possible. Aggressive, adversarial journalism, in the form of tough interviewing techniques and irreverent access shows, may be ways of doing so, in so far as they constitute visible displays of the vulnerability and accessibility of political elites, and feed back to the people images of themselves in the act of debating with politicians. In *Journalism and Democracy* I argued that, for better or worse, for the great majority of averagely active people, 'the media are politics, and politics are the media' (2000a: ix). If that is so (and the UK election of 2001 produced no evidence to suggest that it is not), interview and access formats can be expected to become an increasingly important arena for democratic participation in the age of mediated politics.[9]

Conclusion

The evidence of a decline in voting numbers across Europe and North America certainly requires careful analysis in the years to come, and it may be found that contemporary trends in political communication – whether one means by that the communication practices of the political elites or of the journalistic media which transmit them to the public at large – have a role to play in turning people off that most basic form of democratic participation. I suspect that the reasons why fewer people are voting than have the right to do so will turn out to be more complex than anything said or written by poltical journalists, and are associated with deeper cultural and ideological trends in the development of twenty-first century capitalism. That said, the democratic role of political journalism – especially its interactive, confrontational, even gladiatorial forms – in mobilising popular interest in and engagement with the political process cannot be under-estimated.

Notes

1 My paper on journalism and democracy given at the EPCR's joint sessions of workshops in early 2000 was published in *Journalism Studies* (McNair 2000b). Rather than reprint it here, the editors of this volume invited me to revisit both it and the book on *Journalism and Democracy* of which it was a kind of summary (McNair 2000a). I have taken the opportunity to reflect on events since those publications were researched and written, to cover the period up to and including the 2001 British general election.
2 See McNair (2000a and 2001).
3 Mandelson retained his parliamentary seat of Hartlepool in the 2001 general election and so survived to fight another day.

4   I do not claim my arguments as presented here to have the weight of considered scholarly analysis. They are more of an informed first draft, written in the weeks immediately after the 2001 election and before the benefits of hindsight could be felt.

5   For a recent book-length analysis of the intellectual phenomenon of cultural pessimism, see Bennett (2001).

6   See McNair (1998) for a chapter-length discussion of the impact of new information technologies on traditional print media.

7   See review by Granville Williams (2001) *Journalism* 2/1: 109.

8   See review by Michael Bromley (2000) *European Journal of Communication* 15/4: 554.

9   See work on 'mediated access' conducted by the author with colleagues at Stirling University as part of the Economic and Social Research Council's Democracy and Participation programme (project reference L215252016).

References

Barnett, S. and Gaber, I. (2001) *Westminster Tales: The Twenty-first-century Crisis in Political Journalism*, London: Continuum.

Baudrillard, J. (1983) *In the Shadow of the Silent Majorities*, New York: Semiotext.

Bennett, O. (2001) *Cultural Pessimism: Narratives of Decline in the Postmodern World*, Edinburgh: Edinburgh University Press.

Blumler, J.G. and Gurevitch, M. (1995) *The Crisis of Public Communication*, London: Routledge.

Bourdieu, P. (1998) *On Television and Journalism*, London: Pluto.

Carey, J. (1992) *The Intellectuals and the Masses*, London: Faber and Faber.

Chambers, S. and Costain, A. (eds) (2000) *Deliberation, Democracy and the Media*, Boulder: Rowman & Littlefield.

Fallows, J. (1996) *Breaking the News*, New York: Pantheon Press.

Franklin, B. (1994) *Packaging Politics*, London: Edward Arnold.

Hart, R.P. (1987) *The Sound of Leadership: Presidential Communication in the Modern Age*, Chicago: University of Chicago Press.

Humphrys, J. (2001) 'Interviewers aren't really the opposition, whatever they say', *The Sunday Times*, 17 June.

McNair, B. (1998) *The Sociology of Journalism*, London: Arnold.

McNair, B. (1999, 3rd edition) *News and Journalism in the UK*, London: Routledge.

McNair, B. (2000a) *Journalism and Democracy: An Evaluation of the Political Public Sphere*, London: Routledge.

McNair, B. (2000b) 'Journalism and democracy: a millenial audit', *Journalism Studies* 1/2: 197–211.

McNair, B. (2001) 'Public relations and broadcast news: an evolutionary approach', in M. Bromley (ed.) *No News is Bad News*, London: Pearson.

Pavlik, J.V. (1999) 'New media and news: implications for the future of journalism', *New Media and Society* 1/1: 54–9.

Tunstall, J. (1996) *Newspaper Power*, Oxford: Clarendon Press.

Young, H. (2001) 'We too have twisted the truth', *The Guardian*, 1 June.

11 Repositioning the newsroom

The American experience with 'public journalism'

Theodore L. Glasser and
Francis L.F. Lee

'Public' or 'civic' journalism denotes a loosely organised reform movement aimed at getting the American press to rethink its commitment to the ideals of democratic participation. It offers an arguably new approach to political journalism, an informal set of policies and plans animated by what Rosen (1995b: 2), one of its chief architects, views as a key but neglected proposition: 'journalism cannot remain valuable if public life does not remain viable.' Rooted in a concern for what any number of commentators in the United States regard as 'the disreputable state of contemporary democratic dialogue' (Post 1993: 654), public journalism rests on the simple but apparently controversial premise that the purpose of the press is to promote and indeed improve, and not merely report on and complain about, the quality of public or civic life.[1]

As a self-conscious effort to engage journalists in a discussion about what might be done to foster greater citizen involvement in the affairs of the community, the nascent claims of public journalism began to emerge in 1989 when Rosen, then a junior member of the journalism faculty at New York University, spoke in Des Moines, Iowa, at the annual Associated Press Managing Editors meeting. What 'makes news matter to citizens', Rosen said, are the very activities journalists cover but seldom nurture:

> The newspaper of the future will have to rethink its relationship to all the institutions that nourish public life, from libraries to universities to cafes. It will have to do more than 'cover' these institutions when they happen to make news. It will have to do more than print their advertisements. The newspaper must see that its own health is dependent on the health of the dozens of other agencies which pull people out of their private worlds. For the greater the pull of public life, the greater the need for the newspaper. Empty streets are bad for editors, despite the wealth of crime news they may generate. The emptier the streets, the emptier the newspaper will seem to readers barricaded in their private homes . . .
>
> (Rosen 1989: 18)

Pleasantly surprised by the enthusiastic response from at least some of the editors who heard his Des Moines comments, Rosen soon received and eagerly accepted invitations to other meetings, including a fateful conference in New York in 1991 sponsored by the Kettering Foundation and Syracuse University. There Rosen met Davis Merritt, then editor of the *Wichita Eagle,* a small mid-western daily owned by the Knight Ridder newspaper chain. The *Eagle* had just completed a project, 'Your Vote Counts', which Merritt regarded as 'an unabashed and activist effort to restore some role for citizens in the election process' (Merritt 1995a: 3–4). It succeeded in improving readers' understanding of key campaign issues and in increasing voter turnout for the state's gubernatorial election. As Rosen and Merritt spoke at the meeting, each saw in the other a kindred spirit; they understood journalism and its role in society from vastly different perspectives, and yet they shared a sense of urgency about the importance of changing the way newsrooms positioned themselves in their communities. Merritt, an experienced reporter and editor with little in the way of academic credentials, and Rosen, a recently minted communication studies PhD whose newsroom experience amounted to a summer internship with the *Buffalo Courier Express* in upstate New York, began a partnership that would over the next several years devote itself to developing what Rosen (1995a: 22) later described as the three dimensions of public journalism: 'an argument, a practice, and a movement'.

By the end of 1993 Merritt had sought and received an unprecedented sabbatical from Knight Ridder 'to be left totally free for a full year' to think about matters concerning journalism and democracy (Merritt 1995a: 10) – and, as it turned out, to write one of the first books on public journalism (Merritt 1995b). Meanwhile, Rosen had secured a grant from the Knight Foundation to create the Project on Public Life and the Press, a broadly defined research and outreach centre that 'would conduct seminars for journalists, research the relevant experiments, and work out a philosophy for those who wanted to move in a civic direction' (Rosen 1999b: 61).[2] Now eager to put 'the cause' in 'readable form' and tired of calling it 'this thing' (Rosen 1999b: 72), Rosen and Merritt issued a pamphlet (Rosen and Merritt 1994), which they half jokingly called their manifesto, that outlined in two separate essays and a joint introduction the 'theory and practice' of what they henceforth agreed to call 'public journalism'.[3]

The 'manifesto' pointed to the diminished quality of 'politics and public life in America' and invited the press to think about what it could do to improve the situation: 'if changes are necessary for America to meet its problems and strengthen its democracy, then journalism is one of the agencies that must change' (Rosen and Merritt 1994). Careful not to claim too much for journalism, Rosen and Merritt called on journalists to reconsider their role in the community; to find ways to engage readers, viewers, and listeners as citizens with a stake in the issues of the day; and to treat problems in a manner that highlighted the prospects for their resolution. However, Rosen and Merritt stopped short of providing a detailed account of what public journalism intended to accomplish. Indeed, public journalism did not then, does not now, and probably will never exist as a fully formed theory of the press. It instead began and continues to develop around a handful of propositions and a series of open-ended questions. To the satisfaction of some and the consternation of others, public journalism serves more as a compass that points journalists in a particular direction than a map that tells them what path to follow; or, to shift metaphors and cite the rationale for a book devoted to 'doing' public journalism, its purpose is 'to raise consciousness rather than to spell out a faith' (Charity 1995: 14).

The claims of public journalism

Rosen, Merritt and other proponents of public journalism insist that their plans for a better journalism rest entirely on what interested and sympathetic journalists find compelling: 'If public journalism doesn't resonate with journalists then it doesn't really exist' (Rosen 1995a: 23). Unlike other attempts to reform the American press, which too often defined problems and proposed solutions with little or no regard for how journalists might respond, public journalism directed its appeal immediately and directly to everyday journalists.[4] It sought to create and sustain a conversation with them about what could be done in and for newsrooms that had evidently become, in the parlance of public journalism, 'disconnected' from their communities; a conversation that empowered journalists by involving them in decisions about how, then and there, public journalism could be put into practice. From this Merritt (1995b: 124) concluded that any attempt to 'codify a set of public journalism rules' would be an 'arrogant exercise, a limiting one': journalists who accept the challenge of public journalism need to 'develop their own rules over time and through experience'. Rosen, too, expects public journalism to develop from the ground up, which is why he decided to abandon his 'theoretical framework' and instead approached reporters and editors 'pragmatically' with an invitation to participate in an on-going 'experiment':

> I used to be a media critic, and here's how I worked: I would observe what the press does, filter it through my theoretical framework – essentially, my dissertation – and then write about the results. You can discover a lot that way, but there's a problem. Journalists haven't read your dissertation; they don't have your framework. So whatever you discover is of little interest to them. After all, they have deadlines to meet.
> . . . I now employ a different method: I operate almost completely through the medium of conversation. My theoretical framework becomes whatever is needed to keep the conversation progressing.

> Public journalism is something journalists themselves must carry
> forward. What I think it should be doesn't matter as much as the
> version of it I can share with reporters, editors, and news executives
> around the country.
>
> (Rosen 1995a: 23)

This reluctance to define it with any precision leaves public journalism
malleable enough to find some acceptance in any number of newsrooms. It
means that journalists get to decide by themselves and for themselves what
forms of reform, if any, need to be implemented. Yet it also leaves public
journalism open to divergent and even irreconcilable interpretations.
Whatever can be said of the virtues of approaching public journalism as
a public 'adventure', one with 'no fixed goals, no directing agency, no
clear formula for success' (Rosen 1999a: 23), the *idea* of public journalism
remains in a state of disarray. If Rosen's recent book (Rosen 1999b) on the
development of public journalism, written a decade after the movement
began, arrives as what one reviewer calls 'the most intellectually textured
explanation of public journalism', the same reviewer nonetheless finds the
book's chief weakness to be intellectual as well: 'paltry argument, under-
developed principles for dividing public from private, a failure to assess
journalism comparatively, a reluctance to probe public journalism's logical
paradoxes' (Romano 2000: 26). To be sure, the idea of public journalism,
to build on an observation made elsewhere (Glasser 1999: 6–7), endures
the ignominy of neglect: its defenders seldom argue among themselves; too
little has been said about what separates it from other proposals, some now
forgotten, to craft a public purpose for a private press; no one appears to
know whether it replenishes or depletes the journalist's authority; and no
one has taken up the challenge of reconciling its optimistic claims for the
betterment of public life with what Carey (1995: 374) bluntly describes as
one of the chief sources of its impoverishment: 'the ruthlessly privatizing
forces of capitalism'.

The claims of public journalism do not, then, appear as part of a
logically developed, historically informed, and internally coherent theory
or philosophy of journalism. Although they can be distilled into a series of
propositions (see Charity 1995: 10), they properly exist in the context of a
few general *themes*, the most important of which deals with the relationship
between news and community.

News and community

Among the conditions that gave rise to public journalism, none has
received more critical attention than the 1988 US presidential race: 'a
monumentally smarmy campaign', as Carey (1995: 375) appropriately
describes it, 'reduced to a few slogans and brutal advertisements that
produced yet another record low in voter turnout'. To an unprecedented

degree, the American press depicted the election campaign as a contest, a game in which politicians played and citizens watched – while journalists, safe at the sidelines, provided colour and commentary. Gitlin (1990: 19) called it 'horse-race coverage . . . joined by handicapping coverage': day-to-day reports of the status of the race, authenticated by the latest polling data, combined with an 'insider's view' of politics, a fascinating but mostly irrelevant tour 'backstage, behind the horse race, into the paddock, the stables, the clubhouse, and the bookie joints'.[5] It all added up to a kind of news that favoured strategy over substance, a 'schema', as Jamieson among others (Patterson 1980; Hallin 1985) puts it, that invites voters to ask not 'Who is better able to serve as president?' but 'Who is going to win?'

> In the strategy schema, candidates are seen as performers, reporters as theatrical critics, the audience as spectators. The goal of the performer is to 'win' the votes of the electorate, projected throughout the performance in polls. The polls determine whether the candidate will be cast as a front-runner or underdog, whether the candidate will be described as achieving goals or 'trying' to achieve them, and how the candidate's staged and unstaged activities will be interpreted. In the strategy schema, candidates do not address problems with solutions, but 'issues' with 'strategies'. The language of the strategy schema is that of sports and war. The vocabulary lets reporters, candidates, and the public ask 'Who is winning, and how?' The posture invited of the electorate by this schema is cynical and detached.
>
> (Jamieson 1993: 38)

To combat the alienation and apathy associated with coverage of not only the 1988 election but public affairs in general, public journalism calls for more and better 'good news', to invoke the title of a recent and relevant study of press ethics (Christians *et al.* 1993); a plea for journalists to consider ways of conveying optimism about the future and confidence in the community's ability to get there. Public journalism, therefore, stands as a corrective to a language of despair and discontent; it tries to resist the corrosive cynicism that summons derision, not indignation. It resists, specifically, the unmistakably ironic tone that enables journalists to report the news while conveying, quietly and discreetly, their disgust for it. 'Like cops', Rosen observes, 'journalists find bitter irony an attractive pose because, like cops, they are asked to live in the glare of society's contradictions, to witness at close range its stupidities and crimes, to absorb its hypocrisy – its claim to care, its utter carelessness' (1996b: 5).

In journalism as elsewhere, irony works as a disguise. Irony confounds the appearance of language by inviting readers to reject what a text 'obviously' means; it lets readers know, subtly and indirectly, that the facts do *not* 'speak for themselves'. Irony conceals the writer's judgement by submerging it in a language that, taken literally, means just the opposite.

The disguise, however, is wearing thin. What once might have been a clever invitation to 'read between the lines' has now become a pervasive and unrelenting reminder of the improbability, maybe even the impossibility, of making things work. At a time when the theatrics 'of derision, of reversal, and of parody' overwhelm other forms of public discourse and contribute to what Baudrillard (1988: 210) judges to be a 'radical uncertainty as to our own desire, our own choice, our own opinion, our own will', irony in journalism can become yet another act of public disillusionment.[6]

In contradistinction to news that fosters 'a mood of fatalistic disengagement', as one prominent American journalist (Fallows 1996: 243) describes the unintended consequences of not so much what journalists write about but how they write about it, the good news of interest to public journalism focuses on outcomes. Good news takes seriously the likelihood, or at least the possibility, of *good results*. Notwithstanding critics who insist that any emphasis on 'good' news will only encourage journalists to avoid 'bad' news, public journalism has never expected editors and reporters to ignore or gloss over a community's problems. Instead, good news, as public journalism understands it, heightens a community's awareness of solutions, a mode of coverage that frames issues and problems in terms of what can be done about them. It is precisely the approach to reporting that Ettema and Peer (1996) celebrate in their study of the advantages of a 'vocabulary of community assets' over a 'discourse of urban pathology', a study aptly titled 'Good News from a Bad Neighborhood'.

Too many urban neighbourhoods endure a familiar litany of labels: poverty-stricken, violence-prone, welfare-dependent, drug-invested, gang-ruled. Whatever can be said of the accuracy of these labels, communities described by them come to be understood – by residents and others alike – mostly, and often entirely, in terms of their problems. Ettema and Peer (1996) attribute this in part to journalism's habits of mind, which include an uncritically accepted language of urban decay and social pathology. This language depicts the community without reference to its assets; it effectively ignores the 'community-building resources' that manifest themselves in grassroots organisations, local religious institutions, neighbourhood groups, and in other places covered by the press only when someone decides to do an 'uplifting' story.

If the press wants communities to succeed, rather than wallow in their distress, then journalists need a language that can present 'bad' news in a 'good' way, what public journalism regards as a vocabulary that can capture not only the problems a community faces but the community's capacity to confront them as well. What public journalism proposes, then, is a deeper appreciation for the relationship between news and community, a relationship that reveals itself in the language journalists use to render the world intelligible and distinct; it wants journalists to understand that 'there are ways of facing even the darkest facts that leave us open to the task of remaking them' (Rosen 1996b: 6). Thus public journalism's critique of the language of news moves beyond the surface meaning of a text, where questions of syntax and semantics typically receive most of the attention, and involves instead what Ettema and Peer (1996: 837) describe as

> an extended effort to analyze the deep structures of news as a conceptual system – that is to say, patterns of community coverage, definitions of newsworthiness, choices among community sources, selection of story frames, and so on. The identification of journalistic conventions with journalistic language in this way is not merely metaphysical. These conventions, after all, are a system of thinking and writing that embodies a particular conception of the community and its prospects.

By improving the tone, shifting the frame, and broadening the scope of the stories journalists tell, public journalism expects the press to be able to begin to better position itself as a partner in the community, one of any number of local organisations that has a stake in the community's future and therefore an interest in the community's success. However, unlike other local organisations, which have, understandably, substantive interests in moving the community in one direction or another, public journalism calls on the press to play the special role of 'fair-minded participant', to use one of Merritt's (1995b: 94–5) phrases, a moderator of sorts who participates in the affairs of the community by facilitating a discussion among other participants.

Journalism and public discourse

Merritt's 'fair-minded participant' role for the press alludes to an important but contested (Gartner 1998; cf. Glasser 2000) distinction between setting an agenda and finding one. In the tradition of public journalism, the press pays attention to the *community's* agenda, a range of issues that might or might not correspond to what journalists themselves regard as the most salient issues of the day. Without discounting the need to report 'discomforting truths' (Rosen 1999b: 297), even ones that might offend or even alienate the community, the agenda that drives public journalism resides outside the newsroom and beyond the political elite. It exists among citizens who have come together, figuratively if not literally, to discover the shared values that define their community – and to assess the conditions that might threaten or strengthen them.

Promoting a community agenda, rather than setting one for it, amounts to public journalism's limited endorsement of an advocacy role for the press: 'Journalism should advocate democracy without advocating particular solutions' (Charity 1995: 146). By positioning the press as a champion of democratic means but not of democratic ends, public journalism encourages journalists to care about 'outcomes' in general but none in particular: caring about the quality of public life, Merritt (1995b: 116) writes, 'does not mean trying to determine outcomes. But it does mean accepting the obligation to help the process of public life determine the outcomes'. An agenda-setting role for the press, it follows, emphasises process or procedure: 'Public journalism does not apologise for having an agenda', according to Rosen (1996a: 15), so long as the agenda takes the form of 'things like a more engaged and deliberative public, a more workable civic climate, a better political debate'. Just as the press cannot afford to 'pretend to have no investment in the community's welfare, no stake in its on-going struggles, no need to be alarmed when civic life falters or the public climate turns poisonous, no role in making democracy work' (Rosen 1996b: 4), it also cannot afford to pursue 'partisan agendas' or toss 'aside the virtues of an independent press' (Rosen 1999b: 200).

Although critics worry about its apparent disdain for old-fashioned 'objectivity', in fact public journalism neither rejects in principle nor abandons in practice the ideal of neutrality. In recognition of the 'many ways to find a neutral position in the drama of public life', Rosen (1999b) cites the neutrality of the referee, 'keeping order on the field of play'; of the critic, 'judging the scene from a distance'; of the catalyst, 'persuading people to engage one another, then stepping back'. For the press, Rosen (1999b: 258) favours what he terms 'proactive neutrality', a role that honours the importance of being disengaged from any particular issue but very much engaged in efforts to facilitate the discussion of issues in general:

> Public journalism succeeds when it strengthens the political community's capacity to understand itself, converse well, and make choices. Public journalists are animated by a vision of the well-connected community, one that operates at full capacity as it reflects on itself, its future, and its choices. More than mere observers, they are willing to join in creating the well-connected community, in adding to civic capacity. In this sense they themselves become political actors.
>
> (Rosen 1994: 381)

By remaining 'neutral on specific schemes and practical solutions', as Hackett and Zhao (1996: 10) understand Rosen's notion of proactive neutrality, public journalism 'champions itself as a partisan of a particular form of politics, rather than a particular political cause'. Being objective, then, need not prevent editors and reporters from serving their community in the role that matters most to public journalism: as 'civic capitalists' dedicated to improving 'the productivity of the community' (Charity 1995: 11).

To improve a community's productivity, and consistent with its interest in the relationship between the language of news and a community's sense of itself, public journalism calls for a shift from a 'journalism of information' to a 'journalism of conversation', a distinction Carey (1987: 14) uses to underscore the possibility that 'the public will begin to reawaken when they are addressed as conversational partners and are encouraged to join talk rather than sit passively as spectators before a discussion conducted by journalists and experts'. The public needs to be informed, of course, but it also needs to be engaged by the day's news in ways that invite discussion and debate; issues need to be covered as opportunities for citizens to govern themselves rather than as topics subject only to the considered views of the prominent and elite. To do this requires certain changes in the culture of newsrooms, something akin to what journalists at the *Virginian-Pilot* in Norfolk, Virginia, outlined in 'Reporting on Public Life', a presentation they made at a public journalism seminar in 1994 (quoted in Hume 1995: 36):

- Reporters look not just for sources at the opposite extremes of an issue but for moderate views in the middle.
- Coverage is framed in terms of people's daily experiences, instead of treating people as incidental ornaments in stories about official politics.
- Reporters use people's emotions to show how they arrive at their decisions, instead of just as 'colour' to show how people feel about the issue.
- Articles describe the values people bring to an issue, including the grey areas and complexities, rather than simply describing conflict.
- Citizens' knowledge is valued along with experts' knowledge.
- In writing about who, what, why, when, and where, they should also try to explain to citizens why they should care.
- Reporters try to explore how people resolve issues, suggesting that solutions are possible and that readers may have a role to play.

From principles to projects: public journalism in practice

In many ways, public journalism exists as a succession of projects. In the early years of the movement, Rosen's Project on Public Life and the Press kept tabs on these projects and used them to illustrate the quality and diversity of work being done in the name of pubic journalism. Now the Washington, DC-based Pew Center for Civic Journalism, funded by the Pew Charitable Trusts, plays that role through its newsletter, *Civic Catalyst*, which provides a forum for discussion about the principles and practice of public journalism as well as brief summaries of the projects being funded by the Center. Through its annual Batten Award for Excellence in Civic Journalism, named in memory of James Batten, a Knight Ridder executive and an early booster of public journalism initiatives, the Pew Center also recognises, formally and financially, what it judges to be the best work being done in the tradition of public or civic journalism.

No quick summary would do justice to the range of projects completed under the banner of public journalism, except to say that many of them deal directly with election and campaign coverage; and among these most are likely to share the attributes of a recently developed 'operational definition' of 'citizen-based journalism: (i) sponsoring one or more public forums on issues; (ii) using polls to establish issues worthy of coverage; (iii) conducting focus groups with voters to establish their concerns; (iv) forming citizen panels to consult at different stages of the campaign; (v) seeking questions from readers and viewers for use when interviewing candidates; (vi) basing reporting largely on issues developed through citizen contact; and (vii) providing information to help citizens involved in the political process in ways other than voting (Meyer and Potter 2000: 119). Although no formal criteria exist for separating traditional from public journalism, most of the projects and activities in the spirit of the latter will differentiate themselves in three broadly distinguishable areas: the ways reporters interact with citizens and the community; the tools editors use to identify a public or community agenda; and the nature of the stories journalists tell.

Redeploying newsroom personnel

Public journalism offers alternatives to the standard 'beat' system used in most American newsrooms, the prevailing method of deploying journalists in and around the community for purposes of supplying a steady flow of news. Because no newsroom can afford to 'blanket' the community with reporters, the beat system offers an efficient compromise: a 'netlike formation of the dispersion of reporters', to use Tuchman's (1978: 23) frequently cited metaphor, designed to catch 'big fish'. Typically assigned to cover the handful of institutions that make up a community's infrastructure (police, government, courts, schools, etc.), beat reporters operate efficiently in at least two ways. First, if reporters cannot predict tomorrow's news, they can always know where to find it; beats *locate* news among a handful of public bureaucracies staffed by public officials who are often compelled by law to disclose what journalists usually want to know. Second, these officials offer 'bureaucratically credible' (Fishman 1980) statements and documents, and these pronouncements generally do not require further inquiry from reporters. Editors will ordinarily accept as news, although not always as true, what comes from sources who have the social and political authority to know what they know.[7]

The beat system, however, promotes precisely what public journalism wants to combat: a bias in favour of what Gouldner (1976: 122–3) calls the 'managers of the status quo', public officials or their functionaries who provide an inherently conservative account of the community. Moreover, the beat system deals with the community at large only when its stories can be told through one of the covered bureaucracies, which accounts for the familiar complaint from neighbourhoods that the only time the press pays attention to them is when someone commits a crime. The local police department might be one of the most lucrative beats, but many in the community do not regard it as the best or most appropriate source of news.

A number of newsrooms have moved in the direction of public journalism by augmenting or revising the traditional range of beat assignments. Recognising that news 'does not develop along territorial boundaries established within the newspaper's organisation', the Columbia (South Carolina) *State*, for example, reconfigured its beats into a series of 'circles' based on 'broad themes that reflected the newspaper's core coverage franchise':

> Quality of Life, which covered such areas as crime, housing, food/nutrition, health, and the environment; City Life and Governance, which explored issues affecting citizens from town council to Capitol Hill; Community Roots, which explored issues firmly rooted in the Columbia community, such as religion; Leisure, which covered entertainment and related recreational activities; Transactions, which focused on business news; and Passages/Learning, which explored 'cradle to grave' issues including parenting, child care, education, and aging.
>
> (Johnson 1998: 128–9)

Putting reporters from different beats together in the same circle created opportunities for newsroom collaboration, which in turn focused attention on a broader range of issues and sources. Because circles, unlike beats, do not correspond to particular pages or sections of the newspaper, reporters began to think in terms of what each day's newspaper needed rather than in terms of how best to fill the news holes for which they had responsibility.

To encourage its reporters to move beyond their standard repertoire of sources, for quotes as well as for story ideas, the *Anniston Star* in Alabama compiled a database of more than one hundred 'informal community leaders' from civic clubs, church groups, leadership training programmes, civic rights groups and others (Pew Center, Summer 1999: 5). To avoid using new and different sources in trivial ways, the *St. Paul Pioneer Press*, an urban daily serving the capital of Minnesota, gave its reporters time for in-depth interviews. In a project on intergenerational relationships, for example, *Pioneer Press* reporters immersed themselves in the lives of the people they were interviewing; as amateur anthropologists eager to take the time to understand life in a nursing home or the routines of day-care centres, reporters earned a degree of trust that yielded more and better material than the 'superficial soundbite quotes' for which they often settle (Pew Center, July 1996: 4).

'Immersion reporting', as the *Pioneer Press* describes its method of coverage, also characterises the work of New York *Newsday* reporter Jim Dwyer, who in the early 1990s wrote a column, 'In the Subways', based on his acquaintance with, not simply his knowledge about, the world's biggest transit system. Unlike reporters for, say, the *New York Times*, whose approach to stories about the subways usually begins and ends with interviews with officials at the Transit Authority, which has jurisdiction over the subway system, Dwyer – Rosen (1995b: 4) notes approvingly – 'spent most of his time underground, suffering the chronic delays, the panhandlers, the danger and filth', but also experiencing the 'patience and civility' of the people who work for and travel in the subways each day. Significantly, Dwyer's 'immediate, flesh and blood connections to citizens' established his authority as a representative of, or surrogate for, his readers and their interests. Dwyer may end up interviewing Transit Authority officials, but by then 'with some earned authority of his own', which, Rosen believes, addresses what public journalism needs to address when it encourages new routines for reporters: 'Power without authority is the quickest way to arouse public resentment' (Rosen 1995b: 5–6).

Finding a public agenda

Public journalism struggles to strike a satisfactory balance between what the managing editor of the *State* describes as newspapers' traditional 'patriarchal contract with their communities', in which '[n]ews and information was handed down from on high, along with advice on how the community ought to behave' (quoted in Johnson 1998: 141), and the risk, as one steadfast critic of public journalism puts it, of ceding editorial judgement 'to pollsters or, worse, to readers or viewers in focus groups who have no particular knowledge of a state, of politics, or of politicians' (Gartner 1998: 229). Whatever the compromise it might reach between exercising its own discretion and accommodating citizens' presumably shared concern for some issues and not others, projects in the tradition of public journalism maintain a commitment to facilitating and then responding to what it understands to be the *public's* agenda.

Projects under the banner of public journalism typically convene the community and search for a public agenda by sponsoring forums, organising town meetings, arranging focus groups and commissioning polls. A description of a typical project might include a passage like this one from a coalition of news media in Long Beach, California:

> After a poll and more than 75 focus groups – three each held by 25 reporters and columnists – 'Long Beach 2000: The Future of our Community' ran as an eight day series in late fall. Issues that surfaced as community concerns were safety, education, race relations, immigration, neighborhoods and volunteering.
>
> (Pew Center, Spring 1998: 10)

Projects of this kind often discover issues that would have been ignored or neglected by the newsroom. This is especially obvious in the case of election coverage, as the editors of the *Orange County Register*, a major suburban daily published near Los Angeles, realised when they decided to cover the 1996 Republican Convention by focusing on the issues that came to their attention when they established telephone lines for readers to call in, invited letters from readers and organised conversations with civic leaders and average citizens. The aim was 'to provide the paper with a deeper understanding of concerns the system either was not addressing or was treating in such a polarised manner that a majority of people saw no room for themselves', as Rosen (1999b: 113) described the point of the project. By starting with citizens' concerns, the *Register* changed campaign coverage from using the perspective of the political insider, the prototypical source for campaign news, to the perspective of the people who have to make the voting decisions. The coverage no longer centred on the making of the political campaign, the chances of winning, the candidates' images and personalities – the 'strategy schema' – but on substantive issues and the policy positions of the candidates.

By involving citizens in an agenda-setting process that usually remains isolated in the newsroom, editors can begin to redefine not only the range of issues that might need to be covered but the issues themselves. Rather than beginning with a list of issues defined and labelled by journalists, public journalism at its best lets the community itself define the issues; that is, rather than 'pigeonholing' citizens with 'multiple choices', as Charity (1995: 38) describes the benefits of public journalism, the newsroom looks for 'questions and concerns that spring up from them without prompting'. Thus the 'The Front Porch Forum' project organised by the *Seattle Times* and a number of public broadcasters in the region revealed that 'virtually every problem [the citizens] defined could be linked to the effects of the region's rapid growth' (Pew Center, Spring 1998: 10). The 'growth' issue emerged not only as a salient topic but as a way of bringing together in a distinctively meaningful way a variety of related topics and issues. Put a little differently, the issue of growth pointed to a *consensus* in the community that provided journalists with an opportunity to focus coverage on a topic everyone appeared to understand and wanted resolved. It pointed to an area of agreement among citizens rather than the areas of division and disagreement that ordinarily get journalists' attention.

Telling a different story

If 'politics' remains the 'universal speciality' of the American journalist, as Herbert Gans (1979: 132) contends, it is politics understood less in terms of the substance of issues than the intrigue that surrounds them. As such, politics – the politics of struggle – accounts in large part for the dominant story frame in American journalism: conflict. Predictably, a recent study of a diversity of local and national newspapers found that the press in the United States

> shows a decided tendency to present the news through a combative lens. Three narrative frames – conflict, winners and losers and reveal-

ing wrongdoing – accounted for 30% of all stories . . . . The penchant
for framing stories around these combative elements is even more
pronounced at the top of the front page and is truer still when it comes
to describing the actions or statements of government officials

(Project for Excellence in Journalism 1999: 1)

Public journalism abandons the politics of struggle for a different
struggle, what Rosen calls the 'struggle to come to public judgment'. What
all public journalism stories share is the 'excellent drama' of that struggle, a
drama defined by one simple question: 'Will the community succeed or
fail?' (Rosen, quoted in Charity 1995: 85). Parisi puts it a little differently
but reaches basically the same conclusion when he observes that public
journalism wants to replace the 'cynical narrative of conflict and strategy'
and 'reanimate democratic life' by focusing on 'local activism' (1997:
680–1).[8]

Focusing on local activism usually means dealing, specifically and con-
cretely, with what can be done to solve problems. However, for the *Press
& Sun Bulletin* in Binghamton, New York, it also meant setting a tone of
optimism in its coverage of a failing local economy. The first in a series of
stories began with a lengthy sub-head:

> In the last eight years, we've lost thousands of jobs, seen the price of our
> homes plummet and said goodbye to friends and neighbors. There's
> some good news on the horizon but our future is still uncertain. We've
> got to do something to make this community strong again. We need
> good jobs and a future for our kids. That's going to take lots of hard
> work – and lots of good ideas . . . to change things, we need everyone
> pulling in the same direction . . . Our jobs may have left but our dreams
> didn't. This series launches our yearlong effort to help citizens
> recapture those dreams. It'll be a long, hard journey. It begins today.
>
> (Ford 1998: 29)

Wherever a project of this kind takes the community, the test of its success
rests on the 'good results' it brings about. When Jan Schaffer, executive
director of the Pew Center for Civic Journalism, announced the winners of
the Batten awards for 1999, she made clear what counts as good results:

> In Maine, the journalism gave rise to more than 70 study circles on
> alchohol abuse; in the Twin Cities, more than 2,500 people parti-
> cipated in book clubs and discussion groups on poverty amid welfare
> reform; and in San Francisco, thousands of people engaged in an
> online conversation about race relations, and the reporting is in its
> second year.

As a result, in each of these communities, the one-way conversation of traditional journalism became an active dialogue that continued long after journalism wound down.

(Pew Center, Summer 1999: 1, 11)

When the quest for good results turns into a campaign for a particular outcome, however, the press can be criticised for the very partisanship public journalism wants to avoid. When the *San Jose Mercury News* launched a project in 1994 to increase voter turnout in a particular district, the net result – not a very good result, in Rosen's judgement – was to increase the odds of a victory by the Democratic Party in the election. The *Mercury News* 'singled out a particular population' of mostly immigrants and poor people who 'everyone knew . . . were likely to vote for the Democratic party' (Rosen 1999b: 257).

Locating public journalism

Even with scores of workshops, seminars, conference papers, articles, and no fewer than eight books devoted to understanding what it means, public journalism remains an intellectually dislocated project. It makes constant reference to the importance of being democratic, but offers no particular theory of democracy or democratic practice. It wants to revive public life and strengthen community, but fails to define 'public' or 'community' in ways that highlight their essential differences and delineate the nature of the relationship between them. It encourages dialogue and deliberation, but ignores the crucial dissimilarities in the modes of participation they each imply (cf. Thompson 1995: 249–58). It promotes better ways of telling stories, but not within 'a culturally informed theory and practice of feature reporting' that would 'encourage the social solidarity and empathy that make public life possible' (Pauly 1999: 147). It hopes to engage readers, viewers and listeners in a conversation about shared values, but presents no plan to 'capture the attention of the inattentive and challenge the imagination of the disenfranchised' (Hardt 1999: 205). It resists equating the opinions of publics with the opinions of individuals, but relies on polls that do just that (Glasser and Craft 1998: 210–11). It intends to empower ordinary citizens, but says conspicuously little about how the citizenry might influence the resolution of issues on which individuals do not formally vote.

Only a few years ago no one knew just how far Rosen and others intended to go with the claim that public journalism represented a 'grass-roots reform movement' (Charity 1995: 1) that would 'recall journalism to its deepest mission of public service' (Rosen 1995a: 116). Not very far, Rosen now acknowledges. Public journalism can only work within – and cannot be expected to effectively challenge – 'the highly restricted environment in which most journalists labor' (Rosen 2000: 683):

Public journalism is not an insurrection, or even a minor revolt against the structural forces at work. It did not pose and cannot sustain a challenge to the commercial regime in which the American press operates. Precisely because it is a mainstream movement, it is the wrong place to look for a new political economy of the mass media.

(Rosen 2000: 682)

Schudson reached essentially the same conclusion a year or so earlier when he pointed out that public journalism does not offer a fundamentally new model of journalism in democracy. On the contrary, its proposals tend to conserve rather than change the basic elements of the American press:

It does not propose new media accountability systems. It does not offer a citizen media review board or a national news council. It does not recommend publicly elected publishers or editors. It does not suggest that the press be formally or even informally answerable to a governmental or community body. It does not borrow from Sweden the proposition that government should subsidise news organisations that enlarge the diversity of viewpoints available to the reading public.

(1999: 122)

As Schudson implies in his brief account of what public journalism does not propose or support, advocates of public journalism remain remarkably silent on any role for the state in promoting a democratic press. This might be taken as evidence of a narrowly liberal, even libertarian, view of democracy, one where the state maintains its commitment to individual liberty, including the liberty of journalists, by honouring the sovereignty of private transactions. Yet nothing in the public journalism literature suggests any particular allegiance to the tenets of liberalism, certainly nothing that would indicate support for the kind of 'minimal' state that libertarians like Nozick (1974) would prefer.[9] Indeed, given the sprinkling of quotes and citations from the handful of scholars whose work provides what little political theory exists in the public journalism literature, public journalism would appear to favour some form of republicanism, a tradition in democratic thought that rejects the standard liberal proposition that individuals can know their preferences, interests and conceptions of the good independent of, and prior to, any association with other individuals.

With reference to Sandel (1982, 1996), Barber (1984), Putnam (1993, 1995), and occasionally Arendt (1958) and Habermas (1989), public journalism begins to build a case for the political and cultural sensibilities that resonate with one of the core claims of republicanism: 'we can know a good in common that we cannot know alone' (Sandel 1982: 183). Certainly the constant attention from Rosen and others to the exchange between John Dewey (1927) and Walter Lippmann (1922) that took place in the early years of the twentieth century – a 'debate' almost singlehandedly rekindled by Carey (1989) through an influential essay first published in 1982 – conveys considerable enthusiasm for Dewey, 'an exemplary republican' (Baker 2002: 142) who maintained great faith in the capacity of people to govern themselves, and considerable disdain for Lippmann, one of the educated elite who believed that only the educated elite could effectively govern complex societies. What Dewey wanted, and what public journalism finds so appealing about him, is widespread participation in society, participation marked by ideas which are 'communicated, shared, and reborn in expression' (1927: 218).

Public journalism correctly attributes to Dewey an abiding faith in community and communication, a belief that communication 'can alone create a great community' (1927: 142). However, public journalism takes little notice of Dewey's corresponding faith in the state and the government that runs it. Although Dewey knew that only 'through constant watchfulness and criticism of public officials by citizens can a state be maintained in integrity and usefulness' (1927: 69), he also knew that only the state possessed the power and resources needed to 'bring about equalisation of economic conditions in order that the equal right of all to free choice and free action be maintained' (1939: 162). If labels help, Dewey was, like many republicans, a socialist – not in the crude sense of supporting 'a kind of arithmetically fractionalised individualism' but in his preference for 'socially planned and ordered development' over the 'unplanned determinism, issuing from business conducted for pecuniary profit' (1929: 119–20). He was also a Jeffersonian who applauded Jefferson's 'principle of equality of rights without favor to any one', which meant, Dewey wrote, 'giving supremacy to personal rights when they come in conflict with property rights' (Dewey 1939: 162). Specifically, what concerned Dewey but what appears to be beyond the purview of public journalism are the integrative forces he associated with 'aggregated capital and concentrated control' (1929: 37). In a chapter entitled 'The United States, Incorporated', written more than a half century ago, Dewey lamented an American condition that has in recent years worsened considerably: the 'condition of dominant corporateness' and the consequent 'disintegration of individuality' (Dewey 1929: 36, 66). Dewey saw the 'constantly increasing role of corporations' as both 'a cause and a symbol of the tendency to combination in all phases of life' (1929: 36); in passages that could have been written today, he warned about the 'great pressure now brought to bear to effect conformity and standardisation of American opinion', and in general 'the arrest and benumbing of communication' (1929: 83, 86).

Without serious and sustained attention to the one area that apparently stands beyond its reach, namely, the political economy of American journalism, public journalism forfeits any opportunity to confront what most American journalists regard as the biggest threat to the quality of the American press: private gain at the expense of public service. Carey (1999) hardly overstates the case when he reminds us, in an essay written in defence of public journalism, that the 'republican impulse behind public journalism' rests on the belief that 'freedom consists of something more than the protection of rights *against* the society and the preservation of freedom to choose our lifestyles as we do goods in a supermarket'; and the '"more than" entails sharing in self-deliberating with fellow citizens about the common good, and working together to shape the destiny of the political community' (1999: 61). A few pages later Carey identifies the very issue public journalism fails to address: 'Whether the historic meanings of political liberty and a free press can be preserved once the borders separating journalism and business, the corporation and the newsroom, are effectively breached is a central question of the American press today' (1999: 65).

If the press needs to be understood as a fundamentally important democratic institution, as public journalism contends, and if the press defines its democratic obligations in terms of facilitating what Arendt once described as the 'interminable dialogue' self-governance demands, as public journalism further contends, then the press deserves special protection from the state not because journalists have a right to be heard but because citizens have a right to hear. Logically, as Baker (2002: 199) explains in his recent assessment of the relationship between a government's policies and journalism's purpose, this invites consideration of 'positive' roles for the state and, therefore, a rejection of what prevails among journalists who fear *any* role for the state: 'constitutional interpretations that block all media-specific governmental regulation and intervention'. As Baker points out in an argument public journalism needs to consider, if only to reject it, accepting the proposition that the state has no legitimate role to play in promoting or prohibiting an individual's *speech* does not mean accepting the proposition that the state has no legitimate role to play in promoting an institutional design for the *press* that affirms the distinctive and presumably desirable contribution journalists make to a democratic society. In particular and in recognition of the fact that 'not only government but capital can threaten press freedom' (2002: xiii), Baker concludes that freedom of the press should be understood 'to allow the government to promote a press that, in its best judgement, democracy needs but the market fails to provide' (2002: 213).

Notes

1 This chapter draws on several previously published essays (Glasser 1999, 2000; Glasser and Craft 1997, 1998).
2 See Rosen (1994) for a discussion of the origins of the Project.
3 The term 'civic journalism' is favoured by the Pew Charitable Trusts, which in 1993 funded the Pew Center for Civic Journalism, but the term is used more or less synonymously with 'public journalism'.
4 See, for example, the work of the Commission on Freedom of the Press, a panel of scholars funded in 1942 by Henry Luce, the founder and then publisher

of *Time* magazine. Vilified and then more or less ignored by the press, the principal findings of the Hutchins Commission, so-called after the chairman Luce selected, University of Chicago president Robert Maynard Hutchins, are summarised in Leigh (1947). For a worthwhile assessment of the Hutchins Commission and its work, see McIntyre (1987).

5 See Didion (1988) for a similar critique of the campaign and journalists' treatment of it.

6 For a discussion of the logic and consequences of irony in American journalism, see Ettema and Glasser (1994, 1998) and Glasser and Ettema (1993).

7 Within their officially sanctioned domain, Fishman (1980: 92) explains, public bureaucrats appear to daily beat reporters as self-evidently competent and authoritative knowledge holders: 'Information which is bureaucratically organised, produced, and provided is hard fact'; it 'is the stuff that makes up straight reporting'. Unlike investigative reporters and others whose work requires independent judgements concerning the veracity of the information they receive, beat reporters generally 'accept at face value the claims they glean from the beats they cover' (Ettema and Glasser 1998: 159).

8 But Parisi (1997) criticises public journalism for its emphasis on local activism. By focusing entirely on the community and its concerns, public journalism pays little attention to what Parisi regards as genuinely public issues that transcend local communities: public health, for example.

9 Nozick favours what he terms a 'minimal state', one that limits its role to 'protecting all its citizens against violence, theft, and fraud, and to the enforcement of contracts, and so on' (1974: 26). Any larger role for the state, Nozick contends, would only inhibit our freedom 'to choose our life and realise our ends and our conceptions of ourselves' (1974: 333–4).

References

Arendt, H. (1958) *The Human Condition*, Chicago: University of Chicago Press.

Baker, C.E. (2002) *Media, Markets and Democracy*, Cambridge: Cambridge University Press.

Barber, B. (1984) *Strong Democracy*, Berkeley: University of California Press.

Baudrillard, J. (1988) *Selected Writings*, ed. M. Poster, Stanford, Calif.: Stanford University Press.

Carey, J.W. (1987) 'The press and public discourse', *Center Magazine*, March–April: 4–16.

Carey, J.W. (1989) *Communication and Culture: Essays on Media and Society*, Boston: Unwin Hyman.

Carey, J.W. (1995) 'The press, public opinion, and public discourse' in T.L. Glasser and C.T. Salmon (eds), *Public Opinion and the Communication of Consent*, New York: Guilford Press.

Carey, J.W. (1999) 'In defense of public journalism', in T.L. Glasser (ed.), *The Idea of Public Journalism*, New York: Guilford Press.

Charity, A. (1995) *Doing Public Journalism*, New York: Guilford Press.

Christians, C., Ferré, J.P. and Fackler, P.M. (1993) *Good News: Social Ethics and the Press*, New York: Oxford University Press.

Dewey, J. (1927) *The Public and Its Problems*, Chicago: Swallow Press.

Dewey, J. (1929 [1962]), *Individualism Old and New*, New York: Capricorn Books.

Dewey, J. (1939 [1963]) *Freedom and Culture*, New York: Capricorn Books.

Didion, J. (1988) 'Insider baseball', *New York Review of Books*, 19 October: 19–21, 24–26, 28–30.

Ettema, J.S. and Glasser, T.L. (1994) 'The irony in – and of – journalism: a case study in the language of liberal democracy', *Journal of Communication* 44/3: 8–16.

Ettema, J.S. and Glasser, T.L. (1998) *Custodians of Conscience: Investigative Journalism and Public Virtue*, New York: Columbia University Press.

Ettema, J.S., and Peer, L. (1996) 'Good news from a bad neighborhood: toward an alternative to the discourse of urban pathology', *Journalism and Mass Communication Quarterly* 73/4: 835–56.

Fallows, J. (1996) *Breaking the News: How the Media Undermine American Democracy*, New York: Vintage Books.

Fishman, M. (1980) *Manufacturing the News*, Austin: University of Texas Press.

Ford, P. (1998) *Don't Stop There: Five Adventures in Civic Journalism*, Washington, D.C.: The Pew Center for Civic Journalism.

Gans, H. (1979) *Deciding What's News: A Study of CBS Evening News, NBC Nightly News, Newsweek and Time*, New York: Random House.

Gartner, M. (1998) 'Public journalism – seeing through the gimmicks', in E.B. Lambeth, P.E. Meyer and E. Thorson (eds), *Assessing Public Journalism*, Columbia: University of Missouri Press.

Gitlin, T. (1990) 'Blips, bites and savvy talk', *Dissent*, winter: 18–26.

Glasser, T.L. (1999) 'The idea of public journalism', in T.L. Glasser (ed.), *The Idea of Public Journalism*, New York: Guilford Press.

Glasser, T.L. (2000) 'The politics of public journalism', *Journalism Studies* 1: 683–6.

Glasser, T.L., and Craft, S. (1997) 'Public journalism and the prospects for press accountability' in J. Black (ed.), *Mixed News: The Public/Civic/Communitarian Journalism Debate*, Mahwah, N.J.: Erlbaum.

Glasser, T.L. and Craft, S. (1998) 'Public journalism and the search for democratic ideals', in T. Liebes and J. Curran (eds), *Media, Ritual and Identity*, London: Routledge.

Glasser, T.L., and Ettema, J.S. (1993) 'When the facts don't speak for themselves: a study of the use of irony in daily journalism', *Critical Studies in Mass Communication* 10: 322–38.

Gouldner, A.W. (1976) *The Dialectic of Ideology and Technology: The Origins, Grammar, and Future of Ideology*, New York: Seabury Press.

Habermas, J. (1989) *The Structural Transformation of the Public Sphere: An Inquiry into a Category of Bourgeois Society*, Cambridge, Mass.: MIT Press.

Hackett, R.A. and Zhao, Y. (1996), 'Journalistic objectivity and social change', *Peace Review* 8/1: 5–11.

Hallin, D.C. (1985) 'The American news media: a critical theory perspective', in J. Forester (ed.), *Critical Theory and Public Life*, Cambridge, Mass.: MIT Press.

Hardt, H. (1999) 'Reinventing the press for the age of commercial appeals: writings on and about public journalism', in T.L. Glasser (ed.), *The Idea of Public Journalism*, New York: Guilford Press.

Hume, E. (1995) *Tabloids, Talk Radio, and the Future of News*, Washington, D.C.: Annenberg Washington Program.

Jamieson, K.H. (1993) 'The subversive effects of a focus on strategy in news coverage of presidential campaigns', in *1-800-President: The Report of the Twentieth Century Fund Task Force on Television and the Campaign of 1992*, New York: Twentieth Century Fund.

Johnson, S. (1998) 'Public journalism and newsroom structure: the Columbia, S.C., model', in E.B. Lambeth, P.E. Meyer and E. Thorson (eds), *Assessing Public Journalism*, Columbia: University of Missouri Press.

Leigh, R.D. (ed.) (1947) *A Free and Responsible Press*, Chicago: University of Chicago Press.

Lippmann, W. (1922/[1965]) *Public Opinion*, New York: Free Press.

McIntyre, J. (1987) 'Repositioning a landmark: the Hutchins Commission and freedom of the press', *Critical Studies in Mass Communication* 4: 136–60.

Merritt, D. (1995a) 'An editor's perspective', in *Imagining Public Journalism: An Editor and Scholar Reflect on the Birth of an Idea*, Bloomington: Indiana University School of Journalism.

Merritt, D. (1995b) *Public Journalism and Public Life: Why Telling the News Is Not Enough*, Hillsdale, N.J.: Erlbaum.

Meyer, P.E. and Potter, D. (2000) 'Hidden values: polls and public journalism', in P.J. Lavrakas and M.W. Traugott (eds), *Election Polls, the News Media, and Democracy*, New York: Chatham House.

Nozick, R. (1974) *State, Anarchy, and Utopia*, New York: Basic Books.

Parisi, P. (1997) 'Toward a "philosophy of framing": news narratives for public journalism', *Journalism & Mass Communication Quarterly* 74: 673–86.

Patterson, T.E. (1980) *The Mass Media Election: How Americans Choose Their Presidents*, New York: Praeger.

Pauly, J. (1999) 'Journalism and the sociology of public life', in T.L. Glasser (ed.), *The Idea of Public Journalism*, New York: Guilford Press.

Pew Center for Civic Journalism (July 1996), *Civic Catalyst*, newsletter.

Pew Center for Civic Journalism (Spring 1998), *Civic Catalyst*, newsletter.

Pew Center for Civic Journalism (Summer 1998), *Civic Catalyst*, newsletter.

Pew Center for Civic Journalism (Summer 1999), *Civic Catalyst*, newsletter.

Post, R. (1993) 'Managing Deliberation: The Quandary of Democratic Dialogue', *Ethics* 103: 654–78.

Project for Excellence in Journalism (1999) 'Framing the news: the triggers, frames, and messages in newspaper coverage', a study of the Project for Excellence in Journalism and Princeton Survey Research Associates, Washington, D.C.

Putnam, R.D. (1993) *Making Democracy Work: Civic Traditions in Modern Italy*, Princeton, N.J.: Princeton University Press.

Putnam, R.D. (1995) 'Bowling alone: America's declining social capital', *Journal of Democracy* 6/1: 65–78

Romano, C. (2000) 'Who owns the Fourth Estate?', *The Nation*, 24 January: 25–30.

Rosen, J. (1989) 'Newspapers' future depends on shaping trends in how people live', *Bulletin of the American Society of Newspaper Editors*, December: 15–19.

Rosen, J. (1991) 'Making journalism more public', *Communication* 12: 267–84.

Rosen, J. (1994) 'Making things more public: on the political responsibility of the media intellectual', *Critical Studies in Mass Communication* 11: 363–88.

Rosen, J. (1995a) 'A scholar's perspective', in *Imagining Public Journalism: An Editor and Scholar Reflect on the Birth of an Idea*, Bloomington: Indiana University School of Journalism.

Rosen, J. (1995b) 'Where is public journalism? The search for a new routine', paper presented to Project on Public Life and the Press Spring Seminar, American Press Institute, Reston, Virginia, 25 March.

Rosen, J. (1996a) *Getting the Connections Right: Public Journalism and the Troubles in the Press*, New York: Twentieth Century Fund.

Rosen, J. (1996b) 'Public journalism is a challenge to you (yes, you)', *National Civic Review* 85: 3–6.

Rosen, J. (1999a) 'The action of the idea: public journalism in built form', in T.L. Glasser (ed.) *The Idea of Public Journalism*, New York: Guilford Press.

Rosen, J. (1999b) *What Are Journalists For?* New Haven: Yale University Press.

Rosen J. (2000) 'Questions and answers about public journalism', *Journalism Studies* 1: 679–83.

Rosen, J. and Merritt, D. (1994) *Public Journalism: Theory and Practice*, Dayton, O.H.: Kettering Foundation.

Sandel, M.J. (1982) *Liberalism and the Limits if Justice*, New York: Cambridge University Press.

Sandel, M.J. (ed.) (1986) *Liberalism and Its Critics*, New York: New York University Press.

Schudson, M. (1999) 'What public journalism knows about journalism but doesn't know about "public"', in T.L. Glasser (ed.) *The Idea of Public Journalism*, New York: Guilford Press.

Thompson, J.B. (1995) *The Media and Modernity: A Social Theory of the Media*, Stanford, Calif.: Stanford University Press.

Tuchman, G. (1978) *Making News: A Study in The Construction of Reality*, New York: Free Press.

Part IV
Conclusion

12 Trends in news media and political journalism

Jeremy Tunstall

Although European and world politics have been greatly transformed in recent decades, the media – including political journalism – may have changed even more. Many media changes have been triggered especially by linked developments in deregulation and technology which have then generated increased competition. Deregulation has affected the entire world economy since 1980 as the USA and various European and other countries have transferred public sector entities into commercial ownership and control. In much of Europe, for example, a predominantly public radio/television system changed into a commercial radio/television/cable/satellite/video system with a much bigger total programme output.

Radical changes in technology have, of course, occurred alongside deregulation. Space satellites and broadband cable played a large part from the 1960s onwards, with small European countries as world pioneers in cable. Computerisation has had an enormous impact in many areas of the media. Already in the 1970s the American telephone giant AT&T was anxious to get into the data business and in 1982 agreed to give up its telephone semi-monopoly in return for permission to provide data. In the 1990s the internet eventually brought about the much predicted data revolution, first for big businesses and then for the media and the domestic consumer.

Political journalism in an era of transnationalised news inflation

More media, more news: more political journalism?

The news business and political journalism have now experienced such radical changes as specialised news, financial news and sports 24-hour cable/satellite services. News is now also available on computer screens from a huge number of general news, financial news, sports news and other news websites. Although these changes are significant, their biggest impact on national political journalism may have been their indirect part in beefing up political news in 'old media' such as terrestrial television and newspapers.

Some of the biggest changes have occurred in newspapers, subsequent to the newspaper computerisation revolution of the 1970s and 1980s. The newspaper industry now uses more pages than ever before; many newspapers have doubled or trebled their pagination since the 1970s. Although some types of light material may have hugely expanded, political coverage has also increased. Radio also expanded its total news output after 1980 and although it mostly carries music, the drip-drip of radio news – even two minutes on the hour – reaches many people at some point during the day. Many politicians and journalists carry both a radio and a mobile telephone with them wherever they go.

Big changes have also occurred in the news agencies, which have always been journalism's pioneer of new technology. A revolution in the quantity, spread and sophistication of fast agency news means that today's journalists, and not least political journalists, now have a radically different core supply of 'hard news'. This supply now includes a much bigger flow of semi-political, international and financial news. Prior to the computer revolution, agency up-dates arrived at forty words a minute in a special area of the newsroom; some updates and pictures were delivered to newspaper offices by messengers. The agency material was split up and relevant sections distributed to senior news executives, while most journalists sat by their typewriters without any flow of agency matter. Political journalists hovered around the national legislature and were not easy to reach even on the telephone. Today all of this is different, as even a junior reporter can summon up endless supplies of agency news on their screen. Political reporters, at their previously isolated legislature locations, can now dip into a huge stream of fast-flowing fresh news.

One consequence of this fast-flowing river of agency matter is that all journalists – both within the same organisation and across the competition – have the same extensive supply of perpetually updated agency hard news. In conditions which most journalists experience as more competitive than before, competition occurs first to extract from this common flow and second to comment on, and find exclusive details about, the basic river of hard news. Political journalism, of course, lends itself especially easily to this second type of competition; the partisan character of democratic politics and the variety of individual politicians facilitates much competition for exclusive details and comments. Another consequence is to diminish interest in set-piece political speeches and published documents, summaries of which are available on all journalists' computer screens. More interesting to journalists are leaked details and extracts before the formal deadline time of delivery or publication. As politicians leak details of their own speeches before the time of delivery, opposing politicians can be asked to comment on speeches which have not yet been given.

Political journalism has no single definition. Even in 1970 it was evident that political journalism happened not just in and around the national legislature but in a variety of other political, or semi-political, fields. (Tunstall 1971). These semi-political fields have become even more important in recent decades. National elections often focus on policy areas such as education, health, law and order, and employment. One semi-political field – finance and business – has become especially salient; most politics is about money.

Most genres in television (or newspapers) have a political element. If one thinks in terms of television genres, or thematic television channels, even sports has some political ingredients – perhaps 5 or 10 per cent. The proportion of political content rises with travel, fiction, comedy, documentary, history, public affairs, local news, and national news. Perhaps a higher political percentage is to be found in non-news special series, such as the political interview or political biography. The very highest political percentage may be found in a short television series on a political topic such as the 1991 BBC series, *The Second Russian Revolution*.[1] This series – about 90 per cent of which was either news film or interviews with leading Russian politicians – was even described by some critics as 'too political'.

This BBC political television series may have justified its cost, because it was sold to thirty other countries. But the general rule about 'purely political' journalism has always been that it needs subsidy. Purely political journalism has traditionally been subsidised for prestige and/or partisan reasons. Public service broadcasters covered a lot of news and politics, because they were legally required to do so. Today's weighty newspapers subsidise their 'narrow politics' coverage with broader or semi-political coverage; fields such as education and health attract not only readers but also advertisers. Much the same probably happened one hundred years ago and before. Lacking contemporary readership research, we cannot be sure; but the long political speeches which appeared in newspapers in the 1890s may have had fairly few readers.

Most news media of the 1890s – even the popular and successful ones – were subsidised. The large sales of some French newspapers in the 1890s were subsidised by other business activities. William Randolph Hearst bought newspaper market leadership in New York with his father's huge silver fortune. The news pioneers of recent times have lost a lot of money. Both CNN and *USA Today* lost money for a decade or more. Similarly, most of the all-news offerings in Europe and elsewhere were also predicted to lose plenty of money, and typically lost even more than predicted. The demand for non-stop news, let alone political news, is limited. This latter point is relevant to the fact that discussions of political news in Europe tend to focus on the nation-state level. There are, however, other levels both below and above the nation-state level. Much news and politics also exist at a local level (such as a small city) and the national-regional level. In the opposite direction, there is the world-region level (Europe, for instance), and finally the much mentioned global level.

Trends in national/European news

While Western Europe has gone a long way towards a single economy, its political news – and news generally – remains stubbornly national. Television channels in foreign languages attract very small audiences. Newspapers remain overwhelmingly national (or national-regional). Nevertheless there are plenty of common factors across Western Europe's mainly national media. Following the linked revolutions (deregulation, commercialisation, computerisation) there is a widespread assumption that the media in general, and political journalism in particular, have got worse, have 'dumbed down', gone tabloid and sensational, become more entertainment-driven, and are now more beholden to advertisers. Also common across Europe is a lack of supporting evidence for this thesis. There is evidence of less news coverage of national legislatures, and more news coverage of the economy, industry and finance. But that change is based on a genuinely significant movement in the location of power.

One of the weaknesses of the 'dumbing down' thesis is that the larger quantity of media output inevitably leads to changes in audience behaviour. In the winter of 1899–1900 the London *Daily Mail* was perhaps Europe's most commercially successful newspaper; the October 1899 audited daily sale was 797,000 copies. The *Daily Mail* consisted of eight pages, three of which were made up of advertising. Readers who wanted additional news had to buy a second newspaper. Today the available choice (especially if the consumer has access to cable or satellite) is vastly greater. The difference is similar to that between the 1900 corner grocery store containing a few dozen separate items and the present-day supermarket with its thousands of brands and packages. But does this situation mean that the supermarket has been 'dumbing down'?

Today audiences use the media rather as consumers use the supermarket. From the huge range available they mainly stick to a few preferred brands, but they may also do a bit of impulse buying. Newspaper loyalty now depends heavily on whether the reader subscribes to home delivery; those who pick up the newspaper on the way to work can and often do vary their purchase from day to day. In Germany, for example, where home delivery is high, newspaper readers are more loyal than in France, where there is no tradition of home delivery, except in the case of some regional newspapers such as *Ouest-France*.

The television viewer with a remote control – and especially the viewer in a multi-channel household – is now accustomed to zap between channels. The 'loyal' or 'regular' viewer of a particular series may watch only every second week. Similarly, few viewers watch the same television news every evening; viewing the same news three or four times a week is now an indication of atypically strong loyalty. An individual who is quite strongly interested in politics may follow a complex weekly mix of print, radio, television, cable and internet; increasingly the precise pattern may be difficult to remember and thus even more difficult to research. It is, of course, because of this zapping pattern or media promiscuity, that the channels and publications now promote and package themselves so aggressively; but melodramatic opening titles and music, or big front-page headlines and pictures, may be only the glossy packaging around more serious political and semi-political content.

Perhaps it is not surprising that – against this more volatile media and news background – there are complaints across Europe about the declining standards of political journalism. Yet at least in Britain – where tabloid journalism was and remains prominent – neither content analysis (McLachlan and Golding 1999) nor comments by a social-science-inclined prominent journalist (Walker 1999) support the 'dumbing down' thesis. There is evidence from a range of countries that more and better educated journalists are being employed (Weaver 1998). While individual journalists do feel insecure about their employment prospects, this is scarcely new in the history of journalism. On the whole the evidence seems to suggest that across a range of countries and media, political (and other serious) journalists have become more central to political coverage and more significant in the provision of financial news (Tunstall 2001: 229–91). There is now less deference shown to politicians by journalists. For example, even in France, the kind of journalist deference and subordination which existed under President De Gaulle in the 1960s no longer prevails today. Around the world, more (not fewer) politicians than ever before go in fear of certain categories of journalists.

While political journalism across Europe maintains its heavy focus on the national level, the resulting political journalism differs radically between countries and thus defies easy generalisation. For example, the differences between Germany and Greece in both politics and journalism are enormous. Germany has high advertising expenditure, still quite strong public broadcasting, Europe's highest circulation newspaper press and a big magazine sector. It also has Europe's strongest cable television and Europe's biggest collection of major commercial channels. In contrast, Greece is very low on advertising spend and has weak public broadcasting, while its newspaper press is very small and consists mainly of afternoon tabloids.

France is also very different from Germany. While French public broadcasting has declined, there remains much state subsidy and much protected monopoly across the French media including the press. Italy is unique. Indeed, in many respects Italy's television and media are more comparable to those of South America than northern Europe. Spain also has its own distinctive media structure. Spain is quite West European in its highly partisan press, but is unusual in the relatively recent ending of dictatorship. It is also special in that its newspapers were nursed back into democratic health with the help of substantial state subsidies.

Three simple variables appear to underlie many of the national media differences across Europe. The first is total media advertising expenditure.

Only Germany and the UK have big advertising spends and these are the only two Western European countries each to possess as many as five elite newspapers. Second, there are huge differences in the significance of the split between the national and regional levels. In Germany the regional level is important in politics and even more important in the media. However, in the UK or the Netherlands, the media, politics and political journalism are highly centralised. A third obvious difference is between north and south. In southern Europe all the media (and especially newspapers) are weak. In contrast, the Scandinavians tend to be world leaders in both democracy and in the consumption of old media (such as newspaper) and new media (such as the internet).

The stuff good stories are made of . . .

The explosion of new video channels and the spread of politics across so many genres and outlets seems to pose almost impossible challenges for content analysis. Yet perhaps we can suggest (or hypothesise) that several categories of 'good stories' for political journalists have emerged across most West European countries. All of these stories can be said to contain mainly national plots, but may include some significant European sub-plotting. Three variations on the 'good story' theme are considered here: the parallels between politics and football, whereby politics is treated by the media in terms reminiscent of the European Champions' League; new dimensions of political coverage such as the economy, food and ethnicity; and a telenovela approach to the coverage of scandals.

First, in many respects politics is like football. Football has 'got bigger' because it now attracts more television coverage and more money and because it is more European (and global). The national domestic leagues may have lost some of their former glamour but each nation has its stars and leading teams, who are prominent nationally because they are prominent in Europe. The same is true of politics. The national level of politics is seen by citizens and media to be less important because of European (and global) changes. However, some national politicians have 'got bigger' because they are political stars on both the national and the European political playing fields. Even a larger European country, like France, has only a few of these star or superstar politicians – typically the president, prime minister, finance minister and perhaps two or three other prominent national politicians.

Political journalists in Europe are not exactly 'the boys on the bus' (Crouse 1973), those journalists who follow American presidential election candidates across the continental USA. In Europe it is more a matter of the 'hacks on the airbus', the senior political journalists who follow their national presidents and prime ministers to those numerous meetings in Brussels, Paris, Rome, Berlin, Madrid, London and other political (and football) national capitals. Below this stellar level there are many semi-political journalists who accompany their national ministers of education, telecommunications, trade and industry, health, or immigration to their specialised meetings across Europe. These political and semi-political journalists can all claim that frequent airbus journalism generates 'good stories', while also providing an opportunity to build relationships with the senior politician and their travelling team of lesser politicians and specialist civil servants.

Second, there are new dimensions of political coverage. Economic journalism is to the fore. When dramatically expanding its financial news and data activities in the 1960s, the Reuters news agency argued that big political stories (such as the 1963 assassination of John F. Kennedy) were also economic stories. As the Cold War retreated and the European Union expanded, political stories focused more on the economy, both national and European. In political journalists' diaries of forthcoming events financial/economic events are now more salient. The financial world has speeded up its flow of significant news announcements. Companies which not long ago were nationalised industries and issued only annual reports are now commercial companies which announce quarterly results, profits and predictions. The quarterly results of a large company can now be a leading national (and possibly European) political story.

Food is a massive source of stories, especially if one includes British (mad cow) beef and stories about French farmers protesting at prices. The food 'news peg' allows for reporting on some quite complex international economic stories. For example, the 1999 banana story brought in the WTO, the EU, the United States banana lobby in general, the US Chichita (formerly United Fruit) company and its cheap production on the large plantation farms of Central America, and the British and French governments who gave their support for small (and higher cost) peasant banana producers in Caribbean ex-colonies. Food is also a significant news theme because the (French-led) Common Agricultural Policy has been the EU's major item of expenditure and because food-and-agriculture leads on easily into environmental, nuclear, climate change, bio-engineering and other stories. The European media can perhaps claim that their coverage of the genetically modified (GM) foods issue – helped by the environment lobby – has been their greatest success. Some might say that it also shows important limitations. One can attract wide-scale attention for a complex political-consumer-environmental story only if there are super-sensational levels of human interest and a US company (Monsanto) which foolishly fits the stereotype.

Ethnic minorities both old and new are another focus of national semi-political stories, in which the European dimension is seen to be increasingly significant. Europe has several historical layers of national minorities. Some minorities were forcibly incorporated into new nineteenth-century states; others came from newly independent colonies in the 1950s and 1960s; yet others have arrived more recently. These ethnic minorities and related issues are significant in national politics and constitute (in some countries) an important field of semi-political specialist journalism. While it is increasingly claimed that 'European solutions' are required, ethnic minority issues are present in several other important semi-political fields such as employment, crime, education, health and food. Ethnic issues are also especially significant at the local and national-regional levels.

A final example of newish trends in political stories is the tendency to turn certain stories into a long-running melodrama of daily episodes. Some such stories are like those endless five-episodes-a-week afternoon soaps. More common is the daily political soap which runs for perhaps nine months. This more closely resembles the Latin American telenovela, often of about 200 episodes in total. The US telenovela-isation of politics was initiated on the media side by the arrival of themed 24-hour channels (such as CNN, launched in 1980) requiring huge quantities of cheap material for those 168 hours of airtime per week.

On the political side were the massed forces of attack publicists eager to 'raise the negatives' of their political opponents. Sensational hearings before Congressional Committees had sometimes done this previously, as had the troubles of the incumbent president and, of course, the year-long presidential election campaign. Then CNN achieved huge ratings boosts with the Gulf War (1990–1) and the Anita Hill Senate hearings. But CNN also had to look to murder trials as available telenovela material – the O.J. Simpson case had huge audience appeal. However, what could CNN use to fill in the audience lows between the sensational human interest highs? Answer: Bill Clinton. More generally the Watergate events of the 1970s led Congress to introduce the Ethics in Government Act in 1978 which established a Special Prosecutor (later Independent Counsel) system intended to prevent another Nixon/Watergate set of events. In the last two decades there has been about one such new Washington investigation launched per year. This was the system which led to Kenneth Starr who pursued Clinton and dominated the news for many months. Money in the form of the Whitewater affair was the first Starr theme. This eventually led to the sex angle in a combination of two old and reliable news themes in political journalism.

Like many other trends, the daily political telenovela spread from the United States, via the UK, to Europe. Britain's biggest contribution to the semi-political real life telenovela was Charles, Diana and the rest of the UK royal family during nine months in 1992. This year of multiple royal disasters was referred to in December 1992 by the Queen as her *Annus Horribilis* (mocked by *The Sun* newspaper as 'One's Bum Year'). As a media format the semi-political telenovela has acquired distinctive nationally idiosyncratic features within different countries. In Britain an important part was played by national daily tabloid papers. However in 1992 Rupert Murdoch's Sky News (launched in 1989) was still in the early (and un-

profitable) years of its 24-hour news task and grateful for the royal opportunity. As 24-hour news channels have proliferated across Europe, a parallel
development has been the growth of the semi-political telenovela 'running
story'.

Europe as both news and news producer

Europe as world-region: gaps and bias in European political news

Given that political journalism and news reporting generally in Europe
remain predominantly national, there are inevitably significant gaps in
European political coverage. Examples include the coverage of Brussels
itself, of communications and media policy, and of national scandals.

The European Community/Union was not designed with public understanding or national political journalism in mind. Public opinion polls
indicate a lowish level of comprehension across Europe. It is confusing to
have several key European bodies called 'Council' and to have so many
DGs dealing with trade, competition, finance, taxation and industry. How
many Europeans know which bits of Europe are located in Luxembourg
and Strasbourg? It seems all too clear that until 1994 many Brussels-
based foreign correspondents focused heavily on Kohl and Mitterrand as
the 'giants' of Europe. In doing so, they too easily ignored Kohl's and
Mitterrand's own corrupt behaviour and also the corruption and in-
efficiencies which led to the removal of the Santer Commission. Yet the
'complexity' of Brussels, emphasised by some Brussels correspondents, can
be exaggerated. The total size of the Brussels operation (buildings, numbers
of people, money) is quite modest compared with what confronts correspondents in Washington DC, New Delhi or Beijing.

Communications and media have become big policy fields at the
European, as well as the national, level. Many people have argued that so
long as Europeans all have their eyes glued to national media, they will
not behave as Europeans. During the 1990s Brussels (and Brussels-based
journalists) did become much more active in telecommunications and
related new technology areas. But media policy remained little covered.
For instance, very little attention was devoted to the major lobbying effort
conducted in Brussels by the newspaper and advertising industries (Tunstall
and Palmer 1991: 85–101).

An obvious weakness of European and national political journalism in
recent decades has been a failure adequately to cover political scandals.
Europe is not alone in having big public scandals; indeed, some major
scandals span, for example, a French oil or armaments company and a
French former colony. In the years 2000–1 alone there were major political
scandals outside Europe in Argentina, Brazil, China, India, Indonesia,
Japan, Nigeria, Pakistan, Philippines, Russia, South Africa and the Ukraine.

Many of these scandals involved bribery to obtain big oil or armaments contracts and the siphoning abroad or laundering of money through Swiss banks and tax havens.

Yet some of these non-European countries' journalists seemed to have a better record in exposing corruption than did their European colleagues. The Indian Bofors scandal – a thirty million US dollar commission paid in 1986 on the sale of Swedish heavy guns to the Indian army – reverberated through Indian politics for the next fifteen years. The scandal coverage was led by Swedish radio and by *The Hindu* (Madras) newspaper. The negative coverage played a part in Rajiv Gandhi (and the Congress Party) losing the 1989 Indian election. This is not an isolated case; several other Indian cabinet ministers and party leaders have been forced to resign as a result of media scandal coverage since 1989.

All European countries have their political scandals and some seem to be quite well reported at the time by both national and European media. This seems to have been true of numerous killings in Northern Ireland and in the Basque area of Spain. The German media have also revealed plenty of scandals since the 1950s, including scandals which undermined major political figures. Helmut Kohl's corrupt party funding activities were reported rather late, but these were not for personal gain and were minor by international or European standards. The same cannot be said of Italy and France. The gross corruption of several senior Italian politicians, the Berlusconi media monopoly of commercial television/television advertising/film, and the dire performance of Italian journalism, all add up to a major embarrassment not just for Italy, but also for Europe. Foreign correspondents based in Italy have over many years criticised Italian politics and media. That Europe tolerates Italian media arrangements, which would not be tolerated within many other countries around the world, is a reminder not only of European weakness but of the inadequacies of European political journalism.

France is another embarrassment, although a little less extreme than Italy. From the mid-1990s onwards, an avalanche of revelations surfaced about Presidents Mitterrand and Chirac, other former senior politicians and the Elf oil company.[2] These revelations were astonishing for two reasons: first, that large-scale corruption was so widely practised by senior national and city of Paris politicians; second, that this corruption had obviously been known to political journalists but not revealed by them. Even when this large-scale corruption was increasingly made public, many of the revelations did not involve investigations by journalists; some emerged in books. Much of the evidence about François Mitterrand's dubious past was provided by the President himself in confessional public statements shortly before his death.

In the case of François Mitterrand, the dying President and the French media between them appeared to invent a fresh political sub-genre – the retrospective political telenovela. Now at last the great French voting public were let in on the real Mitterrand melodrama. This revealed how Mitterrand had worked for both sides in the Second World War – he was a hero both of the Resistance and the Vichy regime. As Minister of Justice in 1957 he had known in detail about, and condoned, large-scale killing-after-torture by French paratroopers in the 'Battle of Algiers'. Mitterrand, while running for re-election to a seven-year term as president concealed that he had cancer . . . and so on. Finally, as the retrospective telenovela drew to a close, the focus shifted to the president's children. He revealed that (in good soap opera tradition) he had fathered a child out-of-wedlock and out of sight of the French electorate. Then another (soap opera style) errant male – Mitterrand's son – was in trouble; he later went to prison for arms and drugs trafficking in Africa.

It also became increasingly apparent in the late 1990s that the new French President (Chirac) had, while long-time Mayor of Paris, engaged in systematic bribery and kickbacks. This arrangement seems to have involved the invention of fictitious employees and non-existent electors. It also involved a regime of kickbacks by construction companies in return for winning major Paris building projects. Cash from these corrupt contracts went to all political parties in Paris, including the Socialists and Communists. Although some media stories did appear about all this, not enough was revealed to stop the corruption. If French political journalists knew about the Paris and the Elf corruption they failed adequately to report it. If they did not know something already widely known among politicians, they were badly lacking in basic political reporting competence.

Anglo-American news as a European problem

An awkward problem for Europe and European political journalism is that the leading Europe-wide media are dominated by the US and UK, countries whose loyalty to the European Union is less than total. This Anglo-American dominance in European news is exercised by:

- International news agencies: the dominant two in Europe, as in the world, are Reuters (UK) and Associated Press (USA). They lead in general news and political fast news for newspapers and radio, in international video news for television, in still pictures, in graphics (maps, charts and diagrams) and in financial news.
- The main Anglophone newspapers which sell across Europe are the *International Herald Tribune*, the *Wall Street Journal* and the *Financial Times*. The FT also owns *Les Echos* (Paris) and half of *Financial Times Deutschland*.
- Twenty-four-hour all-news channels operated by the Anglo-Americans across Europe include CNN, CNBC and BBC World. In addition much on-line news comes directly or indirectly from US organisations.

'Hard news' as supplied by Reuters and Associated Press (AP) is suitable for a large range of different media outlets because both organisations have for over a hundred years been serving a diverse range of news customers. Increasingly in the twentieth century they went on to supply news to national news agencies and other media in nearly all countries in the world. Because Western Europe is an affluent and attractive market, both AP and Reuters make special provisions for Europe. AP, for example, has a very strong German language operation; Reuters (which operates services in about twenty-five languages around the world) focuses heavily on Europe, with its major languages (apart from English) being Spanish, French, German, Arabic and Mandarin.

American and British journalists are the inheritors of a long continuous tradition which assumes relative political stability. Nevertheless American and British journalists tend to be unrealistically nostalgic about the good (or golden) old days, often about three or four decades ago. Some journalists who write books about the evils of present-day 'spin-doctoring' and public relations manipulation have a weak understanding of their own occupation's history. Some British and American journalists interviewed by this author in the 1990s looked back to the 1960s as a golden age (while television was still quite small). Other journalists also interviewed by this author in the late 1960s remembered the 1930s as a golden age. We are also told that London journalists around 1900 looked back to a golden age of non-sensational journalism in the 1860s and 1870s (Lee 1976: 104–17).

Another trend in European (including British) journalism is selectively to borrow inappropriate terminology from the United States. To this author the term 'spin-doctor' has a strong American accent which does not translate well even into British English, in which (several dictionaries indicate) 'spin' tends to relate to the game of cricket. 'Horse-Race' journalism is another American term which loses most of its meaning when applied to situations in Europe. American journalists and academics may regret this type of news coverage but US elections do at least last a long time, and often involve primaries as well as the main race itself. Moreover, in US elections there are two parallel races, one for votes, the second for money. European elections lack most of these features and have other non-American elements such as multi-party coalition formation.

Europe (not the USA) as world news leader

The final assertion – or more accurately hypothesis – of this chapter is that while Europe has fairly few Europe-wide media, Western Europe (and not the United States) is the true leader in supplying news around the world. This assertion rests upon some possibly controversial subordinate hypotheses. The first of these is that the United Kingdom is part of Europe; while the Anglo-American news machine may lead, the Anglo-European news machine surpasses the American (only) news performance.

Let us deal specifically with some media categories. In terms of general news agencies, Reuters alone around the world probably surpasses AP. Reuters, AFP (France), DPA (Germany), EFE (Spain) and ANSA (Italy) together have a much more weighty world presence than AP alone (UPI having died some years ago). In terms of video news, Reuters, Eurovision, Euronews and BBC World score at least a draw against APTV and CNN. In propaganda radio the US is a big player, but Britain, Germany, France and Spain together are bigger and (along with other smaller European countries) transmit in more languages.

In terms of world-regions, Western Europe is the leading foreign news supplier in Eastern and Central Europe, Africa, the Middle East and South Asia. The USA probably has a news exporting lead in Japan and China. Yet while the US leads in Central America and Mexico, Europe leads comfortably in the whole of South America where EFE, other Spanish media, AFP and Reuters are all strong.

With regard to specific stories of recent years, Western Europe probably led the USA in collecting and exporting news about the collapse of Communism in Eastern Europe, the break-up of the Soviet Union and Yugoslavia, and also the Kosovo–Serbia fighting of 1998–9. During the first week of NATO bombing in Serbia (22–8 March 1999) the Reuters team of correspondents in Yugoslavia filed forty-two stories per day. Another study of twenty-three newspapers (including the *Washington Post*, *USA Today* and *Wall Street Journal*) during October 1998 showed that on average each newspaper credited thirty separate stories to either Reuters or AFP during an eleven-day period (Palmer 2001)

Increasingly, the movement of news around the world involves news travelling by satellite to diasporic communities several thousand miles away. Increasingly, ethnic minorities located in particular cities or suburbs can obtain entire television channels from home, now available on the local cable system. This phenomenon and other sorts of channel exporting and importing are now common in the US. Yet Europe, because of its recent colonial past, has a greater weight and variety of these and other long-distance media connections. Indian channels (like Zee) are available in Britain, as are Indian newspapers and magazines. Similar connections exist between Indonesia and the Netherlands; these connections make Amsterdam a focus for Indonesian news. London is a focus for Arabic, Indian, Nigerian and South African journalism and political news. France has unique news connections with its former African colonies.

The complexity and fast-changing character of these connections pose a severe challenge for academic content analysis. The 'manifest content' of a particular television news package or newspaper feature may superficially appear to be the work of one person. Often 'our own correspondent' has also been assisted by news agency material and by stringers (local part-time journalists). Very often the lone journalist whose name is attached to the story was in fact working in close alliance with a 'competitor-colleague'.

Often foreign stories have been reported jointly by one American and one European who share their information, stringers and hired transportation. Increasingly, these partnerships may be European–Nigerian or European–Asian, whether the location is Africa, Asia or Europe.

Just as political journalism is more than what 'political correspondents' do, so world trade is more than just the World Trade Organisation and the European Union is more than just Brussels. The European Union story (like the WTO equivalent) is complex, stretching out across a number of nation-states, languages, and political and economic issues. This complex story neatly matches the strengths of Reuters, AFP, Associated Press and other major news agencies. Their staffs together have all of the necessary language and specialist skills. Unlike many traditional political journalists (and politicians), many agency journalists have financial expertise and quantitative skills.

A few dedicated researchers have studied these major news agencies (Boyd-Barrett and Rantanen 1998). However, too few political scientists and media specialists comprehend how Europe and the world are reported by these high-volume, high-speed, high-expertise and (deliberately) low-profile organisations.

In order to test the main hypothesis of European world news leadership, research needs to look simultaneously at both 'retail' and 'wholesale' media in perhaps twenty nation-states – both net importers and net exporters of news. National news agencies play a very large part in the total news flow even in such large media systems as those of China and India (two countries which together sell about 100 million newspapers each day). Eight or nine of these very large population countries together make up over half the world's population. This author's hypothesis would be that a content study of these major national agencies, together with the international and semi-international news agencies of the US and Europe, would show Europe, not the USA, to be the world's main source of international news. This hypothesis, if confirmed, implies a paradox. While Europe is the leading supplier of news to the world, European political journalism remains ineffective even in explaining European politics to Europeans.

Notes

1 *The Second Russian Revolution* was an 8 × 50 minutes series produced by Brian Lapping Associates for BBC2 and the Discovery Channel. It was shown on television in thirty-one countries. The accompanying book is: Angus Roxburgh (1991) *The Second Russian Revolution*, London: BBC Books.
2 The Elf oil company, it seems, operated as a kind of parallel French external affairs ministry, through which huge bribes and kickbacks were offered (especially in Africa) for oil contracts and arms procurement. All of this was known to incumbent presidents of the French Republic over several decades. Indeed, each president received a detailed annual report.

References

Boyd-Barrett, O. and Rantanen, T. (eds) (1998) *The Globalisation of News*, London: Sage.

Crouse, T. (1973) *The Boys on the Bus*, New York: Random House.

Lee, A. (1976) *The Origins of the Popular Press, 1855–1914*, London: Croom Helm.

McLachlan, S. and Golding, P. (1999) 'Tabloidisation in the British press: a quantitative investigation into changes in British newspapers, 1952–1997', in C. Sparks and J. Tulloch (eds), *Tabloid Tales*, Lanham, Md.: Rowman and Littlefield.

Palmer, M. (2001) 'The value of the ephemeral: assessing news output about Yugoslavia', in S. Lax (ed.) *Access Denied in the Information Age*, London: Palgrave.

Tunstall, J. (1971) *Journalists at Work*, London: Constable.

Tunstall, J. (ed.) (2001) *Media Occupations and Professions*, Oxford: Oxford University Press.

Tunstall, J. and Palmer, M. (eds) (1991) *Media Moguls*, London: Routledge.

Walker, D. (1999) 'Dumbing down', the Tenth Guardian Lecture, Oxford: Nuffield College.

Weaver, D.H. (ed.) (1998) *The Global Journalist*, Cresskill, N.J.: Hampton Press.

Index

Printed in the United Kingdom
by Lightning Source UK Ltd.
110281UKS00004B/7